# ZBrush 4 Sculpting for Games

## *Beginner's Guide*

Sculpt machines, environments, and creatures for your game development projects

**Manuel Scherer**

[PACKT] PUBLISHING

BIRMINGHAM - MUMBAI

# ZBrush 4 Sculpting for Games
## *Beginner's Guide*



First published: March 2011

Production Reference: 1090311

Published by Packt Publishing Ltd.
32 Lincoln Road
Olton
Birmingham, B27 6PA, UK.

ISBN 978-1-849690-80-5

www.packtpub.com

Cover image model rendering, painting by Manuel Scherer on a starry background from Hubble Heritage Project, NASA

# Credits

**Author**
Manuel Scherer

**Reviewers**
Ryan Bailey
Glauco Longhi
Vivek Ram
Luke M. Steichen

**Acquisition Editor**
David Barnes

**Development Editor**
Susmita Panda

**Technical Editors**
Paramanand Bhat
Namita Sahni
Aditi Suvarna

**Copy Editor**
Laxmi Subramanian

**Editorial Team Leader**
Aditya Belpathak

**Project Team Leader**
Priya Mukherji

**Project Coordinator**
Shubhanjan Chatterjee

**Proofreader**
Linda Morris

**Indexers**
Rekha Nair
Monica Ajmera Mehta

**Graphics**
Geetanjali Sawant

**Production Coordinator**
Alwin Roy

**Cover Work**
Alwin Roy

# About the Author

**Manuel Scherer** is a German game developer who has worked in the games industry and in the fields of visual computing. He is currently teaching real-time visualizations at the Offenbach Academy of Art and Design.

Apart from his beloved work, he writes as a freelance journalist about the games industry from major events such as the Game Developers Conference Europe.

---

First, I would like to thank my parents, especially my father who continuously supported me on the long way of creating such a book. Furthermore, I would like to thank my love for her unmatched amount of support and motivation.

Also the team at Packt did an amazing job on setting everything up, thank you. My special thanks go to my friend and author Felix Kerger who inspired me to write this book. Last but not the least, let me thank Prof. Rolf Schubert and Michael Margraf, Alban Voss, and Fabian Schempp for their infinite amount of constructive feedback and their everlasting good mood.

---

# About the Reviewers

**Ryan Bailey** is a Senior-Level CG Artist working in the Animation and Video Game industry for over six years. Having a talent for art at a young age and parents that supported this, helped to nurture and grow his skills and talents as an illustrator and sculptor. Realizing that the only way to progress as an artist he moved onto the 3D Animation and Visual Effects Program at Vancouver Film School after four years of Fine Arts schooling.

Ryan's work experience includes Lead ZBrush Artist at Electronic Arts Canada, Senior Character Artist at Rainmaker Entertainment Inc., ZBrush Instructor at the Art Institute of Vancouver, and currently, he is working at Tecmo-Koei Canada as a CG Artist for their upcoming title Warriors—Legends of Troy. Even with his busy workload and family life, Ryan still finds time to do freelance work on the side.

**Glauco Longhi** is a sculptor, both traditional and digital, working for the cinema and television industry, also doing some toys and collectible works.

His passion for sculpture started in 2006, when he was working with After Effects for Motion Graphics for TV advertisement. At the studio, he met a guy who worked with something called 3Dmax, and then he fell in love with this brand new world.

After some basic courses, he chose the modeling area. And then, realized that only 3D wouldn't be enough for creating some nice characters, so he started sculpting in clay. After some months, his life was changed.

In the meantime, he worked for several 3D companies and studios, mainly focused on modeling and sculpting, but he decided to get some time and dedicate it to his own life, starting the freelancer living.

Now, sculpting maquettes, garage kits, prosthetic appliances, busts, halloween masks, props, and animatronics, his life is starting to make sense.

"Since I was 10 years old, my relation with arts was zero. I only wanted to be a pro skateboarder, and that was all I cared about. But I was very interested in how everything works—the mechanisms, the fx, the magic, and illusion. Now, working with prosthetic fx, animatronics and so on, it's like I'm putting everything that I always loved together. Everything is starting to make sense—that's awesome! I love this...."

Glauco Longhi is always doing workshops around Brazil. He likes to teach and talk about sculpture and character design, creatures, monsters, and also studying hard. Almost every day, free time is spent, sculpting, drawing, or reading some new stuff.

"My relation with skateboarding can be easily seen through my art and my passion, my study routine. When I was trying to do right some trick, I never stopped until I could do that on the right and style way. Since I was a child, my brain chose this path to see things, and that's what I do with my art. I'm obsessed with human anatomy, so I'm always trying to see things better, but with time, I can see that this is an infinite journey...That's good, so I'll be searching for learning forever, and this will keep me on the right path, hope so."

**Vivek Ram** began his career 10 years ago as a freelancer dabbling in all the various segments of 3D animation. He has worked with Rhythm and Hues as a Senior Digital Artist for a few years before moving on to the Dreamworks Dedicated Unit as a Modeling Lead, where he wore multiple hats and moved between many departments during his tenure. He currently works as an independent animation consultant, again playing the role of VFX Supervisor, Designer, or Art Director on both feature and game projects for a variety of studios and production houses. For more information and to view his gallery of work, please visit `www.markeviv.com`.

**Luke M. Steichen** is a character artist working in the video game industry in Seattle, Washington. He spent four years in the United States Army, which gave him the opportunity to pursue his dream of making video games by letting him attend the Art Institute of Seattle to earn his Bachelors of Fine Arts in Game Art and Design. Through hard work, dedication (and many all-nighters) he landed an internship as a character artist which marked the beginning of a successful career in the games industry.

Luke is currently working at Sucker Punch Productions as a character rigger and assistant technical director on inFamous 2. Previously, Luke worked at WB Games in Kirkland, Washington as an Associate World Artist for "Lord of the Rings: War in the North" and F.E.A.R. 3. Before that he worked as a Contract Character artist at Surreal Software on "This Is Vegas" and "Lord of the Rings: War in the North."

Luke's interests include sculpting, tabletop wargaming, playing guitar, and general geekiness.

Luke would like to thank his amazing wife for all her love and support (and patience).

# Table of Contents

# Preface

Since ZBrush was released, it dramatically changed the way game art is created. It is unmatched in its speed for creating highly detailed models and thus, is widely used in the games and film industry. We could even say that if you want to be a game artist today, ZBrush is considered a standard.

A few years ago, ZBrush was used only for organic modeling. With ZBrush 4.0 this changed dramatically and you can now sculpt mechanical spaceships as well as organic creatures. And that's exactly what we're going to do—in the course of this book we'll complete four modeling tasks, covering the complete range of organic and mechanical sculpting. After you've completed this book, you will know all the techniques necessary to sculpt detailed game assets and view it in a game engine of your choice.

## What this book covers

*Chapter 1, Getting Started,* will cover all the preparatory steps of working with ZBrush. We'll get a quick overview about what we will learn in this book and how ZBrush is used in a model creation process. After that we'll quickly go over the basic terminology and finally talk about working in the field of digital art.

*Chapter 2, Learning the Interface,* will introduce you to the interface and the basic modeling concepts in ZBrush. After we're done with that, we are ready to start our first model in the next chapter.

*Chapter 3, Modeling a Spooky Tree with ZSpheres,* deals with model creation from ZSpheres in ZBrush. This is a powerful technique in ZBrush that's very useful for quickly blocking out volumes for our models. We'll use it to create a spooky tree from scratch and finally prepare it for sculpting in the next chapter.

*Chapter 4, Adding Details to the Tree,* covers the sculpting features of ZBrush. In this chapter, we'll take our tree from a rough model to the final stage. We'll learn about the different brushes in ZBrush and how we can use them to detail our model of the tree.

*Chapter 5, Texturing the Tree with Polypaint,* shows how we can texturize our models inside ZBrush. The cool thing is that in ZBrush we can paint our colors directly onto the model, which is a lot more fun than painting textures in a 2D image editor. We'll also take advantage of all the sculpted details and use them to quickly add color variations to our model.

*Chapter 6, Adding an Environment to the Tree,* will introduce subtools to compose a model out of multiple parts. We'll add a hill for the tree and detail it by adding some mushrooms and rocks.

*Chapter 7, Modeling a Sci-Fi Drone,* will introduce a new workflow, starting a model in an external modeling application such as Blender. We'll then see how we can transfer models between ZBrush and other modeling software.

*Chapter 8, Sci-Fi-Drone: Hard Surface Sculpting,* covers the new mechanical sculpting techniques of ZBrush. In this chapter, we'll finish our second model and learn a lot about detailing mechanical objects with the new brushes.

*Chapter 9, Sci-Fi-Drone: Creating a Normal Map,* discusses the different texture types commonly used in games. After that we'll take our detailed drone from the previous chapter and create a normal map from it so we can view all the fine details inside a game engine.

*Chapter 10, Modeling a Creature with ZSketch,* starts off with our third model—the brute. We'll use ZSketching to bring our character to life. This technique builds upon ZSpheres and allows us to paint muscles on top of a skeleton. This is incredibly fast for organic meshes. Once we're done with that, we'll convert our ZSketch into a mesh for further sculpting.

*Chapter 11, Sculpting the Creature's Body,* discusses the key steps involved in sculpting an organic creature. We'll have a closer look at sculpting anatomical details and will learn how to add additional props to our character, like a belt.

*Chapter 12, Sculpting Fur and Accessories,* introduces alphas to achieve realistic-looking material such as fur or feathers. We'll not only use alphas, but also talk about how to create custom alphas on our own. After that we'll use these custom alphas to add the final polish to our creature.

*Chapter 13, Preparing the Creature for Games,* covers the needed steps to bring our detailed creature from the last chapter into a game. This involves creating a low-poly version of it and transferring the surface details. Finally, we'll unwrap the creature so we can bake a normal map, like we did for the drone in Chapter 9.

*Chapter 14, Modeling the Harvester Ship,* will start off with our fourth model—the harvester ship. We'll start this complex spaceship directly inside ZBrush with a new technique called `ShadowBox`. This allows us to create mechanical shapes in no time, so we can assemble our complex ship. We'll then refine these shapes with the new clipping brushes that allow us to create crisp mechanical surfaces.

*Chapter 15, Detailing the Harvester Ship,* covers the creation of more complex parts like a clamshell with ShadowBox and the clipping brushes. We'll also use Booleans to combine or subtract meshes to create forms that were out of reach before.

*Chapter 16, Finishing the Harvester Ship,* will draw together all the techniques learned before to add the final polish to our ship. We'll also learn how we can grab sculpted geometry and use it as a brush to quickly add fine details.

# Who this book is for

This book is for aspiring (game-) artists who want to dig deeper into highly detailed game model production. It's good if you have a basic understanding of 3D and its possibilities and are also familiar with other 3D-software like Maya, 3D-Studio Max, Softimage, Blender, and others, which are good companions for ZBrush. Also, for someone looking for a more intuitive way of creating 3D models, this book and ZBrush are the right tools to start with.

# Conventions

In this book, you will find a number of styles of text that distinguish between different kinds of information. Here are some examples of these styles, and an explanation of their meaning:

Code words in text are shown as follows: "So we'll concentrate on the `.obj` format, which can be read by almost any 3D application."

**New terms** and **important words** are shown in bold. Words that you see on the screen, in menus or dialog boxes, for example, appear in the text like this: "Pick the **Move** brush and make sure that the fur forms a closed volume around the body, as shown in the next screenshot ".

> Warnings or important notes appear in a box like this.

> Tips and tricks appear like this.

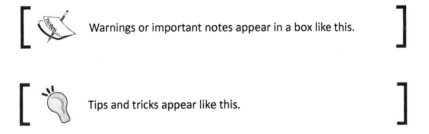

# Reader feedback

Feedback from our readers is always welcome. Let us know what you think about this book—what you liked or may have disliked. Reader feedback is important for us to develop titles that you really get the most out of.

To send us general feedback, simply send an e-mail to `feedback@packtpub.com`, and mention the book title via the subject of your message.

If there is a book that you need and would like to see us publish, please send us a note in the **SUGGEST A TITLE** form on `www.packtpub.com` or e-mail `suggest@packtpub.com`.

If there is a topic that you have expertise in and you are interested in either writing or contributing to a book, see our author guide on `www.packtpub.com/authors`.

# Customer support

Now that you are the proud owner of a Packt book, we have a number of things to help you to get the most from your purchase.

**Downloading the example files and colored graphics for this book**

You can download the example files for all Packt books you have purchased from your account at `http://www.PacktPub.com`. If you purchased this book elsewhere, you can visit `http://www.PacktPub.com/support` and register to have the files e-mailed directly to you.

## Errata

Although we have taken every care to ensure the accuracy of our content, mistakes do happen. If you find a mistake in one of our books—maybe a mistake in the text or the code—we would be grateful if you would report this to us. By doing so, you can save other readers from frustration and help us improve subsequent versions of this book. If you find any errata, please report them by visiting `http://www.packtpub.com/support`, selecting your book, clicking on the **errata submission form** link, and entering the details of your errata. Once your errata are verified, your submission will be accepted and the errata will be uploaded on our website, or added to any list of existing errata, under the Errata section of that title. Any existing errata can be viewed by selecting your title from `http://www.packtpub.com/support`.

## Piracy

Piracy of copyright material on the Internet is an ongoing problem across all media. At Packt, we take the protection of our copyright and licenses very seriously. If you come across any illegal copies of our works, in any form, on the Internet, please provide us with the location address or website name immediately so that we can pursue a remedy.

Please contact us at `copyright@packtpub.com` with a link to the suspected pirated material.

We appreciate your help in protecting our authors, and our ability to bring you valuable content.

## Questions

You can contact us at `questions@packtpub.com` if you are having a problem with any aspect of the book, and we will do our best to address it.

# 1
# Getting Started

*In this chapter, we will discuss who this book is for and what will be covered. We'll also discuss why we use ZBrush and why it is so important nowadays. After that we'll go over the basic terminology and preparatory steps for this book and finally talk about some basics of working in the field of digital art.*

## Who this book is for

This book is for aspiring (game-)artists who want to dig deeper into highly detailed game model production. It's good if you have a basic understanding of 3D and its possibilities and are also familiar with other 3D-software like Maya, 3D-Studio Max, Softimage, Blender, and others, which are good companions for ZBrush. Also, for someone looking for a more intuitive way of creating 3D models, this book and ZBrush are the right tools to start with.

## What we will learn in this book

In this book, we'll focus on learning how to use ZBrush for creating models for game production. We'll start with a quick look at the interface and then immediately start learning by solving little exercises. All these exercises will be based on fictional tasks to explain things in context. This means you'll not only be able to choose the appropriate solution for your task, but also consider the creative process as a whole. This is especially important if you do not only work on your own, but in a team of maybe a hundred or more people.

By the end of the book, you would have finished four complete game-specific modeling tasks, which will walk you through all the essentials of using ZBrush in a game production pipeline. Here's one of the four models we'll create:

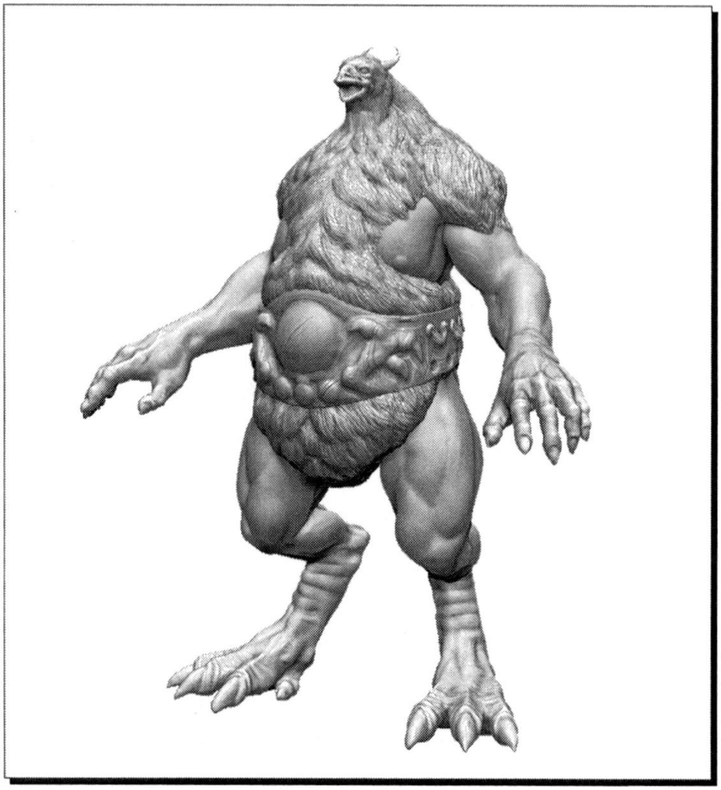

# Why ZBrush?

Why do we use ZBrush and why is it so widely used in the game and film industry? Because it is very good for creating highly detailed models in a very short time. This may sound trivial, but it is very sought-after and if you have seen the amazing detail on some creatures in *Avatar* (film), *The Lord of the Rings* (film) or *Gears of War* (game), you'll know how much this adds to the experience. Without the possibilities of ZBrush, we weren't able to achieve such an incredible level of detail that looks almost real, like this detailed close-up of an arm:

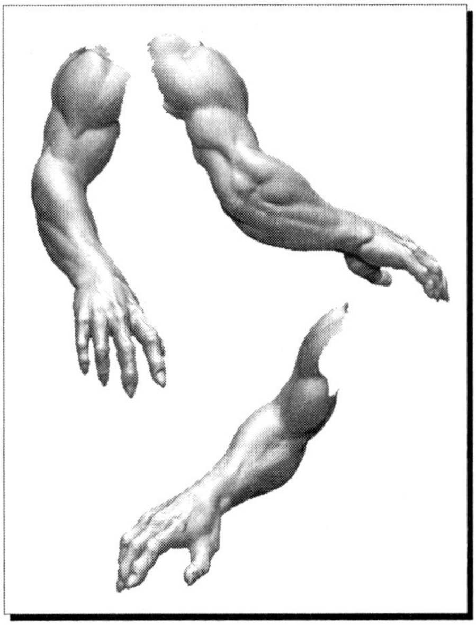

But apart from creating hyper-realistic models in games or films, ZBrush also focuses on making model creation easier and more lifelike. For these reasons, it essentially tries to mimic working with real clay, which is easy to understand. So it's all about adding and removing digital clay, which is quite a fun and intuitive way of creating 3D-models.

Yet it is important to know that ZBrush is a very specialized tool, so it is mostly used in conjunction with other 3D Software to animate or export the models into a game engine, for example. Still, specialization comes along with efficiency and you will be amazed how easily we can realize our ideas with ZBrush in no time.

# How ZBrush is used in a game's production

To better understand the workflow using ZBrush, let's think of a simplified way a 3D model is created to be used in our game. As always, there are many ways of doing the same thing, and many companies do it differently. By the end of this book, you will know some of the different ways of model creation, to blend into an existing workflow or to even create your own.

It all starts with an idea or ideally a concept drawing. This 2D concept is then roughly created in 3D, often in a 3D software such as Maya, 3D Max, Blender, Softimage, and others. Once this is done, ZBrush comes into play to detail the model and finish the digital sculpture, which is the fun part, but may also easily consume most of the time during model creation. After that, you may have something like a very detailed and lifelike sculpture of Caesar, but it has no color variation, it is just stone gray. So you paint it, usually in a 2D application like Photoshop or GIMP. This process of applying color to a model is called **texturing**. Depending on whether you would like to create a stiff statue or a walking Caesar, you may want to animate your creation, which is again done in a 3D software like Maya. With this step done, you're all set to export your model into any game engine you like, to make your own game or just view your model.

So in short, a simplified pipeline of creating a model using ZBrush, Maya, and Photoshop would look like this:

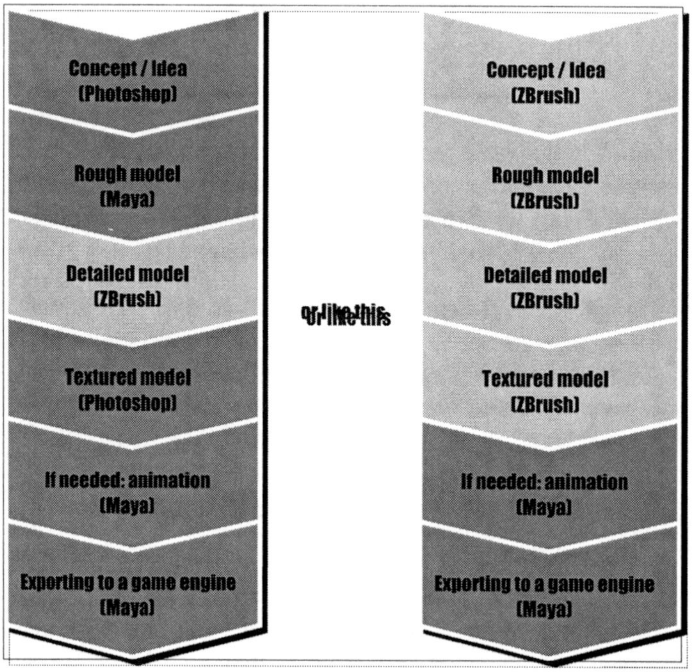


As shown in the previous image, there is more than one way of creating game models. We'll see in the later chapters that ZBrush could even be used for all of the first four steps, covering more than half of the workflow for game model production, as shown in the second diagram.

Here's another highly detailed example we're going to sculpt and view in real time:

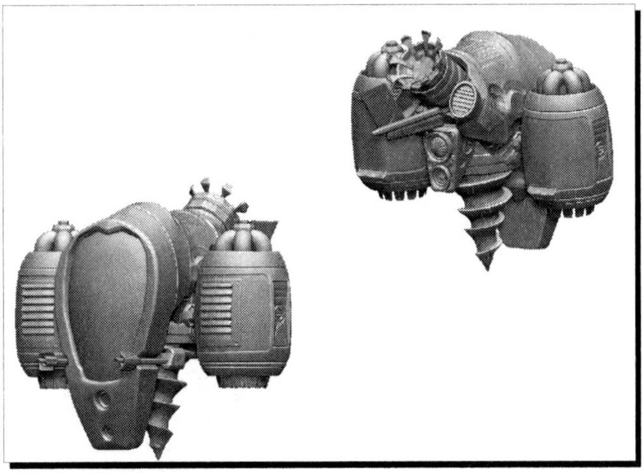

## What you'll need for this book

First of all, make sure, you have at least ZBrush version 4.0 installed on your computer.

> ZBrush is very fast, but still requires a computer with a bit of horsepower. It takes full advantage of multiple cores in your computer or more RAM-Memory, the more the better. Still, a dual core processor with 1 or better 2 GB of RAM will probably be sufficient to work you through this book. If this is all Greek to you, but your computer isn't age-old, it will probably work out well, too.

Another important point to mention are pen tablets. They usually consist of a tablet and a pen, imitating real drawing on your computer. You can still work in ZBrush just with your mouse, but it is highly recommended to use a pen tablet. They are affordable, depending on the working size you choose. Using ZBrush with a pen tablet not only saves you a lot of time, but is also more fun, because it feels very intuitive and natural.

If you ever tried to paint with a mouse, you know that it's a lot faster with a pencil.

> If you think of buying a pen tablet `www.wacom.com` is a very well-known manufacturer.

This book assumes you're working with ZBrush on Windows. So if you're on a Mac, remember that the Control Key (*Ctrl*) we'll refer to is the Command Key (*Cmd*) on your keyboard instead.

# Terminology

There are six terms we will refer to most of the time in this book: **Vertex**, **Edge**, **Polygon**, **Quad**, **Triangle**, and **Mesh**. Let's see, how we can use them to describe a model of a hand, as shown in the following image:

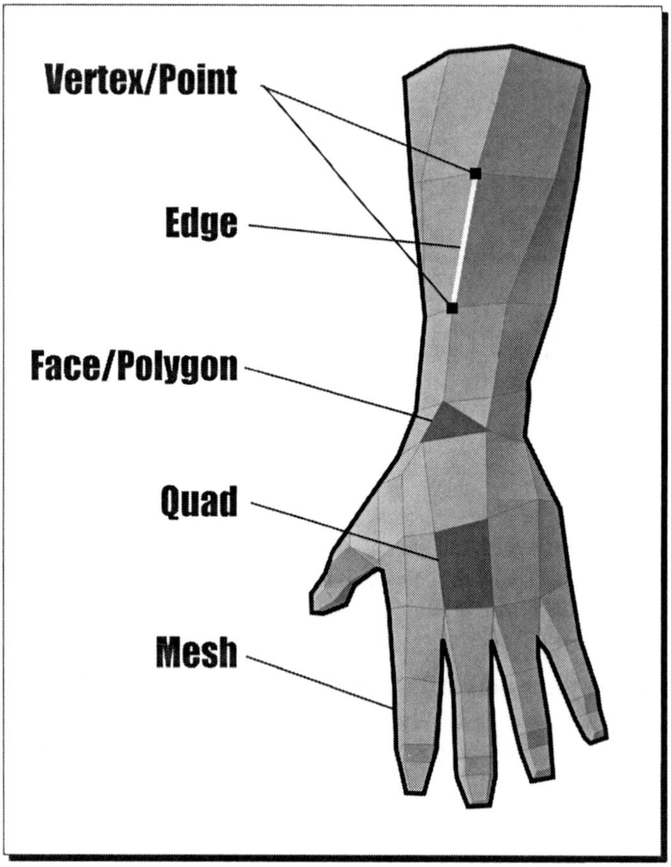


Let's see what they mean in detail:

- A point in 3D space, is also called **Vertex**
- Two connected vertices form a line in 3D space, which is called an **Edge**
- At least three points form a "polygon", which is sometimes also called a **Face**
- More precisely, a polygon made out of exactly three vertices is called a **Triangle**, four vertices form a **Quad**
- The entire hand is composed of several "polygons" forming a **Mesh**

# Working in the field of digital art

The most important thing about working in digital art seems to be very obvious but is often overlooked. It's a form of art and it should also be treated this way. This is something that you should have in mind when working on 3D game models or even concept art, because things such as color and composition will always be part of your work, even if not addressed explicitly.

This doesn't mean that you have to be the world's best painter to start in game art, but just think of your work as art, and also apply the rules of art to it.

Although job positions in game production include the term "artist", for example "concept artist" or "character artist", it is still a field that combines technical and artistic knowledge, and sometimes one outweighs the other.

ZBrush is a very good example of how creating digital art becomes less technical, so more and more people are able to give it a try. As this becomes easier and easier, the real distinction between digital artists will lie in their artistic capability, not their technical knowledge.

If you already have some experience in drawing or painting or even sculpting, it will be even easier for you to use ZBrush. I personally believe that if you can draw it, you can also sculpt it in ZBrush, because both mediums have so much in common.

Like every skill, creating art requires practice. We'll address decisions made out of artistic reasons in this book, so you can decide if you follow them, or alter the examples to your own imagination. Because at the end of the day, it all comes down to being able to give reasons for your decisions.

# The concept

The **concept** is quite an important step in the creative process. Some people like to do it in writing to maybe share it with others, some just do it for themselves. Like the preceding paragraph stated, it's important to be able to explain your decisions. So at first, you need to know the purpose of your 3D-model. Sometimes, you may get such a concept from your Art Director, or you're given the freedom to create your own. To illustrate the latter case, let's imagine a character and do this process in short, so you can see how much this first concept can improve the process and the resulting piece of work.

This example will be written like a really short background story for the character, to give it some personality. Again, there are many ways of doing this and you are encouraged to find the ones that work best for you, because it depends on your personal style of working.

# Time for action – a short example of a concept

Let's imagine we want to create a robot for a game and are given all the freedom we want (which will probably only be the case in personal projects, but it's a good example of how things could work). So we write down short, let's say three, sentences to better define our character.

1. Let's imagine there is not just one, but two robots guarding a city for over a thousand years.
2. Both of them were given orders at the time of creation, but are not to be controlled any further.
3. They haven't moved since their creation, so they probably won't in the future, it's just a tale, right?

## *What just happened?*

Let's see how our imagined robot takes form with each sentence.

"*create a robot for a game*"

At this stage we don't have much of a clue what the robot could look like.

1. *Let's imagine there is not just one, but two robots guarding a city for over a thousand years.*

   Now we could imagine two robots, maybe like brothers in arms, big enough to guard a whole city. They must be strong, but also protective, so that bright, positive colors in combination with white come to mind. Maybe they have features of a knight being loyal beyond death. They could even feature building parts of the city itself as being a part of it. As for the posture, something very calm and resting could fit. Maybe they are sitting opposite to each other, awaiting their call.
2. *Both of them were given orders at the time of creation, but are not to be controlled any further.*

   This may result in a neutral, machine-like expression on their face, following orders, without emotion and questioning, for ages.
3. *They haven't moved since their creation, so they probably won't in the future, it's just a tale, right?*

   This even tells something about their future movement, maybe they move like a child, who has to learn walking and is struggling to keep the balance. It's crucial to bear in mind how the character would move while creating or modelling. Don't waste your time by modeling a character that can't move properly in the end.

The second part of the sentence also implies how others feel or think about the character, giving some hints about the background story and even creating some air of mystery with the uncertainty of their power.

When coming up with concepts for mediums like film or games, which have a high demand for emotions, it's often helpful to also express them in writing style.

This was just the beginning. Depending on the rest of the storyline, especially the period these characters live in or even the target audience, many different robots could arise from this short concept.

However, only three sentences made up a much clearer image of what we would like to achieve. With such goals in mind, you can always step back and check if your digital sculpture serves the same purpose as the concept. This will greatly improve your final work, because every part of it will serve a purpose, defined in the beginning. Searching such a purpose in other digital characters is also a great exercise.

It's also important to notice that a concept not only tells you what to do, but also what not to. Nonetheless, it's just a starting point, and it will evolve during the whole process.

## Have a go hero – imagine your own concept!

Try to write a short concept on your own. Just start with a "thing" and then create a story around it, as shown in the previous example in around three sentences.

# Explore ZBrush on the Web

Now that you're digging into ZBrush, these websites are worth a visit:

`http://www.pixologic.com`. As the developers of ZBrush, this site features many customer stories, tutorials, and most interestingly the turntable gallery, where you can rotate freely around ZBrush models from others.

`http://www.ZBrushcentral.com`. The main forum with answers for all ZBrush-related questions and a nice "top-row-gallery".

`http://www.ZBrush.info`. This is a wiki, hosted by pixologic, containing the online documentation for ZBrush.

# Summary

In this chapter, we've learned quite a lot about ZBrush, how to use it in production, discussed the most important terminology and finally talked about digital art in general and the importance of a concept.

So, now that we've covered all the preliminary steps, let's throw a glance at the interface of ZBrush and create our first model.

# 2

# Learning the Interface

*Before we can start sculpting our first model, we have to talk about some very fundamental interface and modeling concepts in Zbrush so we can work smoothly hereafter. In this chapter, we will cover the basics of ZBrush's interface and will learn how to navigate in 3D space. Especially the interface can sometimes be very frustrating for beginners, so we'll take care of that.*

We will also take a closer look at:

- Navigating in ZBrush and using the interface
- How to customize the interface using the Trays
- The difference between "Documents" and "Tools" in ZBrush
- The difference between 2.5 and 3D in ZBrush

## Interface and navigation

In general, ZBrush's interface is quite different from others, but different does not mean better or worse. I find it very fast to work with, once you get used to it. But, let's try it out so that you can judge for yourself.

If you start ZBrush for the first time, your screen should look similar to the next screenshot:

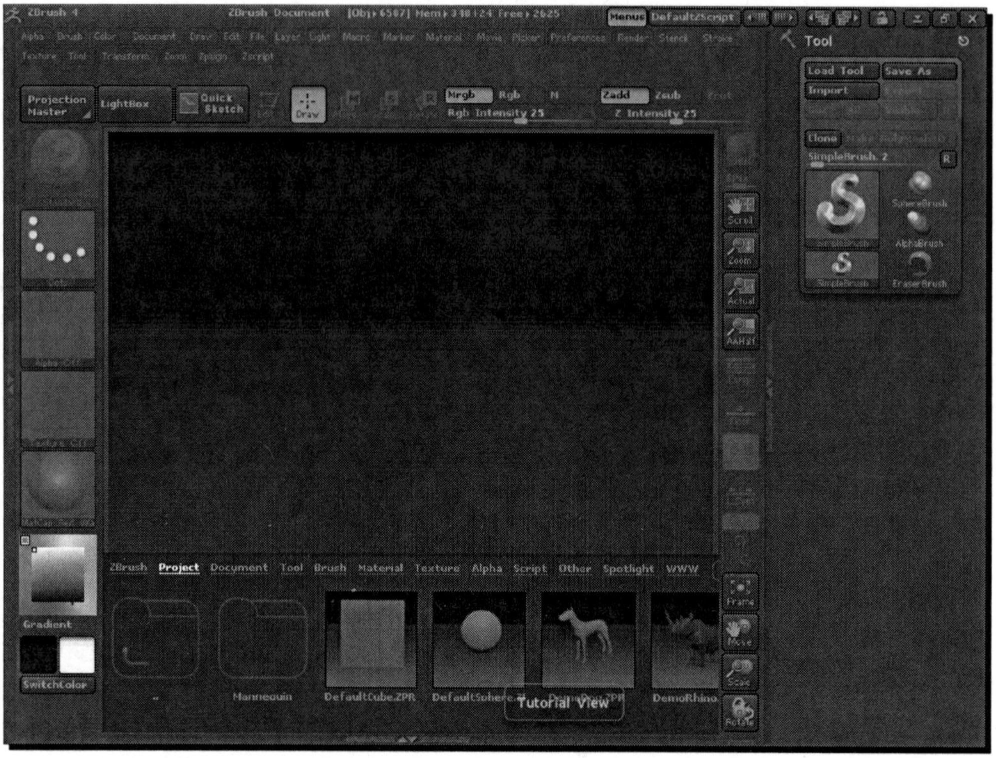


You'll probably notice that the biggest part of your screen is the work area, called the **canvas**, where you sculpt or paint your models. By default, the canvas is empty.

It is surrounded by the **shelf** where the most important functions are located to access them more quickly.

At the top of your window, you'll find the **Palette List**, where every function of ZBrush can be found. Also notice that the palette list is sorted alphabetically, which is not the common way of sorting menus, but is still very effective.

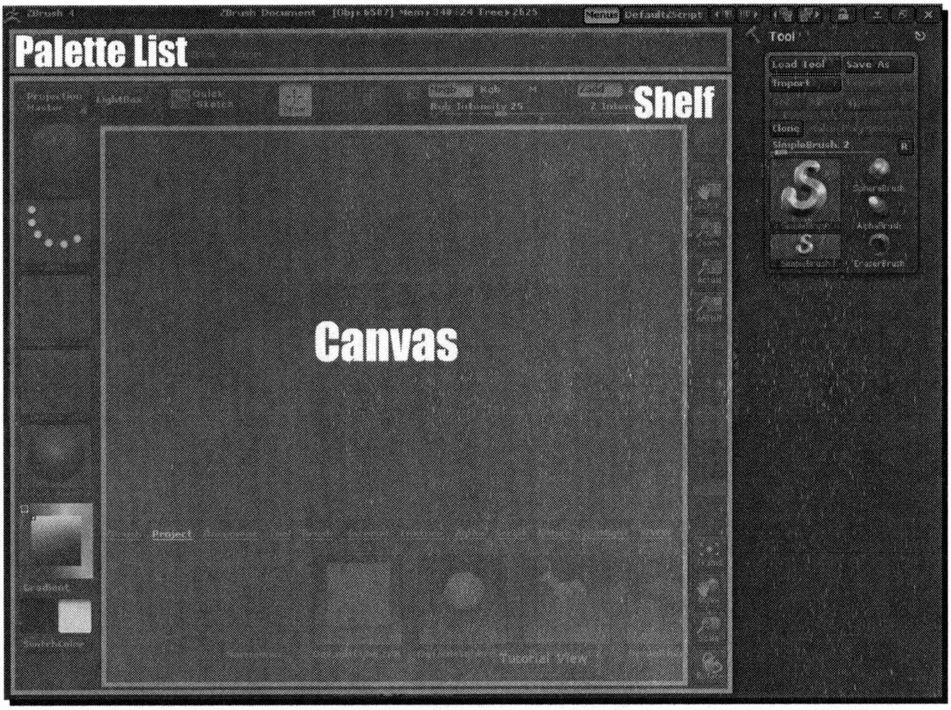


## Time for action – navigating in 3D space

To better learn the controls, let's try to navigate in 3D space. If you're using a pen tablet, a *left-click* means touching the tablet with the tip of the pen.

1. Before we start, we have to load a model to navigate around. Open the **Lightbox** by clicking its button, which is also labeled **Lightbox**, as shown in the next screenshot:

2. In the Lightbox that opens, choose the **DefaultCube.ZPR** by double-clicking on it.
3. If prompted, choose not to save any changes. Left-click anywhere on the cube to start sculpting by pushing the surface outwards.

4. When holding *Alt* while left-clicking, it will inverse the direction and push the surface inwards.

5. Left-click and drag on one of the three buttons **Move, Scale,** and **Rotate** to navigate in your 3D Scene. They are located on the lower right side of the shelf, as shown in the next screenshot.

6. If something goes wrong, just reload the default Cube from **Lightbox**.

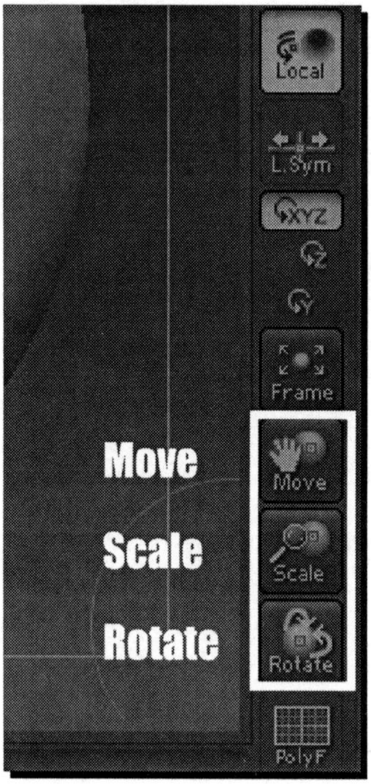


7. Because we'll navigate all the time when modeling in ZBrush, let's see how we can use some hotkeys to speed things up a bit.

    - To **Rotate** your model, left-click anywhere on an unoccupied area of the canvas and drag the mouse.
    - To **Move** your model, hold *Alt* while left-clicking anywhere on an unoccupied area of the canvas and drag the mouse.
    - To **Scale** your model, Press *Alt* while left-clicking anywhere on an unoccupied area of the canvas, which is moving.
    - Now release the *Alt* key while keeping the mouse button pressed and drag.

## What just happened?

We've just learned how easy sculpting and navigating in ZBrush is.

By using hotkeys, we can navigate even faster in our 3D space without having to refer to the buttons on the shelf all the time. As we saw, the *Alt*-key is the main key for navigation.

If your model occupies the whole canvas, you can either use the buttons to navigate, or move your mouse near the border of the canvas into the **navigation area**, to navigate as usual. As an indicator, the cursor switches to a rotation icon when inside the navigation area, as shown in the following screenshot:

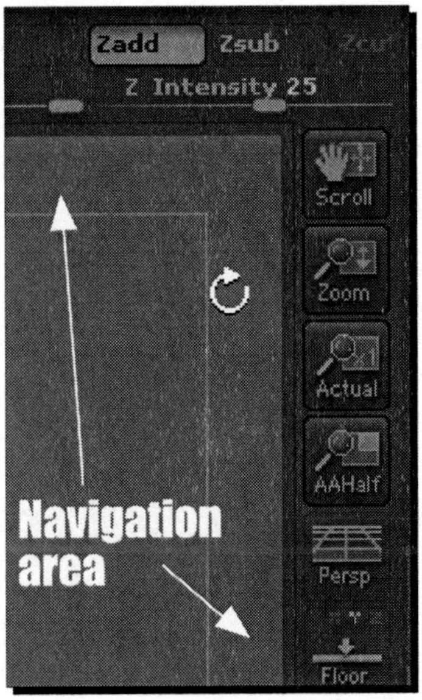

[ Notice that left-clicks can rotate your model, or alter its surface, depending on where the cursor is placed:

When your mouse cursor is placed on the model, left-clicking will alter the surface.

If you left-click outside of the model, on the canvas, you'll rotate the model. ]

The same applies to the *Alt* key. We saw in the first example that holding the *Alt* key when left-clicking on the model inverses the direction of the current brush. The second example showed that holding *Alt* when left-clicking outside of the model will move the model around instead of rotating it.

# More on the interface – The Tray

You've probably noticed that we haven't talked about the rows on the left-hand side and right-hand side of the screen, **The Tray**. By default, only the tray on the right-hand side is open and shows the tool palette. The point about the trays is that you can decide which palette they hold and also hide them to have a bigger canvas area to work with. Let's try that out, as shown in the next screenshot:

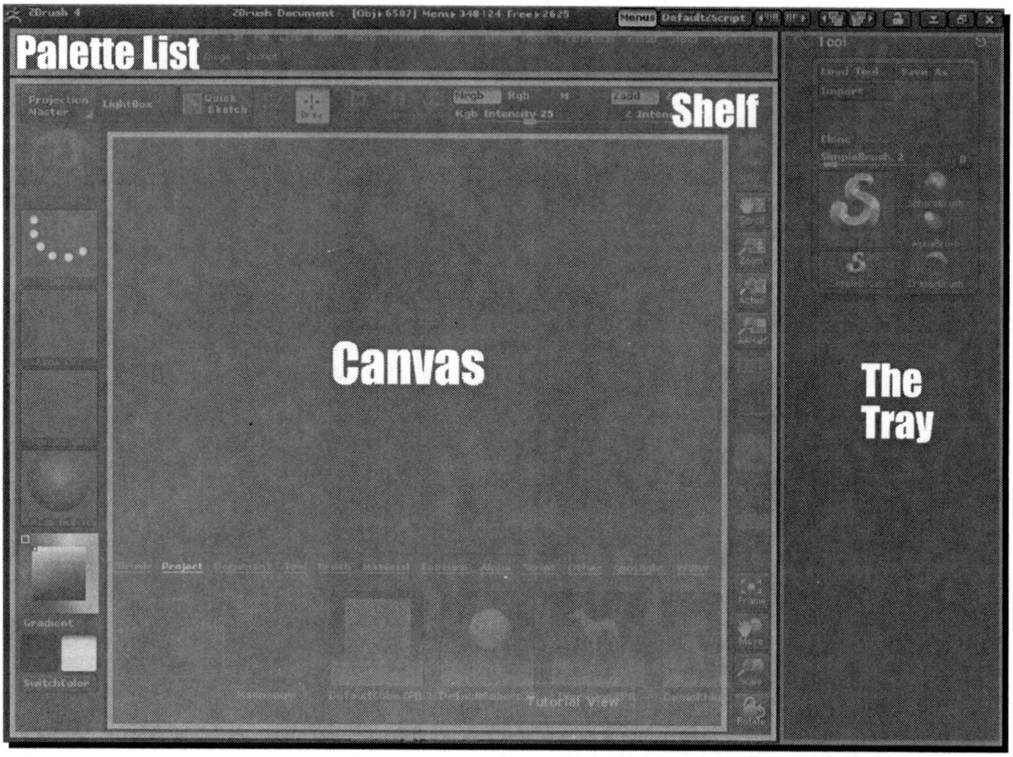


## Time for action – using the Trays

1. Open and close the right tray by clicking on the small arrow symbol on its left border, as shown in the next screenshot:

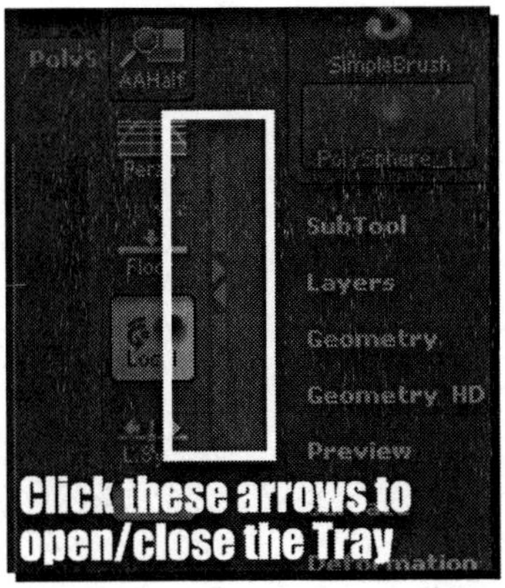


2. Open the hidden tray on the left-hand side of the screen, so that both trays are open.
3. Now let's move the tool palette from the right tray to the left. To do so, click-and-drag the tool palette handle from the right to the left tray.

4. Let's put another palette into our right tray, which is now empty. Open the **Document Palette** from the **Palette List** at the very top of your screen and drag its **palette handle** to the right tray, as you did in the previous step.

5. Your screen should now look similar to the next screenshot with the tool palette docked in the left tray and the document palette in the right:

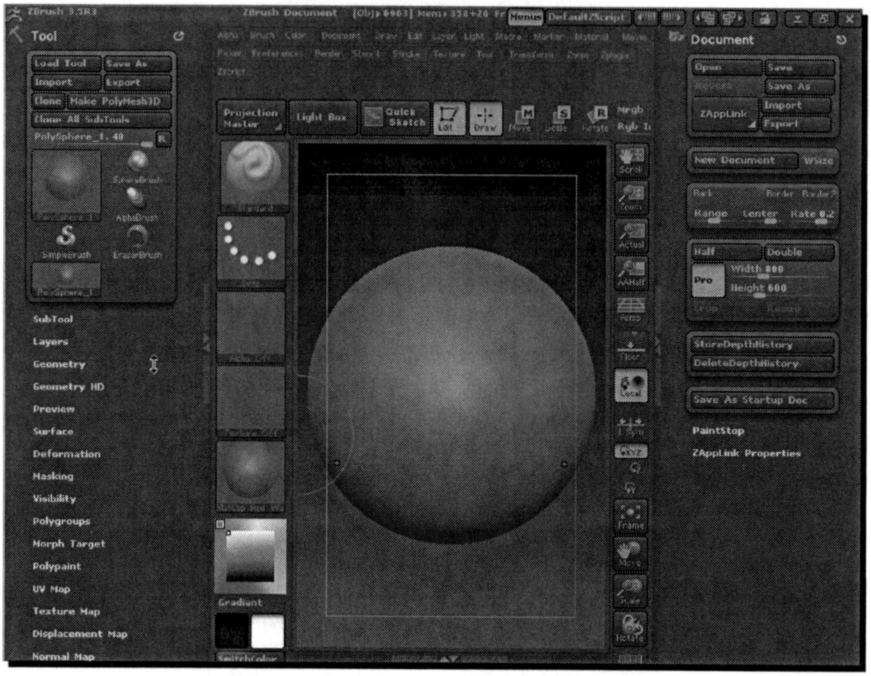


## What just happened?

We've just explored how we can customize our workspace in ZBrush to our liking by using the trays.

# Palettes

If you click on a palettes icon, instead of dragging, the palette will either be thrown out of the tray, or be put into the right tray by default. If you drag a palette from the palette list into a tray, it will still be there in the palette list, only a copy is put into the tray. So you don't have to worry about "losing" palettes.

## Trays

Trays can also have multiple palettes in them. If a palette has more menu entries than your screen can display, or if you have multiple palettes in one tray, you can scroll through them. Scrolling in a tray can be done by left-clicking in an unoccupied area in the tray, as shown in the following screenshot. This is the same principle as for rotating models by clicking in an unoccupied area:

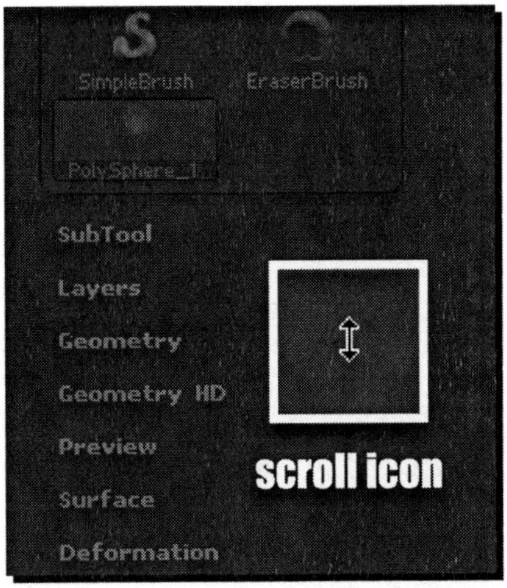


## Have a go hero – exploring the interface

Try exploring the interface more. There's much to be found. These tips will help you on your tour.

1. In the top-right corner of your window, there are two pairs of buttons with **layout presets** and **color presets**. Simply change them to your liking. Different layouts can also be useful for different tasks. The interface "Sculpt01" for example, is designed to efficiently handle sculpting tasks.

2. ZBrush will display the name of the chosen layout in the Note Bar. In the following screenshot, the layout "Sculpt01" was chosen.

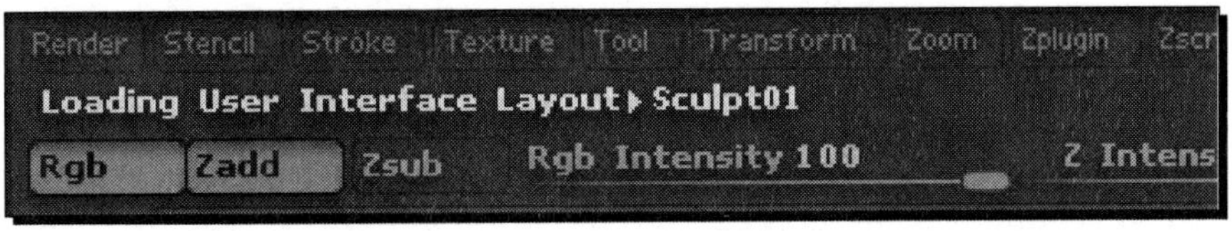

3. If you want to save your screen layout, navigate to **Preferences | Config | Store Config** in the palette list at the top of your window, which will store a configuration file. This will save all your presets, to be loaded on every startup. In the **Preferences**, you can also find many useful options, such as for using ZBrush with a tablet or to take full advantage of multiple cores for displaying your models. Just remember that your changes will be lost the next time you restart ZBrush if you haven't saved a configuration file.

4. The Note Bar is very helpful if you're not sure about the function of any button. Simply place your cursor over it and ZBrush will display a short info about it in the Note Bar at the top left-hand corner of your screen. If there's a hotkey for this function, it will also be shown. No need to read boring hotkey lists anywhere, it's right there under your cursor.

> To get a more detailed tooltip of a function, place your cursor over it and press the **Control Key (*Ctrl*)**. Some of these tooltips even come along with little pictures to explain things better. This allows you to learn new features as you go, which is very handy.

# The difference between 2.5D and 3D in ZBrush

ZBrush is a 2D and 3D program combined in one. This is why they invented the **Pixol**—a mix of 2D and 3D. In this book, we'll mainly focus on the 3D part of ZBrush, since for most games we need three dimensional models only. Nonetheless, to avoid confusion, let's see what makes the difference and how we can take advantage of this.

## Time for action – working in 3D with "Tools"

In ZBrush, 3D models are called **Tools** as opposed to **Documents**, which are 2D or 2.5D images. The main difference is that tools are 3D models that can be rotated or scaled while working with them. Documents, as being images, are a flat representation with optional information stored in them.

- Pressing **Document** | **Save As** will save our 2.5D work as a Document.
- Pressing **Tool** | **Save As** will save our 3D work as a tool.

Let's see how this can affect our workflow.

1. Open the **Lightbox** by clicking on its button. In the Lightbox that opens, switch to the **Tool** tab and choose the **Demohead.ZTL** by double-clicking it.

> As you see, ZBrush's native format of saving 3D models(tools) is `.Ztl`. ZBrush Documents are saved as `.Zbr`.

2. If your **Tool Palette** isn't permanently visible in a **Tray**, open the tool palette in your right-hand side Tray.
3. Notice that the image of the cube in the **Tool Palette** is now replaced by an image of the chosen head. The highlighted and bigger one of these images in the upper left is your active Tool, the others display the last used ones for quick access.

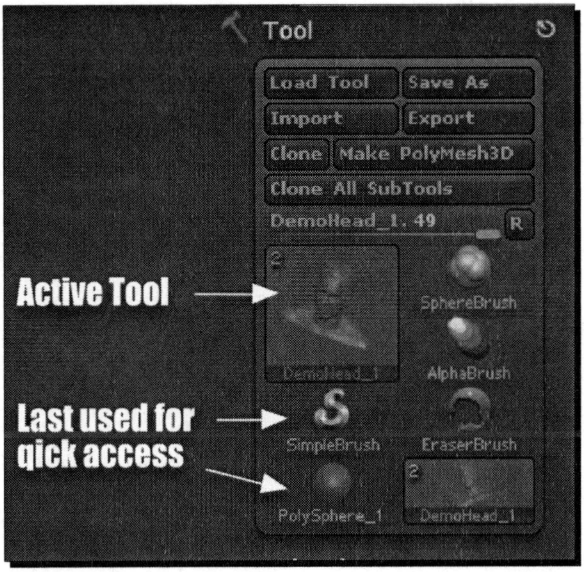


4. Navigate around your model as usual.
5. Now unclick the **Edit** button, or use the hotkey *T* to leave the *edit mode*. The hotkey will also be displayed in the note bar and in the tooltip as you hover over it, as shown in the next screenshot:

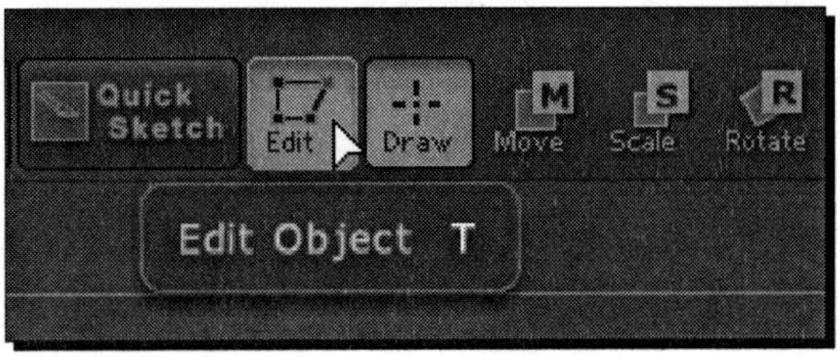

6. Now try to navigate again. As you left-click and drag on the canvas, instead of rotating the model, new instances of it are drawn.

7. Don't worry, your 3D model isn't lost, it's still stored in the tool palette. So all we have to do is create a new document by navigating to **Document | New Document**. You'll then be prompted if you want to save changes to the image or discard it. Discarding will only delete the image, not the 3D model.

8. With a clean canvas, draw the model again on the canvas by left-clicking and dragging once.

9. Now enter edit mode again, by clicking on the **Edit** button like we did before.

10. You can now freely rotate your model again and continue working in 3D.

## *What just happened?*

At the beginning of this section, we've learnt the most important thing: How to save our work.

Instead of saving our model with **Tool** | **Save As** we can also press *Ctrl* + *Shift* + *T*.

# The Edit mode

As we're mainly concerned about 3D, we may sometimes accidentally leave the *edit* mode, and drop our model onto the canvas, but now we know how to solve that.

This may seem like a workaround at first, but it really isn't. The 2.5D mode provides some nice features and is used by illustrators for example.

But what's the difference between 2D, 2.5D, and 3D anyway?

2D digital Images are a flat representation of color, consisting of pixels. Each pixel holds color information. Opposed to that, 3D models—as the name says—can hold 3-dimensional information. A 2.5D image stores the color information like an image, but additionally knows how far away the pixels in the image are from the viewer and in which direction they are pointing. With this information you can, for example, change the lighting in your 2.5D image, without having to repaint it, which can be a real time-saver.

To make this even clearer, the next list shows some of the actions we can perform, depending if we're working in 2D, 2.5D, or 3D:

> 3D – Rotation, deformation, lighting,
> 2.5D – Deformation, lighting, pixel-based effects
> 2D – Pixel-based effects

A pixel-based effect, for example, could be the contrast brush or the glow brush, which can't be applied to a 3D-model.

## How to enter 2D, 2.5D, or 3D mode

The switch for these modes is the **Edit** button. As shown in the earlier example, being in edit mode means we are working in 3D. When leaving the edit mode by unclicking the **Edit** button, our model is then "dropped" onto the canvas with the next action and we're now working in 2.5D. If we save this Document in ZBrush's native format for Documents (`.Zbr`) all 2.5D information will be stored. If we export it as a bitmap (`.bmp`), for example, it will automatically be converted to normal pixels, which can then be read by other applications.

Think of these modes like a hierarchy. A 3D model can always be converted to a 2.5D image by leaving the edit mode, but not vice versa. Also, a 2.5D image can be converted to a 2D image, but no 2D image can be converted to a 2.5D image or a 3D model. It works only in one direction, from more to less dimensions, as shown in the following diagram:

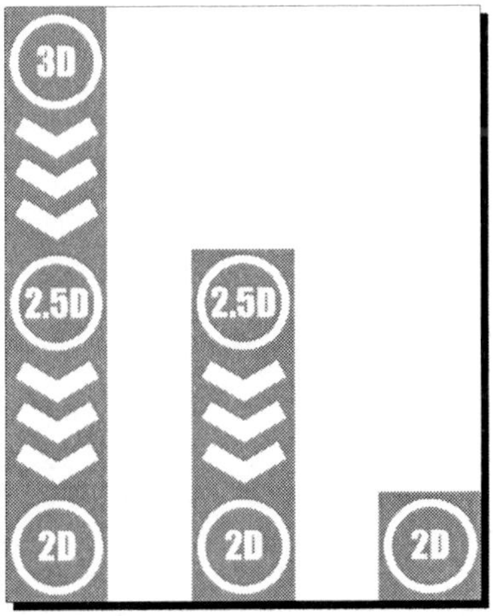

## Have a go hero – using the note bar and the tooltips

Now that we have learned about the dimensions we can work with, let's use the tooltips to figure out some hotkeys for the following useful functions:

- **Divide**, found under **Tool | Geometry | Divide**
- **Activate Symmetry**, found in the **Transform** panel.
- **Draw Size**, found under **Draw | Draw Size**.

## Pop quiz – 2D, 2.5D, and 3D mode

1. How can we switch between 2.5D and 3D mode?
    a. By using the *edit* button
    b. By stopping to rotate in 3D space
    c. By creating a new canvas
2. In ZBrush, a 3D model is considered a:
    a. Brush
    b. Document
    c. Tool
3. What can't be done with a 2.5D Document?
    a. Painting
    b. Rotating
    c. Lighting

# Summary

Throughout this chapter, we became familiar with the interface of ZBrush. We've learned that:

- Our interface is divided into the canvas—where we work most of the time, the palette list—which is our menu at the top, and the shelf—where the most used buttons are placed for quick access.
- We can rotate easily by left-clicking outside of the model or in the navigation area. In combination with the *Alt* key, we can also move and scale our model.
- We can customize and hide our **Trays**, which are located at the left-hand side and right-hand side of our window.

- Learning ZBrush on your own isn't complicated at all, just use the tooltips by pressing *Ctrl* while placing your mouse cursor over any button.
- There's a difference between 2D, 2.5D, and 3D and what each mode can be used for. We could use:
    - 3D mode for sculpting 3D models.
    - 2.5D for creating an image with advanced settings like materials and lighting.
    - 2D for exporting images to other applications.
    - Entering or leaving the edit mode switches between 3D and 2.5D.

# 3

# Modeling a Spooky Tree with ZSpheres

*In this chapter, we will create the rough model for our spooky tree introducing ZSpheres, which is a technique unique to ZBrush. This allows for very fast model creation without having to worry too much about the technical details. After we're done with the rough model,we'll then convert it into a mesh to prepare it for sculpting for the next chapter.*

We'll take a closer look at:

- The workflow when working with ZSpheres
- The edit mode
- Brush settings
- Building the spooky tree with ZSpheres
- Previewing and converting ZSpheres into a polygonal mesh for sculpting
- How to work with draw modes and perspective distortion

In the following chapters, we'll finish our model by adding details and some environment to our tree and finally, paint it using polypaint.

So let's get started.

# ZSpheres workflow

ZSpheres is a technique, unique to ZBrush, which allows us to create a model from scratch directly inside ZBrush. You'll see that this is a very fast way to rough out a model. As ZSpheres have a round shape, this technique is especially useful for organic forms, like a tree or a character, but less useful for modeling more straight forms like a building.

In the first chapter, we discussed different workflows of creating game models. For our first one, we'll mainly rely on ZBrush, as the following image shows:

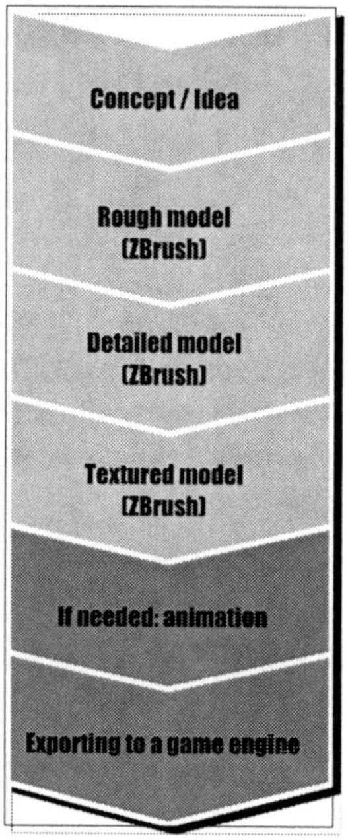


# The concept of the spooky tree

Imagine if we had to create a place for a role playing game, where the players will meet a strong boss monster. So the place has to be recognizable and moody to ensure that the players will find it and have a feeling about it that only something bad could live there.

The following image shows our concept art for the spooky tree. As for the concept, the tree should be spooky and old, which leads to the crooked branches and the slight twist in the trunk. Also, the hard contrast in the moonlight gives the image more power and mood, which leaves the viewer feeling a bit uncomfortable. The entrance of the tree, the pattern of the bark, and also the mushrooms underline the feeling of rough nature, not a place to be for a human being. Viewed in silhouette, the tree forms some kind of claw, reaching for the moonlight.

## Time for action – preparing the spooky tree with ZSpheres

So let's see, how we can realize a rough model to start from with ZSpheres.

1. Open the tool palette either in a tray or via the palette list at the top of your window.
2. Click on the largest image, which is the current tool.
3. Select the **ZSphere** from the pop-up menu, as shown in the following screenshot:

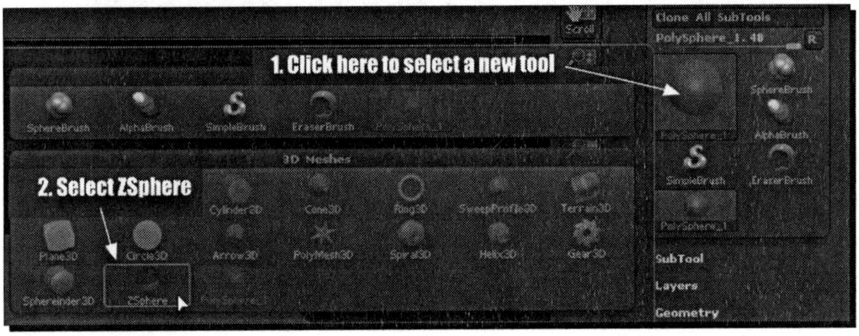

4. If you were in **Edit mode**, when selecting the ZSphere, ZBrush will automatically enter **Edit mode** for the newly selected tool. If not, follow the steps we discussed in the previous chapter. Create a new document, draw the ZSphere on the canvas, and then enter the **Edit mode**.

5. If you hold *Shift* while drawing the ZSphere on the canvas, it will be drawn aligned to the global axis.

> When rotating you can also make use of the *Shift* key to snap your view in 90 degree steps.

6. When working with ZSpheres, we'll only use the **Draw**, **Move**, **Scale,** and **Rotate** buttons, so using their respective hotkeys (see the following screenshot) from early on will make you work much faster:

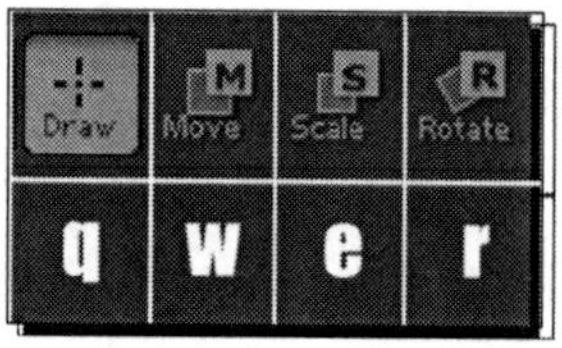


7. Because our model isn't symmetrical, make sure **Transform | Activate Symmetry** is off.

8. Your ZSphere should now look similar to the next screenshot, properly aligned, without symmetry, and in **Edit mode**:

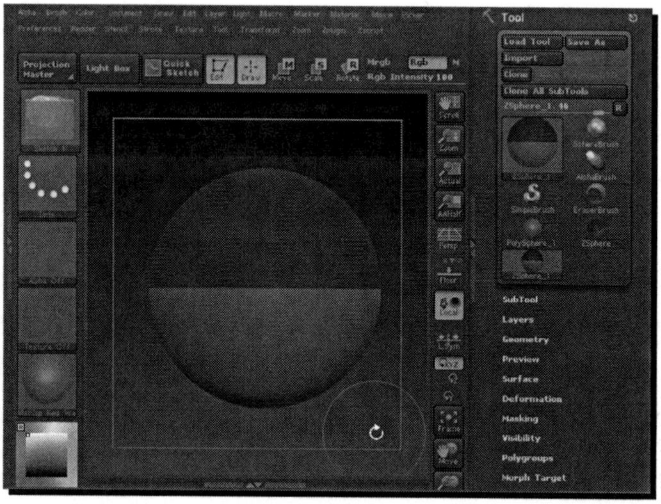

9. It's time to save our tool, so press *Ctrl* + *Shift* + *T*, and give it a proper name, ideally with a number at the end, so we can save in increments (`Spooky_Tree001.ztl`, `Spooky_Tree002.ztl`, and so on)

## What just happened?

We just started our first model by adding and saving a ZSphere.

We chose our ZSphere Tool and made sure that it is in edit mode and symmetry is turned off. Also, we learned that the *Shift* key can be used to align a model or the viewing angle. Using the four hotkeys *Q*, *W*, *E*, and *R* saves us a lot of time, when working with ZSpheres.

Now that we've taken care of all preliminary steps, let's go ahead and form a spooky tree from that.

## Time for action – starting the spooky tree with ZSpheres

1. Enter **Draw mode** by pressing *Q* on your keyboard and draw another ZSphere onto the first one by left-clicking and dragging.

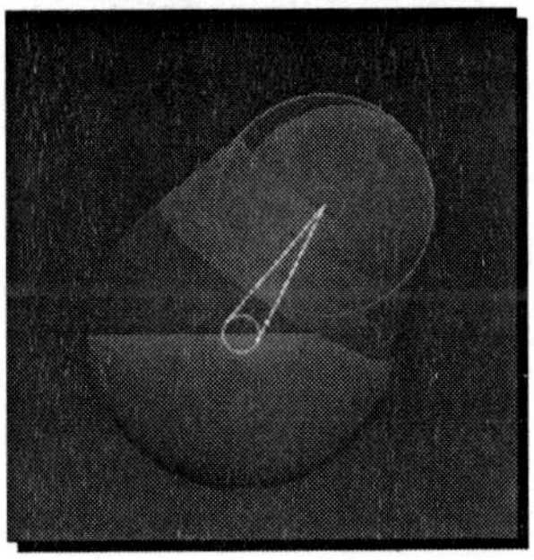

Use **Edit | Undo** (*Ctrl* + *Z*) or **Edit | Redo** (*Ctrl* + *Shift* + *Z*) to revert or redo any changes to your model. In the **Edit** panel, the respective buttons also display how many undos or redos are currently available.

It's easier to work with ZSpheres with your **Draw Size** set to **1**, so you don't accidentally affect any neighboring ZSpheres. You can set your draw size in the shelf at the top, but it's faster to use the hotkeys—*Spacebar* or right-click. This will bring up the **Quick menu** at your cursor, where the most important functions are located, like the **Draw Size**. This menu allows you to do most of the work without needing to refer to the interface all the time.

When creating the first sphere, which is the **root sphere**, bear in mind that it should be somewhere in the middle of the trunk because we can't delete the root sphere without deleting the whole model. This way we can spread out the branches and roots respectively from it and also delete them if we want to.

2. With your **Draw Size** set to **1**, you can now **Draw, Move, Scale,** and **Rotate** ZSpheres by switching to the appropriate modes and create your spooky tree, as shown in the following image:

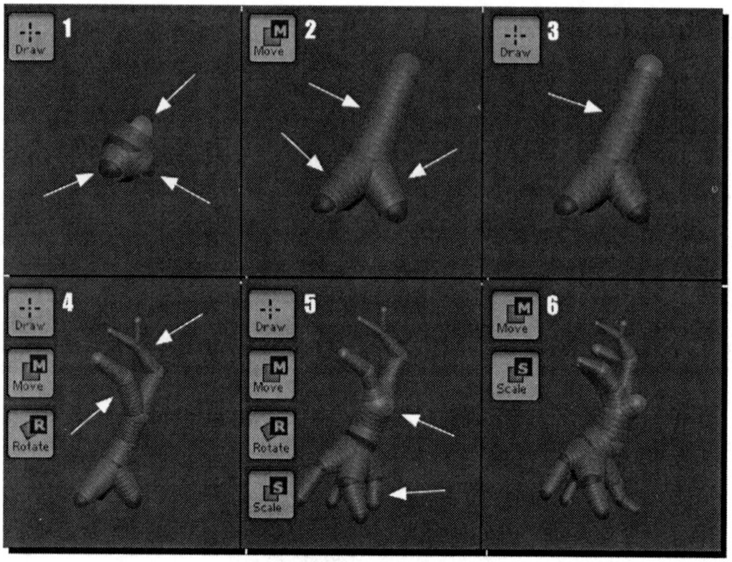


3. In the first step of the previous image, we start by drawing one sphere on the top of our root sphere to be the trunk. Then we draw three additional spheres at the bottom of our root sphere, which will become the roots of our tree.
4. In the second step, we move the newly created spheres into place.
5. The third step shows that we can also insert new ZSpheres between two connected ones with the draw tool, by just left-clicking on the connection.
6. In the steps four to six, we repeat this process over and over again to refine our model, also utilizing the **Scale** tool.
7. We can always **preview** our mesh by pressing the *A* key . Pressing it again will switch back to the ZSpheres.

> Always rotate your model to see if it looks correct from different angles.

## *What just happened?*

We've just learned how fast we can create rough models using ZSpheres. Using the **Draw**, **Move**, **Rotate,** and **Scale** tools, we defined the form of the tree. If we're not pleased with the results, we can use the `Undo` or `Redo` function. We can also define the minimum number of **Undo** steps ZBrush will store, under **Preferences | Memory.** By default, this is set to four, which means ZBrush will save as many steps as there's memory available, but at least four. If the defined memory limit is exceeded, ZBrush will write to your hard disk.

We also made sure that the root sphere is positioned in the trunk because we can't delete it later on. When creating a human character for example, you could place it in a crucial area such as between the shoulders or in the hips.

The **Quick menu** (*Spacebar* or right-click) helps us to change the brush size quickly, even with the interface hidden.

If you only want to affect the draw size, you can also press *S* on your keyboard. Like the **Quick** menu, it will always be located under your cursor. So you can just click-and-drag to change the brush size without worrying about where your cursor is.

When we're finished with the ZSpheres at the end of this chapter, we'll have to convert them into polygons, to sculpt in the fine details. By pressing *A*, we'll get a quick preview of what this converted mesh would look like. Use this preview to identify any irregularities or problems while working. You can also find the settings for this preview under **Tool | Adaptive Skin**.

## Pop quiz – the root sphere and adaptive skin preview

1. Why is it so important where the first (root) sphere is placed in our model?
    a. Because it is so big
    b. Because it can't be deleted
    c. Because the root sphere must be hidden inside the mesh
2. How can we preview what our ZSpheres will look like when converted into polygons?
    a. By opening the quick menue with space bar
    b. By leaving edit mode or by pressing T
    c. By toggling Tool | Adaptive Skin or by pressing A

## Have a go hero – Link Spheres

Let's see how we can control our ZSpheres even better.

When you drew your first ZSphere, you may have noticed the white bone-like lines, bridging the gap between two ZSpheres, the so-called **Link Spheres.** They will be visible when you draw a new sphere, or left-click on an existing one with the **Scale**, **Move,** or **Rotate** tool.

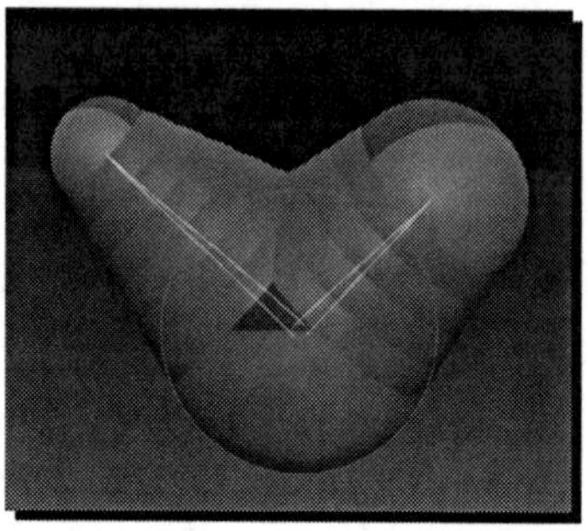

See what happens, if you move or rotate these Link Spheres, instead of the ZSpheres themselves. You'll see that Link Spheres can give us much more control over the model structure.

## Time for action – finishing the tree

Let's finish our ZSphere model and convert it into polygons.

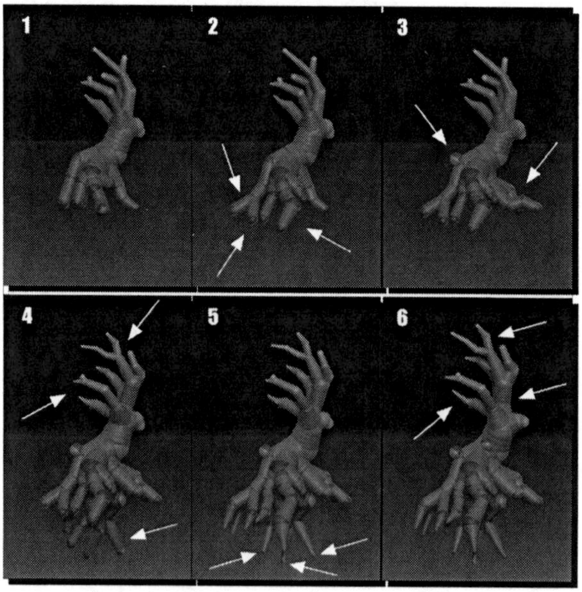

1. The first picture is there for reference, it is where we left off in the last example.
2. In the second step, we expand the roots more, referring to the concept. Make them longer, so we can stick them into the earth when adding a hill for the tree to sit on.
3. In the third step, we take care of the roots on the right side, forming some kind of entrance, following the concept.
4. Also the branches at the top should match the concept more. So here in the fourth step, we're making them more crooked and longer.
5. This fifth step is just for making the model easier to read by scaling the tips of the roots down. These won't be visible in the end, but with this little detail we increase the feeling of a tree. It also helps us in defining the shape of the roots, if we know their length.
6. In the last step, final adjustments are made making the branches a bit larger in relationship to the roots.
7. It's helpful to also check our model in perspective. You can do so by clicking the **Perspective Distortion** button or by pressing its hotkey *P*. Also the **Floor grid** button helps judge the proportions better:

8. Don't forget to save regularly.
9. If you followed the concept, the final ZSphere model should now look somewhat like the next image:

## What just happened?

With just a handful of tools, we created a whole base mesh of our spooky tree. This went quite fast, didn't it?

We also used the **perspective** and **floor** buttons to check our model's proportions. By default, when perspective is off, we're viewing our model in orthographic view, which means, objects that are of the same size won't be bigger or smaller if they are close or far away. For example, if you are viewing a human character from the side, in orthographic view, you can judge if both arms are of the same length.

> Games, for sure, have **perspective distortion**, so we always have to check our model both in orthographic and in perspective view.

## Time for action – converting our ZSpheres into polygons

Now it's time to check our ZSphere structure and eliminate any problems left with the topology.

1. First of all, open your tool palette in a tray and expand the **Adaptive Skin** subpalette. The settings we set in here will determine how our final polygonal model will look.
2. There are two modes of **adaptive skinning**—the newer one, and the classical skinning. Preview the mesh with **classical skinning** unclicked and then with **classical skinning** clicked, to determine which algorithm gives you better results. If both are the same, then ZBrush fails to skin your ZSpheres with the newer method and uses classical skinning as a fallback.
3. If you choose the newer skinning method, use the *Ctrl* key while placing your mouse cursor on the given settings to get more information. For solving topological errors, I would recommend simply pushing the problematic ZSpheres around a little, until the preview is clean, instead of relying on these options. Of course, if you want to control, for example, the density of your mesh, these options are the way to go.
4. To better find any errors in your skin preview, click on the polyframe button on the right side of your shelf or *Shift* + *F*:

5. If you choose the classical skinning method, which I took for the tree, we can see that errors mainly occur in the following two occasions.

   In the classical skinning process, think of a ZSphere as a cube, even if it's hard. If too many ZSpheres are expanding from one side of the parent-cube as in the following example, ZBrush tries to connect both of them to the same side. This results in a mesh where polygons overlap, which should be avoided:

6. The next example shows how we can solve this issue by just moving the child-ZSphere a bit. As you see, one is now connected to the top of the cube and one to the side, which is fine:

7. Here's another example of how we can alter the Zsphere structure to fix potential problems, especially in the roots of our tree:

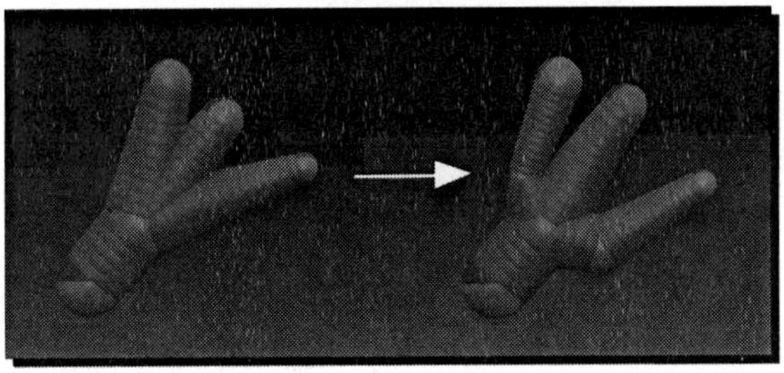

8. If you use classical skinning, correct your tree now, as shown in the previous examples.

9. If you're done, create an adaptive skin, by leaving the preview mode, and clicking on **Tool | Adaptive Skin | Make Adaptive Skin**. The default settings with **Density** set to **2** worked fine for the tree. Don't push the density too high, we can add more polygons later on.

10. Your newly created mesh is then added as a new tool.

11. Finally, save your ZSphere model and your generated adaptive skin separately since you can't create ZSpheres from an adaptive skin, only the other way around.

## What just happened?

We have now created the rough model of our spooky tree with ZSpheres.

We've learned much about the process of **Adaptive Skinning** and how to fix common problems. The **Draw Polyframe** helped us a lot to find errors in our preview mesh. Automatically created Polygroups are another advantage of ZSpheres. With Draw Polyframe enabled we can see that each Polygroup is assigned a different color. We will use them in the next chapter to hide certain parts of our mesh, which is especially useful for interwoven meshes, like our roots.

The next screenshot shows what our final adaptive skin looks like, with **Draw polyframe** enabled:

[ You can also download the example ZSphere model of the tree from this chapter, if you follow the link provided in the preface. ]

# Summary

In this chapter, we've started and finished our rough model of a spooky tree, ready to be sculpted in the next chapter. In this chapter, we saw that :

- We can directly start our models inside ZBrush with ZSpheres, which is fast as lightning.
- Working with ZSpheres mainly relies on four functions: **Draw**, **Move**, **Scale**, and **Rotate**.
- Every time we're not satisfied with an action, we can just undo or redo it.
- Placing the root sphere in a strategic location is important.
- We can convert ZSpheres into a polygonal mesh using the **Adaptive Skinning** method and learnt how to fix topological errors that might pop up.

Now that our rough model is ready, let's start with the sculpting part in the next chapter.

# 4

# Adding Details to the Tree

*In this chapter, we'll learn more about ZBrush's core feature—the sculpting. Starting with the rough model of the spooky tree of the last chapter, we'll now go ahead and detail it. We will learn more about the most important brushes for sculpting and how we can use subdivisions to add all the details we need.*

We'll cover in detail:

- The sculpting interface
- Choosing the right material for sculpting
- Sculpting in ZBrush (in particular the **Standard**, **Smooth**, **Move**, and **Inflat** brush)
- Controlling our brushes with the **Draw Size**, **Z Intensity,** and **Focal Shift** settings
- Hiding parts of the mesh to concentrate on specific areas
- Working with subdivisions
- Adding fine surface details to the tree

[ You can download the mesh of the tree by following the link provided in the preface ]

# The sculpting interface

Remember the screen layouts we tried out in Chapter 1? It's time to review them.

For the sculpting in this chapter, we'll use an optimized screen layout that comes along with ZBrush, the **Sculpt01-layout**. This allows us to handle sculpting tasks more efficiently.

## Time for action – using the interface preset Sculpt01

1. Switch to the interface layout **Sculpt01** by clicking on the interface layout preset button.

2. Our screen should now look like the next screenshot:

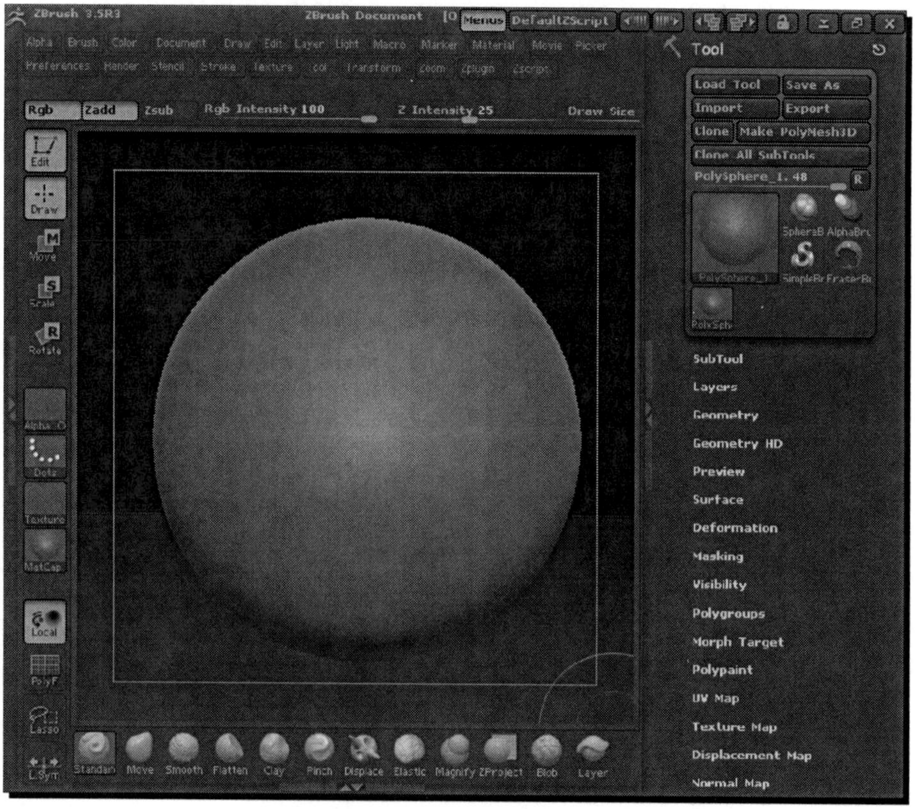

3. The main difference between this layout and the default one is the enlarged canvas and the list of brushes at the bottom. This list holds 12 brushes you can choose from. This way, we don't have to open the brush selection window all the time.

4. Let's change the fourth brush from the **Flatten** brush to the **Inflat** brush. Click on the **Flatten** brush and select the **Inflat** brush from the pop-up list.

> The brush list is quite overwhelming at first. To help find specific brushes, they are sorted alphabetically. You can also filter all brushes commencing with a specific letter by clicking on the letter at the top of the list or just by pressing the respective key.

5. To find the **Inflat** brush faster, open the **brush selection** and press the *I* key. This will only display brushes commencing with the letter I. If you did so, the other brushes will be grayed out and the letter you pressed will be highlighted, as shown in the following screenshot:

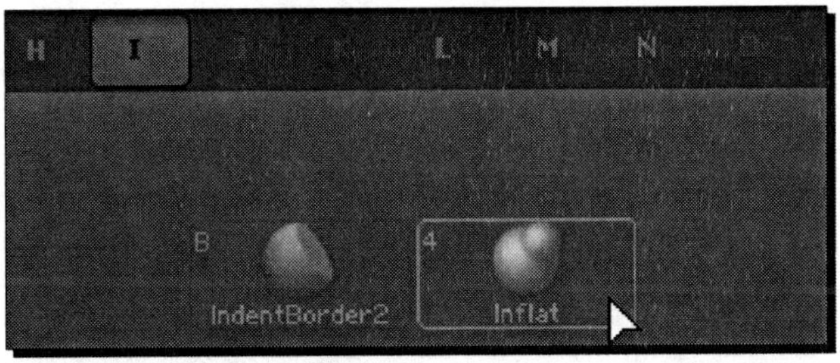


6. Now that you selected the **Inflat** brush, your brush list at the bottom should now look like this

## What just happened?

We've just used a customized interface and put the four brushes, we will use most, in the brush list at the bottom of our window for quick access. Note that this list is only visible in this custom screen layout.

We also learned that by hitting the respective key in the floating brush window, we can narrow our selection to all brushes commencing with the letter we pressed.

Now let's get a suitable material so we can start sculpting.

# Time for action – choosing the right material for sculpting

To know clearly, how the different brushes affect our mesh, let's choose a material well-suited for sculpting.

1. Load your mesh of the tree or the downloaded one. If you want to download the tree from the previous chapter, you can find the download address in the preface of this book. Load the mesh of the spooky tree by clicking **Tool | Load Tool** and then navigate to the respective folder.

2. Left-click on the material icon in the shelf on the left, as shown in the next screenshot. You can also find this material icon in the quick menu (right-click or *spacebar*):

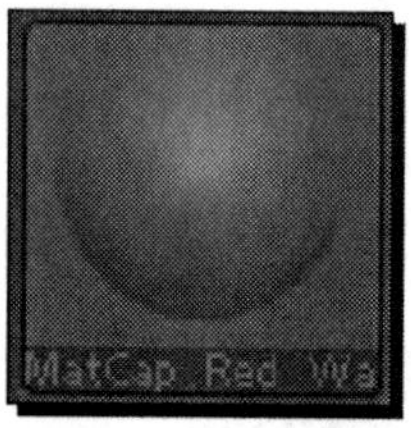


3. Choose a material from the pop-up, as shown in the next screenshot. Everyone has his or her own preferences about what the ideal material for sculpting should be. Some like the default material, some don't. I personally prefer working with **MatCap Green Clay** while sculpting. Find your own favorite!

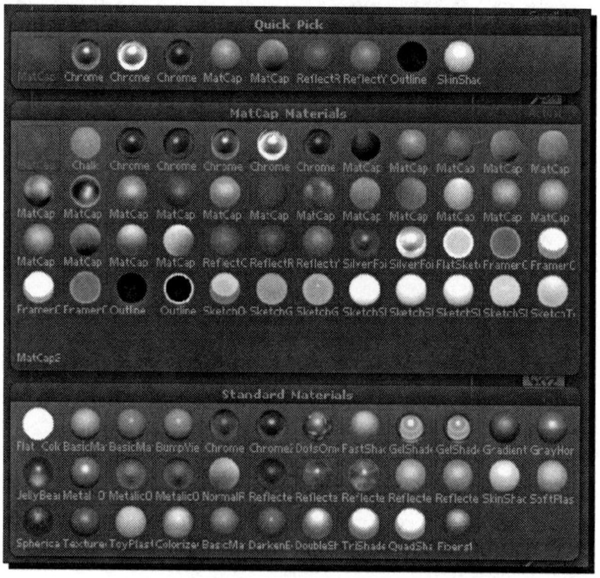

## What just happened?

We've just changed our material to fit our sculpting needs.

As we can see in the previous screenshot, the material pop-up is divided into three sections—the **Quick Pick**, the **MatCap Materials,** and the **Standard Materials**.

The **Quick Pick** is similar to the one we saw in the tools pop-up. It simply shows the last selected Materials.

**MatCaps** are materials that were captured from images. This is why they are named after real world materials like "skin", "clay", or "skeleton". The only thing to notice is that **Mat Cap** materials have predefined lighting stored in them, so we can't change the lighting direction or color. But this won't bother us most of the time, because for games all materials are defined by the game engine, so these are only for visual representation of our sculpt and will be ignored when exporting. As most of them simulate materials with very good lighting, these are very useful for sculpting, without having to set up the lights all the time.

**Standard** materials offer a wide range of customization. Opposed to **MatCaps**, they can be combined, lit by different light sources and have advanced effects, which are only visible when rendered.

## Pop quiz - materials

1. Which materials come with predefined lighting?
    a. Standard materials
    b. MatCap materials

## Have a go hero – download more MatCaps

On `www.pixologic.com`, in the download section, Pixologic offers a library of MatCaps created by ZBrush users, which are ready to download. Experiment with these or just have fun flipping through them.

If you want to use a downloaded **MatCap**, extract the `.zip` folder so you get a `.ZMT Material` file, which is ZBrush's Materials format.

Now let's see how we can open the `Material` file in ZBrush.

Open the material palette by clicking on the material icon, like we did before, and click on the **Load** button at the bottom of the pop-up window, as shown in the following screenshot.

In the dialog that opens, navigate to your `.ZMT` material file and click on **Open**.

The loaded material will replace the one currently active. When restarting ZBrush, all replaced materials will be restored, but we also have to load our material again.

If we want our material to be included permanently in our Material Library, we can just put it in our `ZBrush\ZStartup\Materials` folder. By default, the installation path is `C:\Program Files\Pixologic\ZBrush 4.0\ZStartup\Materials`. Because we placed the material in the startup folder, it will be loaded on every startup hereafter, so we have to restart ZBrush once for the changes to take effect.

## Time for action – using brushes

Now that we have our material ready for sculpting, let's directly jump in and talk about how to sculpt our model, using the **brushes** available in ZBrush.

1. With your tree model still open, select the **Standard** brush.
2. Draw on the surface. By default, the Standard brush will elevate the surface in one direction, as shown in the next screenshot:

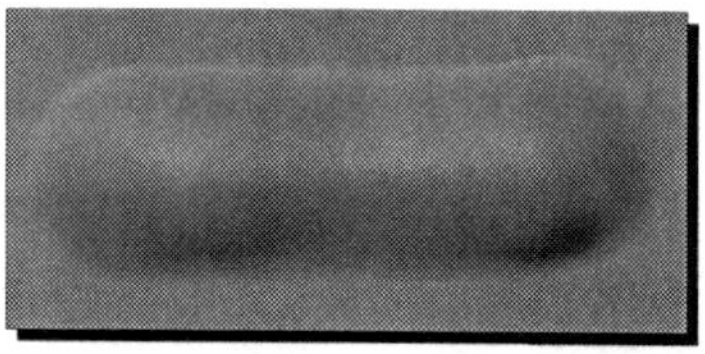

3. Hold down *Alt* while drawing. This will invert the direction of your brush, as the next screenshot shows:

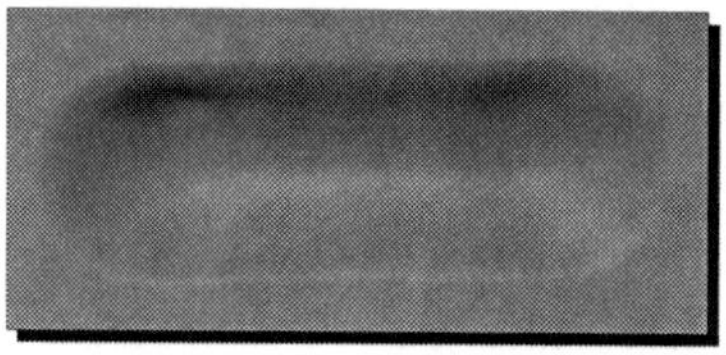

At the top of the shelf, you can find the three most important settings for every brush when sculpting, **Z Intensity**, **Draw Size**, and **Focal Shift**.

- The **Z Intensity** determines the strength of the brush effect.
- The **draw size** alters the size of your brush, which widens the area of effect.
- **Focal Shift** affects how soft or hard the falloff of your brush is at its border.

4. Experiment with the **Z Intensity** settings of the selected standard brush. The next screenshot shows three strokes with the standard brush with Z intensity set to 30, 60, and 90. Note that if you're working with a tablet, the brushes are still pressure-sensitive:

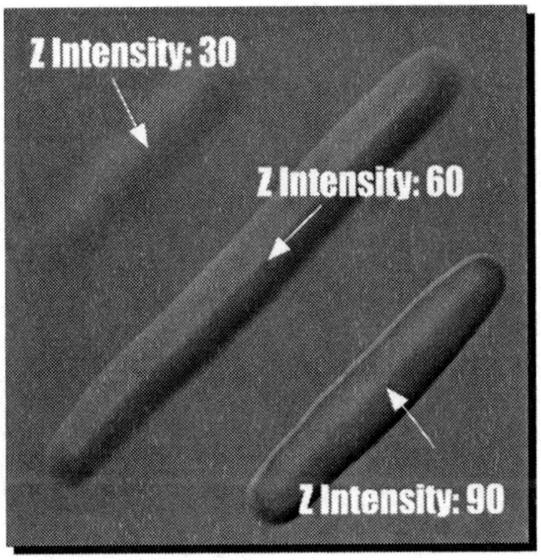


5. The **Draw Size** is quite self-explanatory, but there is one little trick to use it. The size of our cursor is relative to the canvas, not to the object. So if we scale our model up, the cursor keeps its size and thus is now smaller in relation to the object. So if we're sculpting in little details and scale our model up, our cursor automatically becomes smaller in relation to the object, as shown in the next screenshot. Try it!

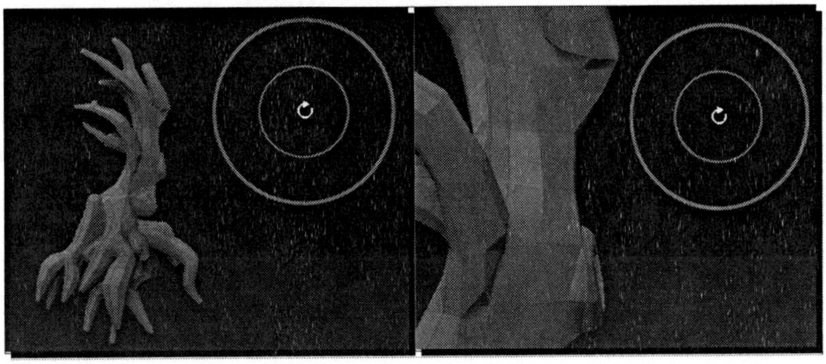

6. The **Focal Shift** sets the falloff of the brush. Too high or too low values can cause artifacts when drawing.

> As for visual representation, the outer circle of your cursor represents the draw size, whereas the inner one shows the Focal Shift.

7. Now that we're familiar with the brush settings and also the Standard brush, let's see what the other three brushes do. Pick the **Move** brush, and move some parts of the tree into shape, like the roots, as shown in the next screenshot. Alter the Z Intensity to strengthen the effect and the draw size to move more vertices at once:

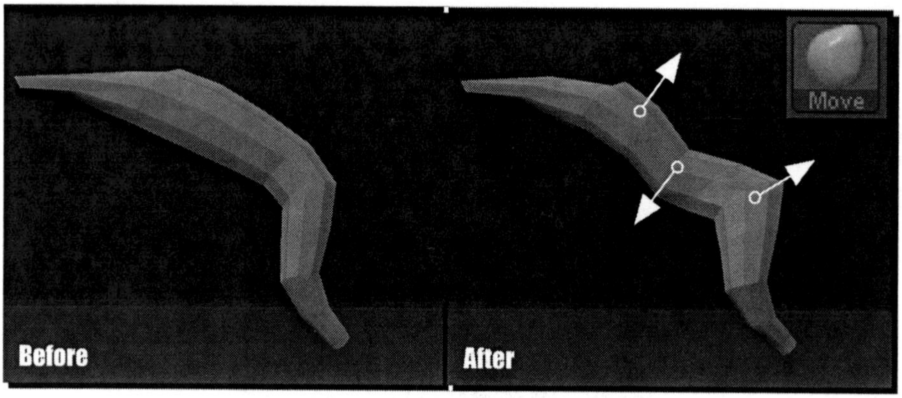


> When using different brushes, we can quickly switch to the **Smooth** brush by holding *Shift*. When releasing *Shift*, ZBrush will automatically switch back to our last selected brush.

8. Switch to the **Smooth** brush by holding down *Shift* and draw on your model to see the effect. It relaxes the polygons where it is applied. By default the Smooth brush can be quite strong. If you'd like to change that, hold down *Shift* and adjust the Z intensity.

9. When smoothing objects like the roots, they may look like spikes afterwards. We can use the **Inflat** brush to push the surface outwards again, as shown in the next screenshot. Opposed to the **Standard** brush, which pushes only in one direction, the **Inflat** brush pushes each polygon along its normal. This effect is similar to blowing up a balloon:

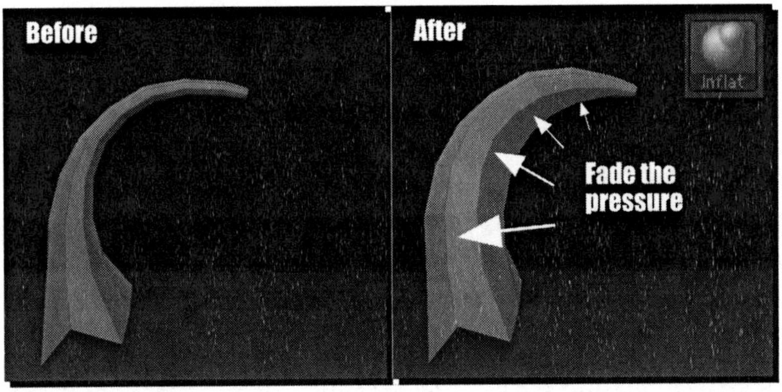


## What just happened?

We've seen how we can invert the direction of the Standard brush using the *Alt* key. This applies to most of the brushes in ZBrush.

The **Smooth** brush: The Smooth brush is bound to the *Shift* key, but why not the Standard brush, for example? This is because smoothing out the last done stroke is used frequently, so drawing and smoothing take turns all the time. As we've noticed, the Smooth brush is accessed exclusively by the *Shift* key, so its Z Intensity can only be altered while holding *Shift*. We've also found out that the draw size of the current brush also defines the draw size of the smooth brush.

# Controlling the brushes

To control the brushes more, we've seen how the **Z Intensity** affects the strength of the brush effect, how the **Draw Size** changes the area of effect, and also how the **Focal Shift** softens or hardens the falloff of the brush. Just remember that the draw size also affects the strength of the brush. This is because ZBrush assumes that if you want a bigger brush, you want a bigger effect, too.

Finally, we've learned about the four main brushes we'll use for sculpting the tree: The Standard, Move, Smooth, and Inflat brush.

## Pop quiz - brush settings

1. What key do you have to press to invert the direction of your brush?
    a. Alt
    b. Space bar
    c. Shift

2. What happens with your cursor if you zoom in on your model?
    a. It becomes bigger in relation to the model.
    b. It keeps its size in relation to the model.
    c. It becomes smaller in relation to the model.

## Time for action – shaping the spooky tree

Equipped with our four brushes, **Standard**, **Move**, **Smooth**, and **Inflat**, we'll now shape our tree.

At this early stage, our job is to establish the right form and silhouette. For this old and spooky tree we're looking for a kind of broken shape with a lot of contrast in form, like roots normally have, changing their direction often. Viewed from the left, the branches also form some kind of claw.

1. In the **Transform** palette, you can find two useful options, **Local Transformations** and **Rotate On Y Axis**. Turn on both, as shown in the next screenshot:

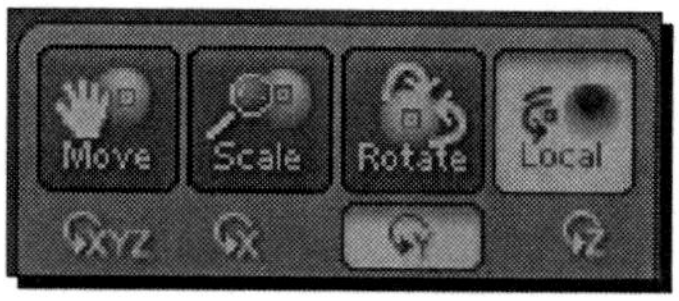


2. The ZSpheres gave us quite a good volume to begin with but a too rounded shape. Use the **Move** brush to transform the rounded shape into an old and crooked one, as shown in the next image:

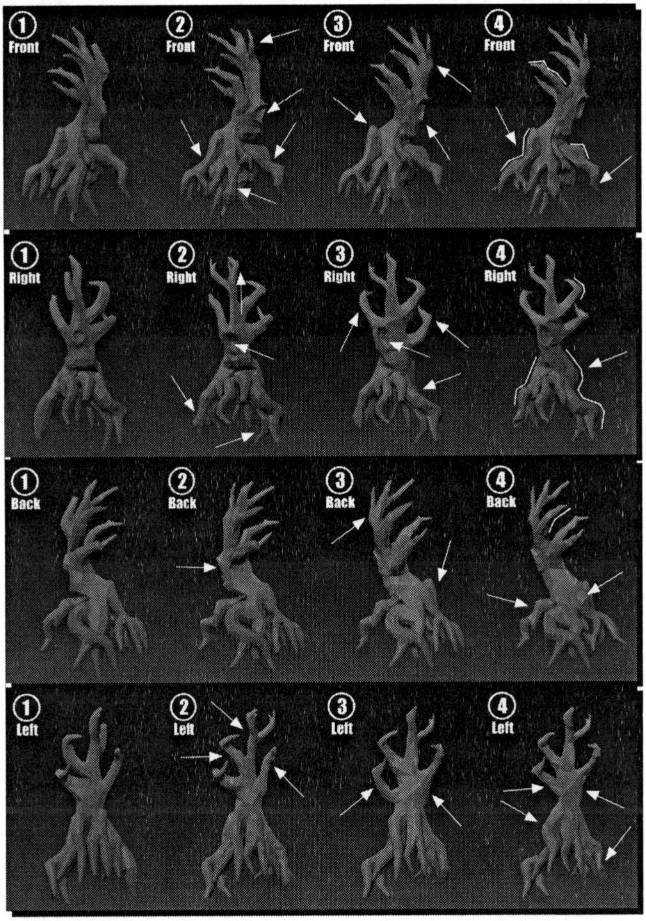


## What just happened?

We've just established the rough form of our tree, which is a crucial step in the modeling process.

# Local transformations and rotations

**Local transformations** are activated by default. If clicked, all transformations are done around the last edited point. This means, when sculpting the tip of a branch, it will also rotate around that point, which is very convenient.

**Rotate On Y Axis** is an option I prefer to have on, when working. This is closer to the navigation in other 3D programs. For sure this can also be the X or the Z axis, depending on which axis of your model points upwards. By default, XYZ rotation is enabled. Try whichever setting you like better for rotating your model.

# Time for action – isolating parts of the tree with Polygroups

In the last chapter, we've touched on having automatically generated **Polygroups** of our ZSphere model. We can use them for isolating parts of the mesh.

1. Load the model of the tree.
2. Activate **Draw Polyframe** by clicking on its button in the shelf on the right. You can also use the hotkey, which is *Shift + F*.

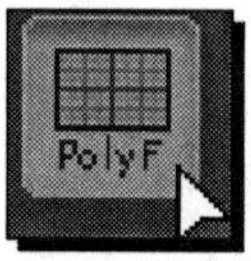


3. Our mesh now appears colored. Each color represents a **Polygroup** that ZBrush created from the structure of our ZSpheres.
4. We can now isolate polygroups to reveal roots, which are partly hidden by others. To do so, hold *Ctrl + Shift and* left-click on a Polygroup to isolate it. This will hide all other Polygroups.
5. To make everything visible again, *Ctrl + Shift* + left-click on an unoccupied area of the canvas.

## What just happened?

We've just found another advantage of working with ZSpheres, automatically generated Polygroups! This is very handy if the mesh has overlapping forms, like our roots do.

Note that hiding parts of the mesh can simply be **undone** by pressing *Ctrl + Z.*

We won't go into detail with this, just know that Polygroups are not exclusive to using ZSpheres. They can also be generated later on, if we didn't start from ZSpheres but imported a mesh, for example. At the moment, we can simply enjoy that ZBrush did this for us.

# Have a go hero – isolating several parts of the mesh with Polygroups

When isolating a root, like we did in step 4 of the previous example, we can invert the visibility by *Ctrl + Shift* + left-clicking and dragging a rectangle on an unoccupied area of the canvas. This way we're hiding the root, instead of isolating it.

Now we can keep on hiding parts with *Ctrl + Shift* + left-click.

With several parts hidden, try inverting the visibility again. You'll see that for isolating three roots, it's quicker to hide these and invert the selection than hiding everything else.

# Time for action – working with subdivisions

Now that we've moved our tree into shape, let's use **subdivisions** to add more polygons to sculpt.

When we created our **Adaptive Skin**, we set the density to **2**, which created a mesh from our ZSpheres with two subdivision levels. Let's see what we can do with them.

1. Load your mesh of the tree.
2. Navigate to **Tools | Geometry**. Ideally the **Tool** palette is permanently open in a tray.
3. In the **Geometry** palette, we can find a slider and a display of the current level of subdivision above it, stating that we're currently at subdivision level **2**. Use the slider to switch between subdivision levels and see the difference.
4. Let's add another level of subdivision by clicking on the **Divide** button. The small **Smt** button next to it determines if our mesh is smoothed when subdivided. For now, leave this option on. As you can see in the **Geometry** subpalette, ZBrush will automatically switch to the new subdivision level.

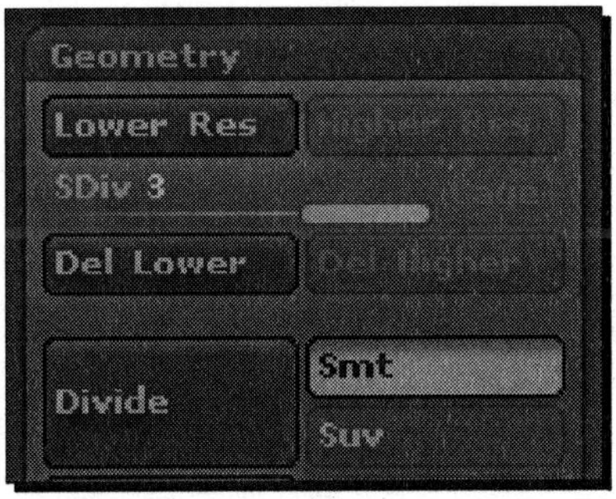


> **Subdivision hotkeys**
>
> As we will subdivide and switch between subdivision levels quite often, it's good to know the hotkeys from early on:
>
> Subdividing the mesh can be done with *Ctrl + D*.
>
> Switching to a higher level of subdivision is done by pressing *D*.
>
> To switch to a lower level of subdivision press *Shift + D*.

## What just happened?

We've just explored how to add millions of polygons to our mesh to sculpt all the details we need. Nonetheless, this has to be handled with care. It's best to finish the work on a lower level of subdivision first and then add another level.

The reason for this is, when subdividing, each quad is divided into four. This means four times the polygons, but also four times the work. Your model will always benefit when you work from low to high, not vice versa.

If you're already familiar with another 3D program, you're probably also familiar with subdivisions. The great thing about working with subdivisions in ZBrush is that we can work on every subdivision stage, not just at the lowest or highest.

What ZBrush does is applying every change made on one subdivision level, to the others. So if we want to make larger changes to our model, we can apply these on a low subdivision level, while preserving the detail of the higher levels.

For example, if we finish our tree consisting of millions of polygons, we decide to make the trunk thinner. This would be quite complicated, having to push thousands of points around. So we just switch back to our lowest subdivision level– which has around 500 polygons– and apply the changes. When stepping up in subdivision levels again, all our sculpted detail on the bark will be preserved, but the overall form has changed.

> Since for games it's always interesting to know how many triangles our mesh is made up of, we can look that up by hovering our mouse over the tree model in the **Tool** palette. The pop-up displays the **polygon count**, as shown in the next screenshot:

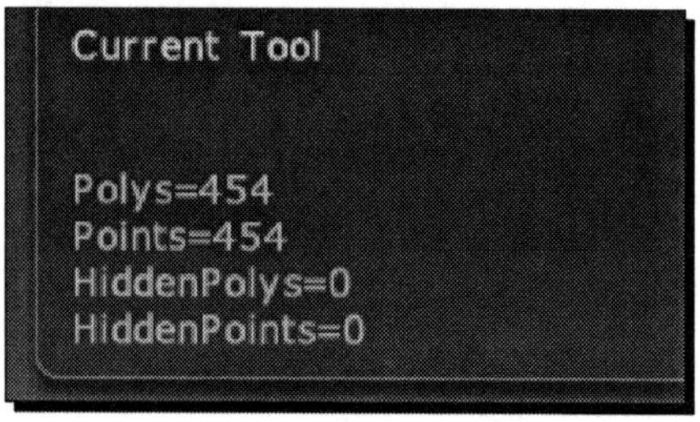


> Beware that both a quad and a triangle will be counted as a polygon. As a rule of thumb, the triangle count is roughly twice as high as the point count.

## Pop quiz - subdivisions

1. If you add another level of subdivision to your model, by how much will this increase the polygon count?
   a. two times
   b. four times
   c. eight times

# Finishing the sculpt

With subdivisions, we can now finish our first sculpture. We'll push the details further and when finished step up in subdivision. Working from a low resolution to a high resolution mesh, gets us better results and saves us time.

## Time for action – sculpting the tree on the next level

1. If you haven't already added the third subdivision level to your tree, do so now by clicking on the **Divide** button under **Tool | Geometry**. Leave the **Smt** option activated, since some smoothing at this level is just fine. Our model should now look somewhat similar to this:

2. Use the **Clay Tubes** brush to define the flow of the roots more. Compared to the **Standard** brush, the Clay Tubes brush builds up more flat volumes, like the next figure shows. We'll use this brush quite a lot, especially for building up the bark structure at a higher subdivision level. When holding *Alt*, the Clay Tubes brush also gives nice flat holes, ideal for snags:

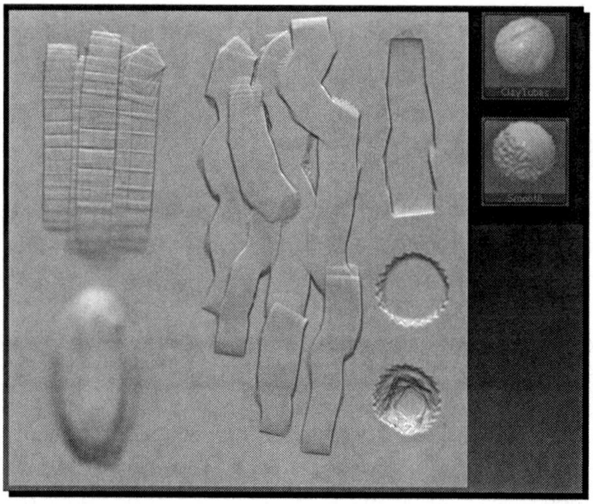

3. If we want to narrow a crack for example, we can use the **Pinch** brush, as shown in the next screenshot:

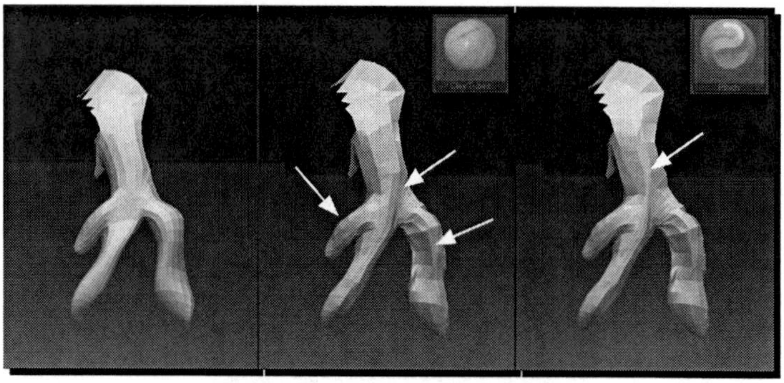

4. Build up hierarchies of roots to define where the surface (the flow of the bark) will be broken.

**5.** Use the **Move** brush to define the tips of the branches, so they look broken. The detail of the branches is crucial for the overall impression of our model, like hands are for a human sculpture.

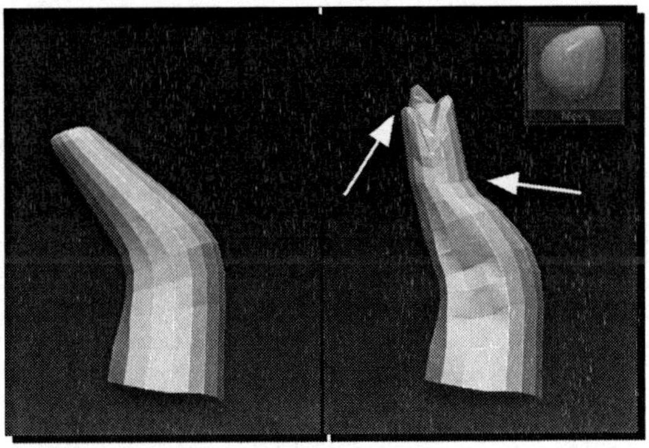

6. Push the sculpture as far as you can at this subdivision level. The next screenshot shows the model before adding another level of subdivision. Compared to the final image, we can see that the overall form is already set at this low resolution stage.

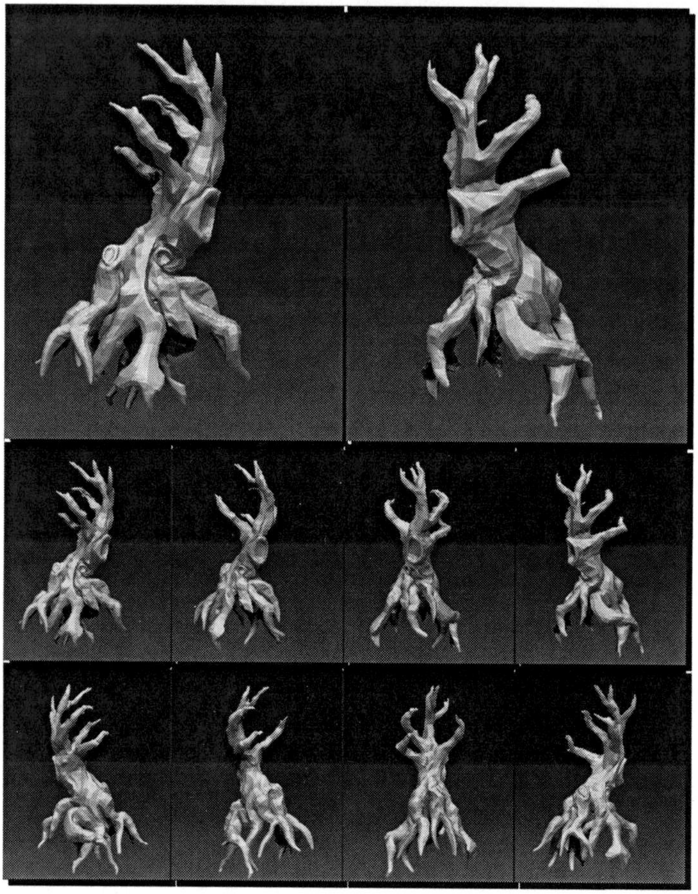

## What just happened?

We added a new subdivision level and defined the form of the tree more. We also added the Clay Tubes brush and the Pinch brush to our repertoire.

As we saw, The Clay Tubes brush is very powerful, since it gives us sharper edges than the Standard brush. With those two, we can do most of our sculpting work.

As we saw, the Pinch brush helps us in narrowing cracks or sharpening borders.

The most important thing we did was pushing the model as far as we could at this subdivision level.

## Time for action – finishing the sculpt

1. We'll now repeat this process over and over again. Pushing it as far as we can and then adding a new subdivision level.
2. The next screenshot shows the models at their respective subdivision levels, before stepping up to the next one:

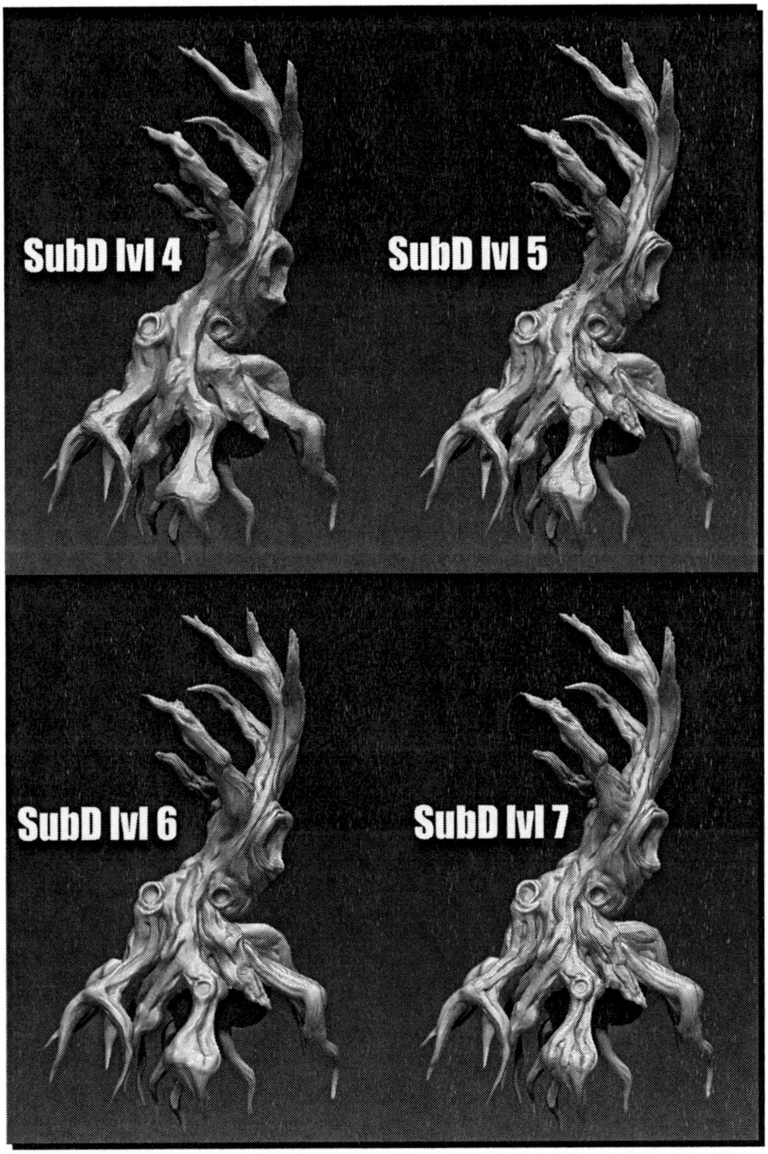

3. Around Subdivision Level 5, there are enough polygons to start defining the structure of the bark. I did the bark basically with only two brushes—the Clay Tubes and the Slash3 brush.

4. The **Slash3** brush, as its name says, slashes into the surface like a knife. This results in narrow, but deep cuts, which is ideal for our bark. By default, the Slash3 brush has the **Lazy Mouse** feature turned on. This can be found under **Stroke | LazyMouse** and averages out your strokes, to make them more rounded and even.

5. This is quite useful for ornaments, but for our bark, we need shaky broken lines, so let's turn it off by pressing *L*. The next screenshot shows the Slash3 brush with LazyMouse turned on and off: (LazyRadius at 30)

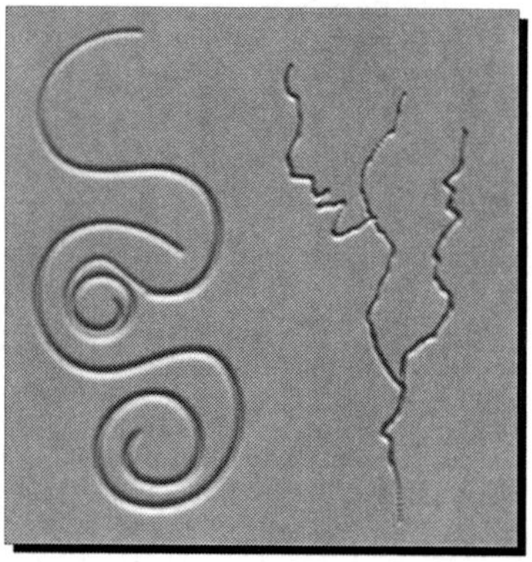

6. With these two brushes, let's start creating the bark, as shown in the next image. Start with strokes of Clay Tubes. Ideally, vary the pressure while drawing if you're using a tablet. Then deepen the cracks and add some holes with the Slash3 brush and LazyMouse turned off. Finally, add smaller Clay Tubes strokes to give it more surface detail:

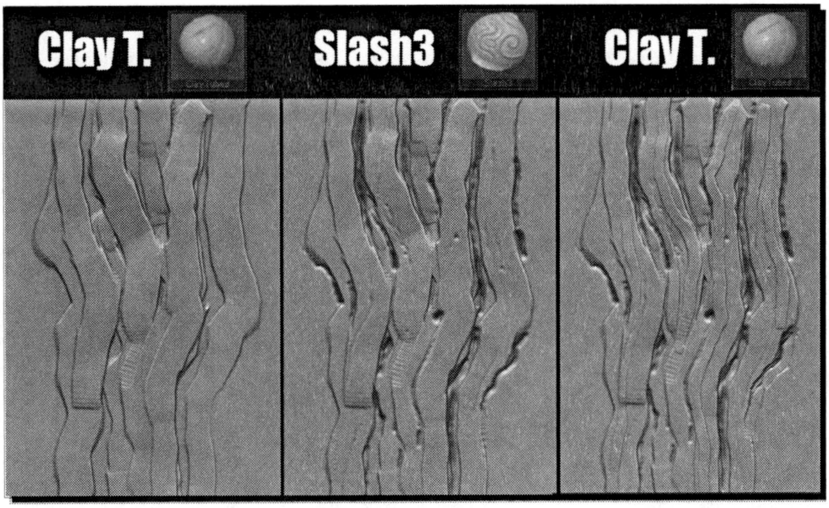


7. When stepping up to subdivision Level 7 or 8, consider turning the **Smt** option off (**Tool | Geometry | Smt**) when adding another subdivision Level if you already have very fine details in some spots and don't want to lose them when dividing.

8. That's pretty much all there is to finish our spooky tree. The next screenshot shows the final mesh with the MatCap white cavity material to emphasize the surface structure:

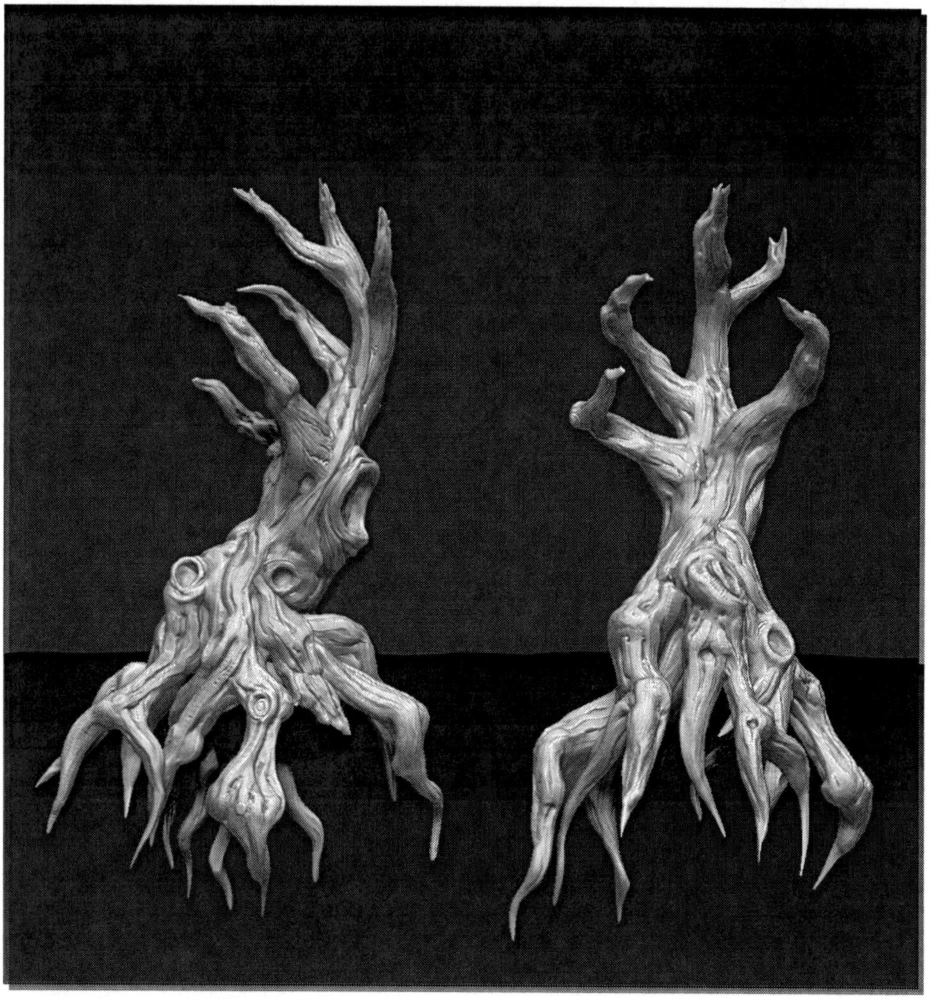

## What just happened?

We've now worked our way through all of the subdivision levels we need, to display even the smallest cracks on the surface.

We used the Slash3 brush, to carve in the details and finished it with the Clay Tubes brush.

Working with millions of polygons in ZBrush is quite straightforward, isn't it?

## Lazymouse

As we saw in the previous example, Lazymouse can be used to smooth out our shaky, hand-drawn lines. Some brushes, like the Slash3 brush do have it turned on by default. What really makes the difference is the **Stroke | LazyMouse | LazyRadius** setting. This determines how far away the actual stroke is from your cursor and thus how much it is being smoothed.

### Have a go hero – the icing on the cake

Try using the **Rake** brush with a low Z Intensity on the roots and partially on the trunk to add smallest scratches.

To make the tips of the roots even sharper, experiment with the **SnakeHook** brush.

# Summary

We've finally finished our first model in ZBrush from scratch—the spooky tree.

In detail, we covered:

- During the whole modeling process, we only needed a handful of brushes, mainly the Standard, Smooth, Move, Inflat, and the Clay Tubes brush.
- To fully control the brushes, we explored the Z Intensity, Focal Shift, and Draw Size settings.
- Our most used brushes can be arranged in the Sculpt01 Screen layout preset for quick access.
- MatCap Materials include predefined lighting, whereas Standard Materials offer more flexibility, for example, changing the light direction. MatCaps are very practical for sculpting when setting up lights would just take up too much time.
- Subdivision Levels add more polygons so we can put in more detail. To make larger changes, we can switch back to a lower level of subdivision. When stepping up again, all the high level detail is preserved.
- Working from low to high polygon count saves a lot of headaches.
- To create ornaments or rounded patterns, we can use the Lazy Mouse feature.
- The Slash3 and the Rake brush can be used to carve in fine scratches or damages.

# 5

# Texturing the Tree with Polypaint

*In this chapter, we are going to texturize our tree with Polypaint, allowing us to paint colors directly onto the model. Opposed to normal 2D-texturing, this will give us the freedom to see the color instantly on the model. This is much more intuitive and lets us use all the details we already sculpted as a guide for the colorization.*

We'll cover in detail:

- How to enable Polypainting
- How to apply color to our tree with Polypainting
- Using Masks for Polypainting cavities and peaks
- Painting with different brushes
- Using Auto Masking to finish the Polypainting
- Adding final shading with Ambient Occlusion

## What is Polypainting?

**Polypainting** lets us apply color onto our model on a per vertex basis. This is also commonly referred to as **vertex colors** in other 3D programs or game engines.

When using Polypaint, each vertex holds color and material information we can paint. This means the amount of detail we can paint depends on the amount of vertices we have.

For example, in a texture map, each pixel holds color information similar to each vertex we can paint. A typical game texture size would be 1024 x 1024 pixels, which is around one million pixels in total. So if we want to cover the same amount of detail as a 1024 x 1024 texture, we would need at least one million vertices. This is the reason why we always polypaint at the highest level of subdivision where we have the maximum amount of vertices available.

> Remember, you can just hover over your active tool in the tool palette to view the vertex- and polygon count.

## Time for action – setting up our model for Polypainting

Let's do the preparatory steps to start Polypainting:

1. Load the mesh of the spooky tree.
2. If not done automatically by ZBrush, draw your mesh on the canvas and enter **edit mode**.

> If you're in **edit mode**, but your mesh is somewhere off the canvas, you can simply press *F* to **frame** it back again. Holding *Alt* and left-clicking on an unoccupied part of the canvas does the same.

3. Make sure the tool is at its highest subdivision level by checking the slider under **Tool | Geometry** or by pressing *D* until it reaches the highest level.

4. Choose a material that gives a nice and *neutral shading*, not a pre-colored one that mixes with the colors we paint. I chose the **MatCap White01**.
5. Activate **Tool | Polypaint | Colorize** to enable **Polypainting** on the mesh.

6. Let's choose a brownish color from the **Color Selector**, located in the shelf, as shown in the next screenshot. The **Color Selector** has two areas. The little square on the outer rim determines the hue, the little inner square determines the value and saturation. This is quite similar to what most 2D painting programs use.

7. Below the **Color Selector**, we can find the **Secondary** and **Main Color**, which are black and white by default, as shown in the previous screenshot. We can switch between them by pressing **Switch Color** or *V*.

> Choosing a color from the Color Selector can sometimes be hard due to its very small size. What we can do is hold down our mouse while choosing, so we can see immediately which color is chosen if we release the mouse button. Opening the color palette in a tray or using the quick menu (*spacebar*) also gives us a bigger Color Selector.

8. To fill our object with the brownish color we selected, make sure to turn off **Zadd** and to turn on **Rgb** in the shelf at the top.

9. Also set the **Rgb Intensity** to **100** (percent), as shown in the next screenshot:

10. Fill the object with the selected color by pressing **Color | FillObject** from the color palette in the palette list at the top of the window.

## What just happened?

We just enabled **Polypainting** for our mesh and set up a proper material.

We also explored the **Color Selector** in detail and learned how to fill an object with selected colors, which gives us a good start for texturing.

When turning **Zadd** off, we made sure that drawing accidentally on the mesh won't alter the surface, but just the color of it. This is why we turned on **Rgb** instead. Next to the **Rgb** button, there's a button labeled **M** for material. If this is switched on, we would paint materials instead of colors onto our model. With the **Mrgb** button, we could do both at the same time. But since we can't export ZBrush materials to game engines, we'll skip that for now and focus solely on the Rgb color information.

As mentioned earlier, the Rgb slider works like a percentage. So filling an object, with a red color selected and Rgb set to 60 will add 60 percent red to the existing color.

Let's talk about masks and how we can use them to color our tree in no time.

## Pop quiz – Polypainting

1. What option should be turned on for polypainting?
    a. Zadd
    b. Zsub
    c. Rgb
2. Why do we always polypaint at the highest level of subdivision?
    a. Because the resolution of Polypainting depends on the amount of vertices available
    b. Because we can't polypaint at the lower levels of subdivision.
    c. Because the resolution of Polypainting depends on the amount of pixels the object covers on the canvas.

## Time for action – using masks for Polypainting

You may know masks from 2D Programs, such as the layer masks in Photoshop. In ZBrush, they work in a similar way, preventing a masked area from being affected. Like in 2D, masks can have smooth transitions, so an area can be masked by anything between zero and a 100 percent. Let's use this to create a basic color scheme for our tree.

1. Make sure you have done all the steps mentioned earlier. Opened the tree, applied a neutral material, enabled Polypainting and filled the object with a brownish color.

2. Also make sure your model is at its highest subdivision level to capture all the details.

3. If not already the case, put the tool palette in your right tray and open the **Tool | Masking** subpalette.

4. Here, we have plenty of options how to create masks. For now we'll focus on the cavity masking, so click on the **Mask By Cavity** button now. The default settings for the (Cavity) **Blur** `at` **10** are fine, but we probably need more contrast in the mask, so set the (Cavity-) **Intensity** to **30** and click on **Mask By Cavity** again.

> There are many sliders in ZBrush, such as the **Cavity Intensity** or even the draw size. We can drag them with the mouse, but we can also type in the values after left-clicking on them. This is especially useful when the sliders are very short in length.

5. Just to see the masking better, switch to the **Flat Color Material**, which is listed under the **Standard Materials**. This Material displays only the flat color or masking of your model without any shading.

6. To better see the difference, we can toggle the **Tool | Masking | View Mask** button in the masking subpalette. The darker a vertex, the more it is masked, the lighter a vertex, the less it is masked.

7. Now that we've masked the cavity, which are the cracks in our barks, let's invert the mask to be able to darken the cracks. To invert the mask, *Ctrl* + left-click on an empty part of the canvas or hit **Tool| Masking | Inverse**.

> Remember *Ctrl + Shift* was the hotkey combination for hiding Polygroups, whereas *Ctrl* is used for masking operations.

8. Select a darker brownish color from the Color Selector. Opening the **Color Palette** in the left tray makes it easier to access and also gives us a bigger Color Selector.

9. Click **Color | FillObject** to darken the unmasked cracks in the bark with this color.

10. Don't forget to **hide** or **clear** your masking in the masking subpalette to judge the colors because with the mask still visible, it darkens areas that are much lighter.

**11.** If you're satisfied with the colors, save your work.

> By the way, it's always better to save your work at the lowest level of subdivision to prevent errors. Press *Shift+D* to **step down** and *D* to **step up** in subdivision.

## What just happened?

We've just established a basic color scheme for our tree. Now that you know how to do it, it's just a matter of minutes if you have to do it again. Fill it, mask it, fill it, done.

This masking can also be applied to sculpting. So if you want to sculpt everything except the deep cracks in the bark, you could go for cavity masking too.

The **Flat Color** material is great for checking colors, masks, or silhouettes of a model, since it displays no shading.

So now that we did the basic coloring, let's finish it by painting it.

## Pop quiz – masking

1. What does masking do?
    a. Masking hides parts of the mesh
    b. Masking protects parts of the mesh from actions such as sculpting or painting
    c. Masking colorizes parts of the mesh, such as painting

## Have a go hero – creating your own color scheme

With the cavity masking option, you can now alter the color scheme to your own wishes quickly.

Will it be a magical tree, so the colors could be desaturated reds with glowing cavity colors?

Will it be a burnt tree, so the cavities are black, while the outer bark appears ash-gray?

Does the tree stand in a moist place, so will the cavities be partly covered with greens?

Create your favorite color scheme like we did in the previous example; the possibilities are endless.

# Brushes for Polypainting

With our color scheme ready, let's explore how we can paint onto our model using the same brushes we used for sculpting.

> To **Polypaint** with a brush, just disable **Zadd** and enable **Rgb**, like we did in the previous examples. Because ZBrush remembers these settings for each brush, we have to switch from **Zadd** to **Rgb**, once for every brush we want to paint with. The settings for the **Smooth** brush can be accessed exclusively when holding *Shift*.

The following image shows that the brushes behave in a similar way when used for Polypainting.

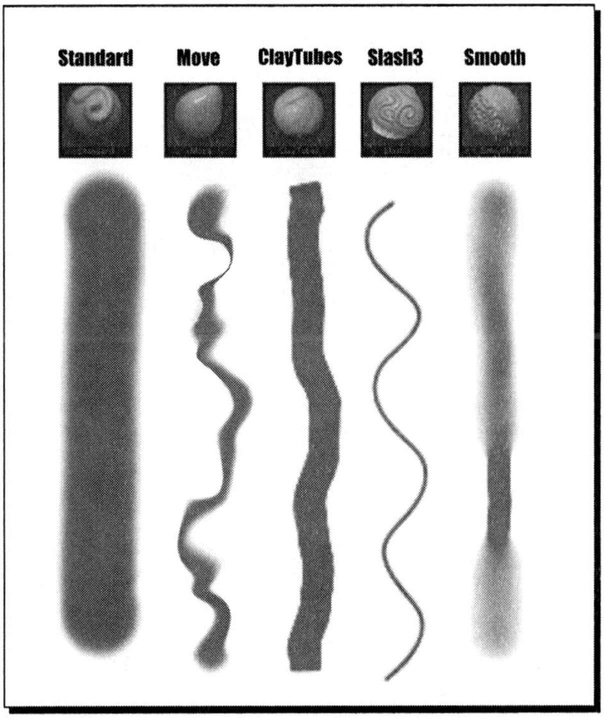


We can use the **Rgb** slider to set the opacity of the stroke. Remember that with a pen tablet, the strokes are still pressure sensitive. So even with **Rgb** set to **100**, painting with very low pressure can give very faint colors.

Let's see how we can paint with these brushes onto our mesh, without losing the cavity colors we set in the previous example.

# Time for action – using Auto Masking to finish the Polypainting

Now that we created our basic color scheme with cavity masking, let's use the brushes to paint the final details. We could also continue using the cavity masks for painting the colors, but there's a handy feature, that masks the cavity on the fly, which is called **Auto Masking**. Let's see how painting the tree becomes a no-brainer with this feature.

1. Open the brush palette in the left tray and expand the **Auto Masking** subpalette.
2. Enable **CavityMask**, as shown in the next screenshot:

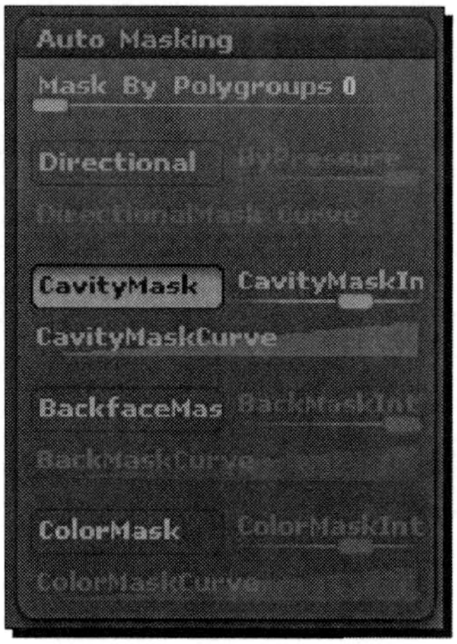


3. Next to the **CavityMask** button, we can find the **CavityMaskingIntensity** slider. Set it to **10**, choose a lighter color and brighten up the bark a bit while keeping the masked cavity colors, as shown in the next screenshot:

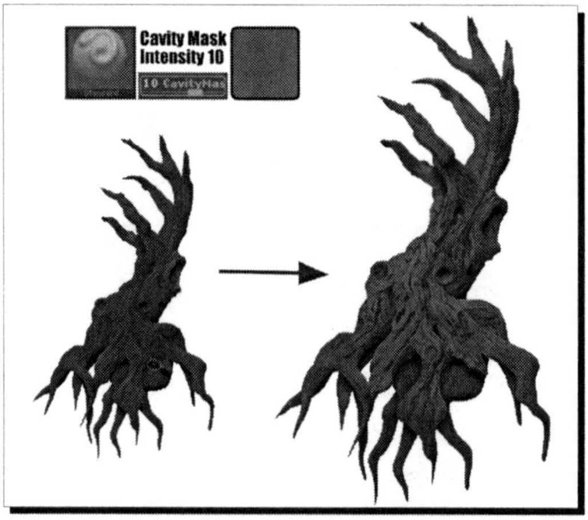

4. Set the **CavityMaskintensity** Slider to **-10** and choose a darker color to darken some cavities and add variation to the texture.

5. Try establishing some kind of gradient from the bottom to the top because the roots are darker or more saturated in color than the bark. This helps to make the object more realistic and easier to read. Deeper cracks should also have darker cavities than shallower ones.

We can pick any color under our cursor by hitting *C*, including colors from the canvas and even from the interface. Note that this picks the pure color under the cursor, which is unaffected by any material shading or lighting conditions. If you want to pick the shaded color, click on the active color icon and drag while holding *Alt*.

6. Check the Polypainting on your whole model by framing it by hitting *F* or *Alt* + left-click on an empty part the canvas.

7. Now we've got all the tools we need for finishing the texture of the tree. Don't forget to turn off cavity masking sometimes, to prevent the texture from looking too monotonous. Also consider which parts of the tree would look more weathered than others. The finished tree could now look similar to the next screenshot:

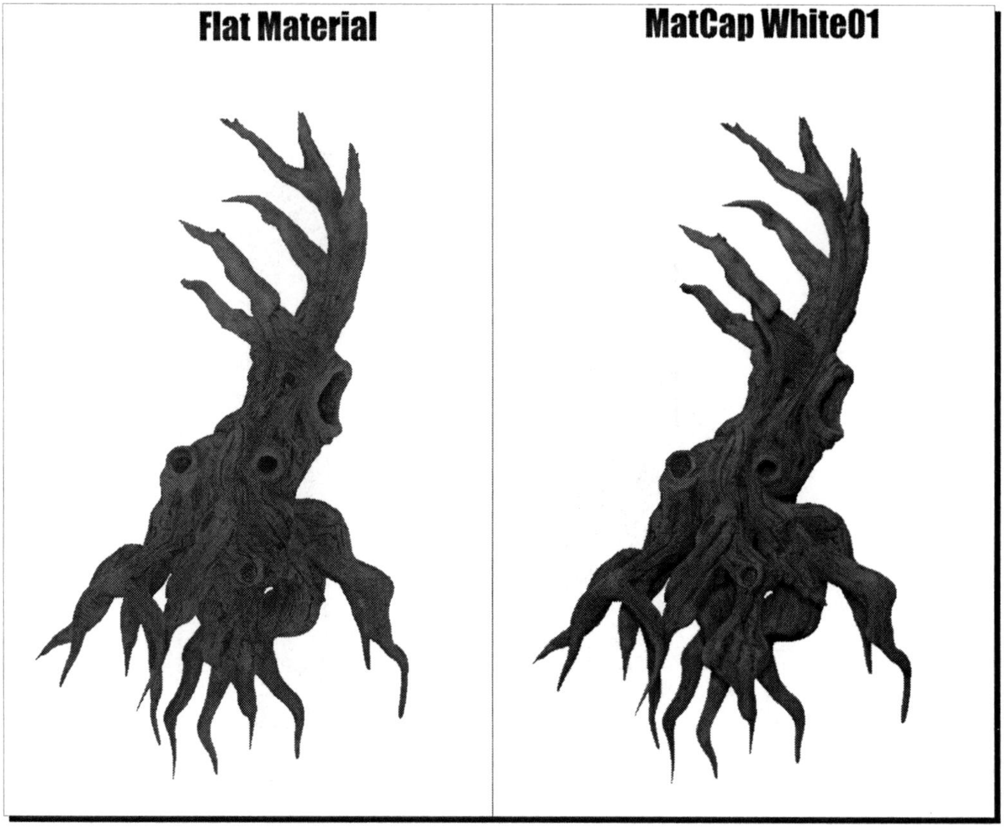


## What just happened?

We have just finished modeling and texturing our first mesh—the spooky tree. As we saw, Polypainting is just as easy as sculpting because the brushes are all the same. When Polypainting, we can use the **Rgb slider** like the **Z Intensity** slider to control the amount of color that is applied onto our model.

With the color picking accessed by pressing the hotkey *C*, the canvas becomes our color palette, where we can pick added and mixed colors from.

## Auto Masking

To not lose any previously assigned colors, we used the **Auto Masking** feature to mask or unmask cavities of our tree on the fly while painting. The **CavityMaskIntensity** slider gives us full control over the Auto Masking. Setting it to a positive value allows us to paint only the peaks, while masking the cavities. A negative value will let us paint only the cavities.

In the **Auto Masking** subpalette, there are also other very useful options such as the **BackfaceMasking**, for example. With this enabled, it automatically masks polygons facing away from our view. This comes in handy when editing very thin objects, where sculpting on one side would also affect the other due to the brush size.

## Have a go hero – adding final shading with Ambient Occlusion

In the **Tool | Masking** subpalette, we can find another masking option, **Mask Ambient Occlusion**. The next screenshot shows how **Ambient Occlusion** and **Cavity Mask** differ. To put it simply, the Ambient Occlusion masking gives more of a global masking, taking into consideration which parts of the mesh occlude others, whereas the Cavity Masking shows the contrasts between peaks and valleys on our surface, ignoring the overall mesh structure.

Note that both calculations are independent from any lighting, as their calculation depends on the mesh only.

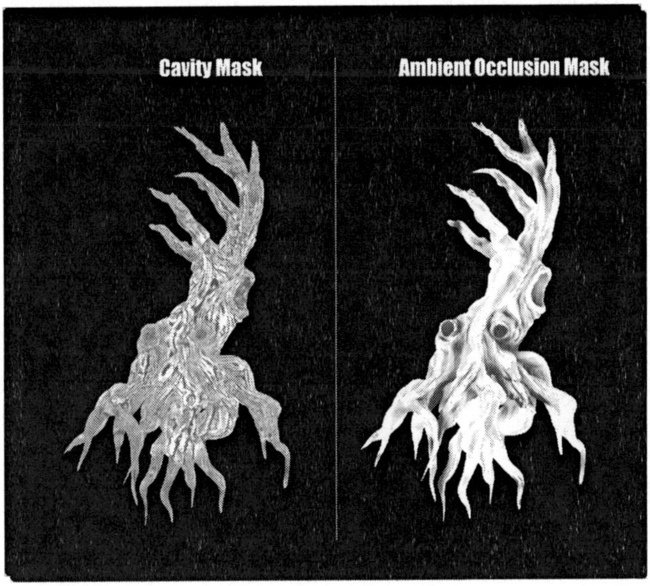

As we can see, the cavity masking highlights the smaller surface details, whereas the Ambient Occlusion masking enhances the shading by clarifying the overall mesh structure for the viewer.

We already used the Cavity Masking for the small structures, so let's add some final shading with Ambient Occlusion masking:

1. Masking Ambient Occlusion can take quite a long time, so you may want to step down one level of subdivision from the highest one.
2. Open the **Tool | Masking** subpalette.
3. Set the **Intensity** to **10** and increase the **AO Scan Distance** to **0.8**. Leave the **Aperture** at **90**. Note that increasing the **AO Scan Distance** mainly influences the time needed for the calculation.
4. Click on **Mask Ambient Occlusion**. The **Note Bar** shows the time already passed and the estimated time left, as shown in the next screenshot. If this takes too long, press *ESC* to abort and either step down one level of subdivision or decrease the AO Scan Distance Value.

5. Invert the mask by hitting **Tool** | **Mask** | **Invert** or by holding *Ctrl* + left-click on an unoccupied area of the canvas.
6. If you stepped down one level to calculate the Ambient Occlusion mask, step up again to the highest level now. Fill the unmasked areas with a color of your choice. I chose a slightly bluish color and kept the **Rgb Intensity** at a lower value, something around 30.
7. Go to **Tool | Masking | Clear** or **Tool | Masking | Hide** the mask to judge the colors. Finally, you may want to correct some parts of the Ambient Occlusion color by hand.

> If you like, you can download the final colored mesh of the spooky tree from the link provided in the preface.

# Summary

We've finally finished our spooky tree by texturing it. This was even easier than sculpting the tree, wasn't it?

Let's see what we've covered in this chapter:

- We saw that Polypainting relies on vertices, thus the amount of detail depends on the amount of vertices available.
- Choosing a non-colored material helps us see the polypainted colors better. The **Flat Material** displays colors only, which helps us judge the color range better.
- By masking areas of our mesh, we can exclude parts of it from our painting or sculpting.
- We can take advantage of our sculpted details using the **Mask by Cavity** option. This way we can quickly establish a basic color scheme for our meshes.
- The brushes behave quite similar when used for Polypainting. Simply turn off **Zadd** and turn on **Rgb** instead to polypaint with them.
- The **Rgb Slider** determines the opacity of the color that is applied when filling or painting the mesh.
- We can make use of the masking features on the fly with **Auto Masking**.
- Finally, we used **Ambient Occlusion** to add final shading to our object, increasing its believability and readability for the viewer.

Let's create the environment for our tree in the next chapter.

# 6

# Adding an Environment to the Tree

*Complex objects or places are made of multiple objects called subtools in ZBrush. This is very useful to keep things organized. If it comes to mechanical objects that are made of many small parts, the advantage of subtools is even more obvious. In the course of this chapter, we'll finish the model of the tree by adding some environment to it.*

We'll cover in detail:

- How to change the document size to fit your screen
- Adding objects to the tool using subtools
- The Transpose tool for moving objects
- Using 3D "primitives" in ZBrush
- How to create one mesh out of two
- Using radial symmetry to sculpt round objects

## Changing the document size to fit your screen

Before we start, let's make sure our document is the right size. Especially if you're utilizing a big monitor, you'll experience that the canvas does not fill up the whole screen. Let's fix that.

# Time for action – setting up the canvas size

1. Open the **Document** palette from the **palette list** at the top of your window.
2. Activate the **WSize** button, as shown in the next screenshot, and click on **New Document**:

3. If prompted to save changes, click on **Yes**, if there is any 2.5D work on your canvas you want to save, otherwise click on **Don't save changes**. Creating a new document will only clear 2D and 2.5D information. All 3D models are still stored in the **tool palette**.
4. Still in the **Document palette** hit **Save As Startup Doc** to save the current document size as default to be loaded on every startup.

## *What just happened?*

We just maximized our working space and saved it as a default, so we don't have to change it all the time. Clicking on **WSize** adjusts the resolution of the new document to fit the available screen space, not hidden by the interface. Now we're all set to start adding some environment to our tree.

# Adding objects with subtools

Until now, we've always edited a single object only. To add additional ones, like a ground floor or rocks to the scene, we can use **subtools**. We'll always use subtools, when it makes sense to split objects to be able to edit them separately. For instance, when modeling different outfits for a hero character, you would like them to be appended as subtools, so you can switch them on and off. A good example would be a knight with his armor appended as a subtool.

Once we have several subtools appended, we'll use the **Transpose tool** to put them into place. Let's see how this works:

## Time for action – stand your ground

1. **Load** your model of the polypainted tree and make sure the model is drawn onto the canvas and in **edit mode**.
2. **Save** the tool under a different name.
3. Make sure the **Tool palette** is permanently open in one of the trays for quick access.
4. Open the **Tool | SubTool** subpalette, which is the topmost in the list.
5. Click on **Tool | SubTool | Append**. From the inventory list that opens, choose the **Circle 3D Tool**, located under 3D Meshes, which will become our hill.
6. Now that we've added the circle as a subtool to our tree, the subtool subpalette should list two meshes, as shown in the next screenshot:

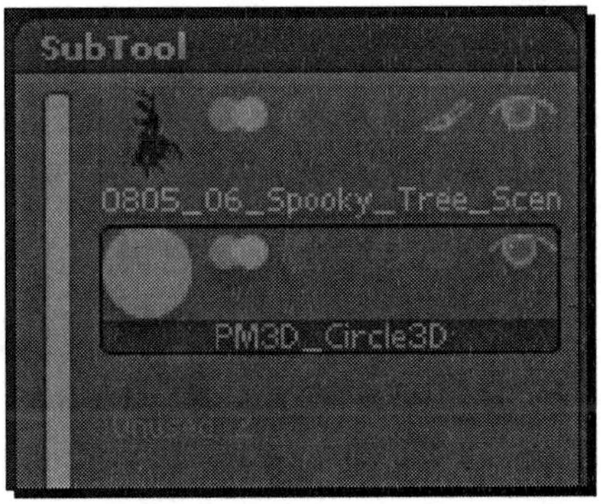


## What just happened?

We've now appended another object to our tree as a subtool. With this technique we can compose much more complex meshes out of several simpler ones.

We saw that when appending, we can simply choose any mesh from the tool list. So we could also add more trees or anything else we can import as a tool into ZBrush from other applications.

Note that there's always one **active subtool**, which is indicated by its thin black border, like the **PM3D_Circle3D** in the previous screenshot. Only the active subtool can be edited. Inactive subtools appear darker on the canvas, similar to the masking effect.

> We can also use the little eye icon of each subtool in the list, to toggle the visibility.
>
> Clicking the eye icon of the active subtool hides all other subtools.
>
> Clicking the eye icon of an inactive subtool only toggles its own visibility.

## Pop quiz – subtools

1. What can we add to our model as a subtool?
    a. Brushes
    b. Images
    c. Meshes
    d. ZSpheres

# The Transpose tool

To move, rotate, or scale objects in ZBrush, we can use the **Transpose tool**. This helps us to arrange objects like our tree and the ground. Getting familiar with it at this early stage is important because we will use it a lot later on when we have to arrange dozens of subtools. Let's see how this works.

## Time for action – moving the ground floor with Transpose

Now that we've appended our ground floor, let's use the Transpose tool to move it into position.

1. Under **Tool | SubTool** click on the newly appended circle to make it the active subtool, as shown in the next screenshot. The tree should now appear darker and the circle, lighter:

2. Activate **Transparency**, which can be found either in the shelf of the default screen layout or in the Transform palette **Transform | Transp**. This renders all inactive subtools semi-transparent, revealing the active subTool, which is of great help when working with overlapping subtools.

3. Now let's rotate the circle, so it looks more like a ground floor, than like a traffic sign. Open the **Deformation** subpalette from the Tool palette. Here we can find a slider to **Rotate** our object.

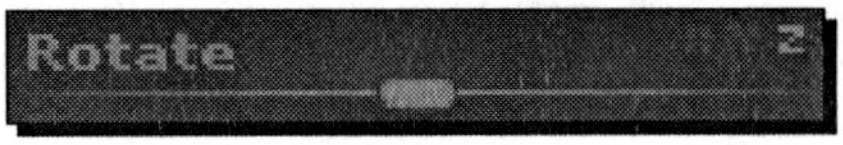


4. We can specify on which axis the rotation will be applied by using the three toggles for X, Y, and Z on the right hand side. Since we want to rotate only around the X-Axis, **switch X on** and **Z off**, as the next screenshot shows.

5. Click on the Rotate-slider, enter **90** and press *Return* to rotate the circle around the X Axis by 90 degrees. Make sure not to drag the slider accidentally when clicking on it.

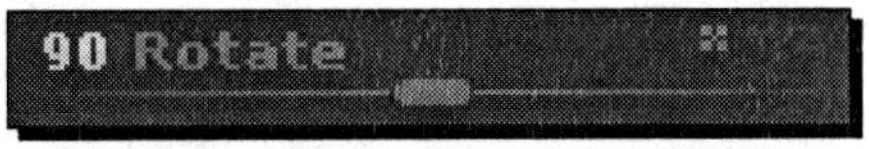


6. Switch from **Draw** to **Move** by clicking the **Move** button in the shelf, or just press the hotkey *W*. You can also find the Move Button in the **quick menu**, available by right-clicking or by pressing *spacebar*.

7. By switching to the move tool, we are presented with a new tool, the so called **Transpose tool**, with an **Action Line** for visualization. By default, the Action Line is quite short in length, so let's create a longer one by left-clicking and dragging **onto** our circle. Drawing a new action line will replace the previous one.

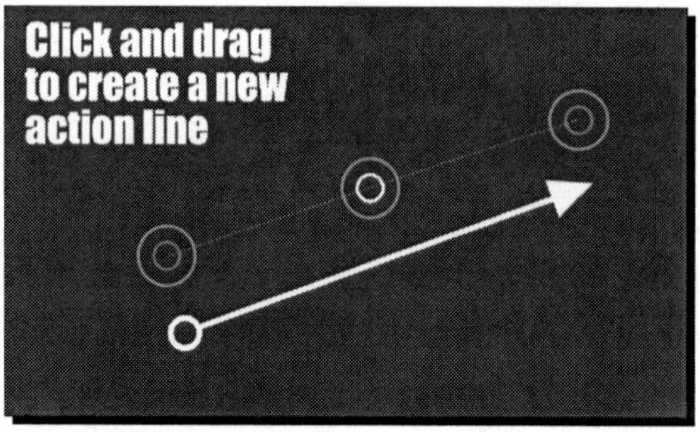


8. Rotate around the Object and snap the rotation by holding *Shift*, so you see the tree from the side. The Circle won't be visible from the side, since it is too thin, but that doesn't bother us, since the Action Line we need is still visible.

9. To move the circle down, click the **inner circle** of the middle point, as shown in the following screenshot:

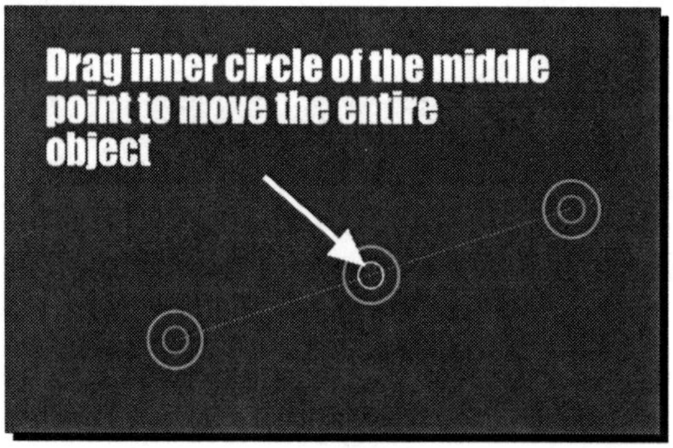


10. Now that we've rotated and moved our circle, let's scale it up with the Transpose tool. Click on **Scale** or press the hotkey *E*.

11. Draw a new Action Line onto the circle and drag the inner circles of the outer points to scale it up, as shown in the next screenshot. You may have to scale it several times for it to reach a reasonable size:

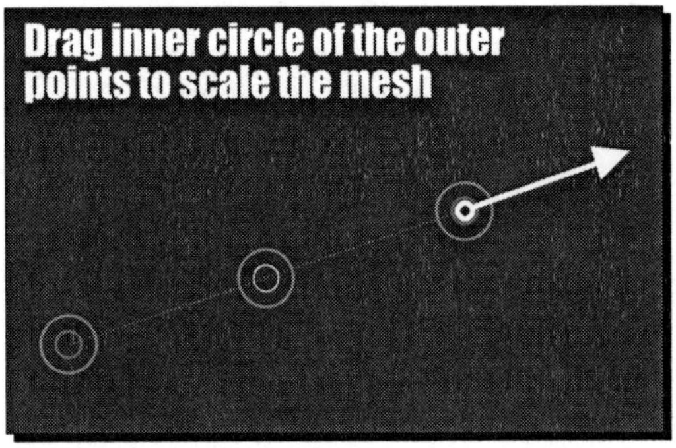


## *What just happened?*

We just saw how easy moving or scaling objects can be with **Transpose**. We could even have rotated our circle with Transpose, but rotating around 90 degrees is done quicker using the **Deformations subpalette**.

Drawing a new Action Line will work in Move, Scale, and Rotate mode.

Activating **Transparency** helps us when working with complex, overlapping forms.

## Transpose

When using Transpose, we pressed the same buttons and hotkeys, like we did when working with ZSpheres, but were presented with a different tool. The **Action Line** from Transpose will only show up when working with polygons, since Move, Scale, and Rotate work differently with ZSpheres.

As we've seen, the Action Line will always snap to the surface it is drawn upon. We can adjust the position by dragging the outer circles without surface snapping.

> Dragging inner circles of the Action Line will result in deformation; whereas dragging the outer circles will reposition it.

It's important to understand that moving the object with Transpose is always dependent on the current camera view. To move objects exactly along one axis, we snapped the rotation, so we view the object exactly from the side to move the circle up and down accurately.

In the Deformation subpalette, we found plenty of options to play with. Note that this palette will never display any deformation applied to the object. So after rotating the object by 90 degrees, the slider won't display 90 degrees, but rather jump back to 0.

## Single-sided polygons

Maybe you wondered why the circle we added is only visible from one side. This is because polygons are normally only drawn on one side, because it saves performance. The same applies for games. If we had a closed mesh of a horse, composed out of polygons, who would bother to view it from the inside? Since most of the meshes are closed and only viewed either from the inside or from the outside, this is on by default. Nevertheless, we can force it to be displayed **double sided** by going to **Tool | Display Properties | Double** (-sided). Note that this option will only change the way objects are displayed inside ZBrush and will be ignored when exporting the model to other applications.

## Time for action – roughing in the hill

1. We'll now quickly rough in the hill to place props onto.
2. Start with the **Move** brush and a big draw size to shape a rough form of a hill from the circle, as shown in the next screenshot:

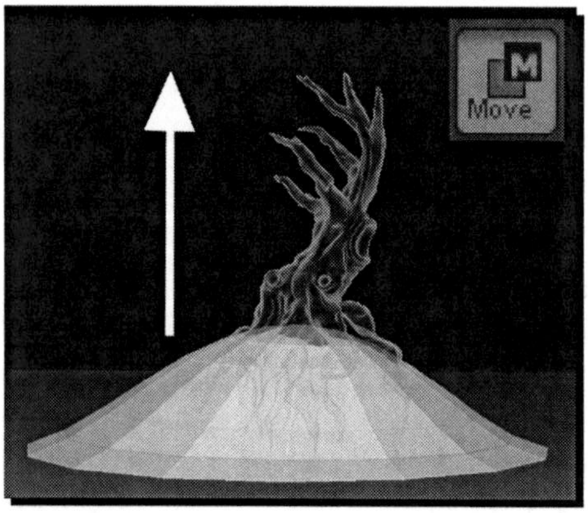


3. Continue to work your way up through the subdivision levels. Use the **Clay Tubes** brush to establish the overall form, as shown in the next screenshot:

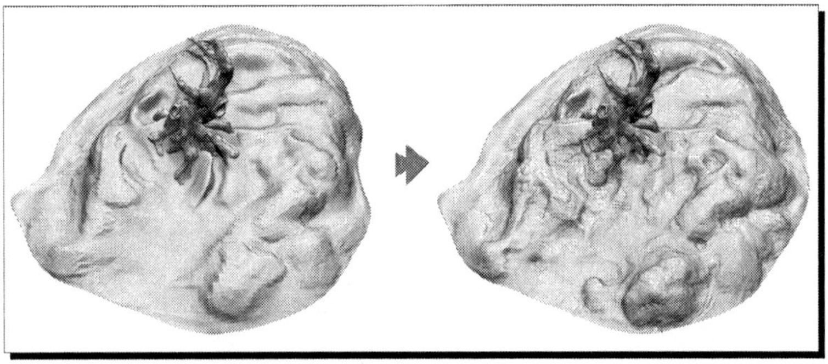

4. Finalize the structure with the **Fracture** and **Crumple** brush, as shown in the next screenshot. Both are sensitive to the direction of your stroke. Drawing circled shapes with the Fracture and criss-cross with the Crumple brush produces nice patterns for stone:

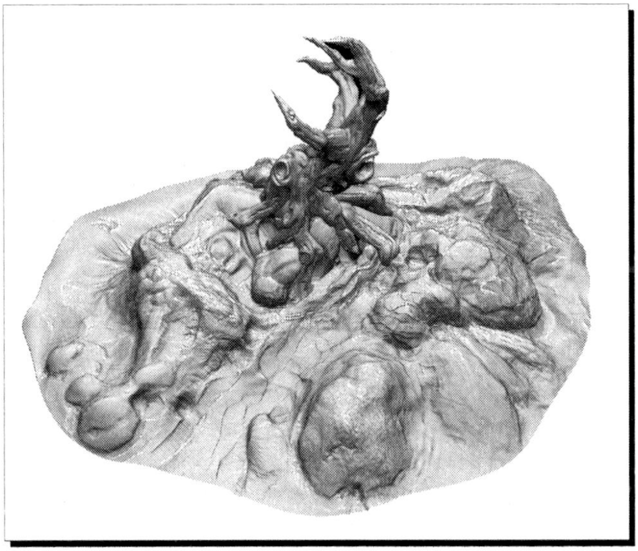

5. Also, think of the relative size of the hill compared to the tree. As you can see, in the next screenshot, I've decided to make everything more compact, so I simply stepped down in subdivisions and moved the borders inwards. As for the theme, it's up to you, if you're building a rocky-dusty hill, or a more rounded one, which will be covered with grass in the game engine:

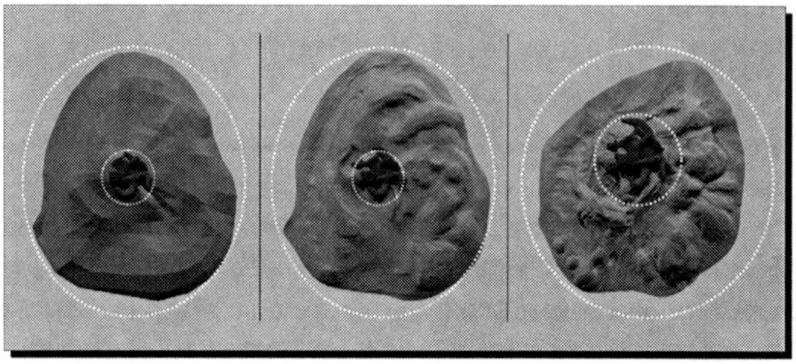

## What just happened?

We've now created a hill for our tree to stand upon exploring two new brushes, the Fracture and the Crumple brush.

When working with a game engine, there are two ways of creating landscapes, like a hill:

- Firstly, if your engine supports advanced terrain editing, you could paint the hill for the tree to stand up on in your level editor. When the ground floor is made out of one piece, this has several advantages, for example: There's no texture seam to be covered where the hill penetrates the ground floor it stands upon.
- The second one is to sculpt the hill in ZBrush, place all props like the tree, rocks, mushrooms, and export everything to your engine. A hill modeled in ZBrush will probably be more detailed and individual than one painted in a level editor, but also consumes more resources.

Either way, we still would need to rough in the hill in ZBrush, to know where to place our rocks and mushrooms, which we will do in the next step.

## Have a go hero – sculpting a rock

With the **Fracture** and **Crumple** brush we've just explored, try building a rock as a separate subtool. As we saw, drawing circled shapes with the Fracture and criss-cross with the Crumple brush produces nice patterns for stone. Using the Slash1 Brush also gives nice scratches for rocky surfaces.

If you model all sides of a rock, it can be used multiple times in a game engine by rotating and scaling it, which saves performance. Here are some examples of how the finished rocks could look:

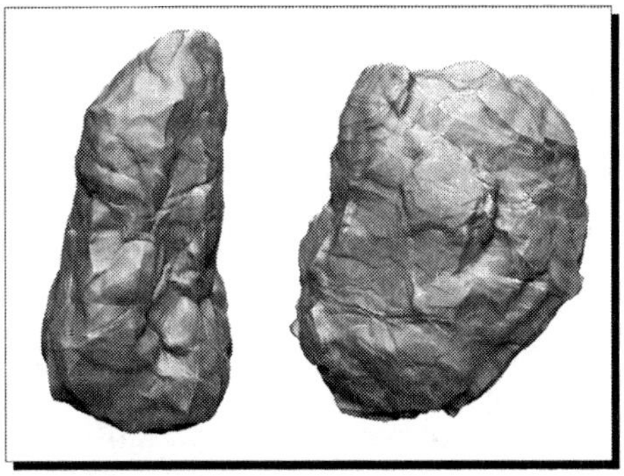

## Time for action – creating a mushroom

Let's create a mushroom that can stand next to the tree. To do that, we'll combine a cylinder and a cone. Let's see how this can be done:

1. Click on your active tool and choose the **Cone3D** from the inventory list that opens.
2. Open the Initialize subpalette from the **Tool palette**. **Tool | Initialize**
3. Lower the **Z Size** to **60** so that the head of our mushroom isn't that high anymore.
4. Click the **Tool | MakePolymesh3D** button, located at the top of the **Tool palette**.
5. Click on your active tool and choose the **Cylinder3D** from the inventory list that opens.
6. Under **Tool | Initialize** set the **X Size** to **20** and the **Y Size** to **20** to thin the cylinder.
7. Navigate to the **Tool | MakePolymesh3D** button again.
8. Open the **SubTool** subpalette and go to **Tool | SubTool | Append** and choose the **PM3D_Cone3D** object, which will become our trunk. Your mushroom should now look similar to the next screenshot:

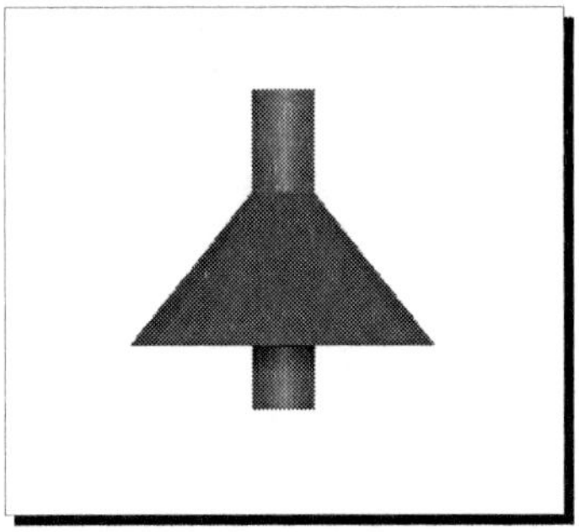

9. The only thing left to do is move the cylinder subtool upwards. Click on the cylinder subtool to make it the active one.

10. Rotate your mushroom while holding *Shift* so that you view it exactly from the side.

11. Now activate **Transpose** by clicking on **Move** and draw a new Action Line onto the cylinder object.

12. Now move it upwards by clicking the middle point's inner circle of the Action Line. Try to keep everything aligned, so that the head of the mushroom does not float in the air and isn't shifted too much to the right or left.

13. Your mushroom should now look pretty similar to the next screenshot, with the head properly aligned with the trunk:

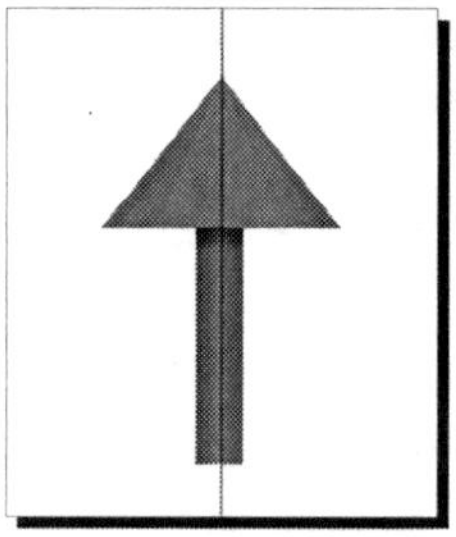

14. **Save** your tool.

15. To combine both primitive objects press the **Remesh All** button in the subtool subpalette, shown in the next screenshot. The default settings are fine:

16. This should add the freshly combined mushroom as a subtool. If you saved the tool before clicking on **ReMesh All**, you can now delete the two other subtools by clicking on **Tool | SubTool | Delete** and save again under a different name.

## What just happened?

We've just combined two meshes to become a mushroom.

As we saw, we can start with a 3Dmesh like the Cone3D Object in ZBrush. Those "primitives" come along with the initialize settings, where we can set things like size, or even make a hemisphere out of a sphere. As long as they have initialize settings, they can't be sculpted. If we want to sculpt them or use tools like Transpose, we have to convert them into a PolyMesh3D first.

When appending such a "primitive" as a subtool, ZBrush will automatically convert it to a Polymesh3D Object.

After aligning the trunk and the head, we used the **Remesh** function, which creates a new mesh out of all visible subtools. The advantage is that we now get a mushroom with a continuous surface. Before remeshing, the cylinder was stuck into the cone, but their surfaces weren't connected. Remeshing even creates Polygroups for us, so we can still work on the head and the trunk separately. Click on Polyframe or *Shift + F* to see it.

So let's sculpt the mushroom now to finish the environment for our tree.

## Pop quiz – 3D primitives

1. What would you have to do, to sculpt a 3D primitive?
    a. Nothing
    b. Enter Edit mode
    c. Convert it to a Polymesh3D

## Time for action – sculpting the mushroom with radial symmetry

Given that we took care aligning the head and trunk of the mushroom properly, we can make use of the radial symmetry feature.

1. Open the **Transform palette** in the right-hand side tray by clicking on the Transform palette's handle.

2. Activate symmetry by clicking on **Activate Symmetry**. Deactivate the X-Axis and Activate the Z-Axis and click on the **(R)** button to activate radial symmetry, as shown in the next screenshot:

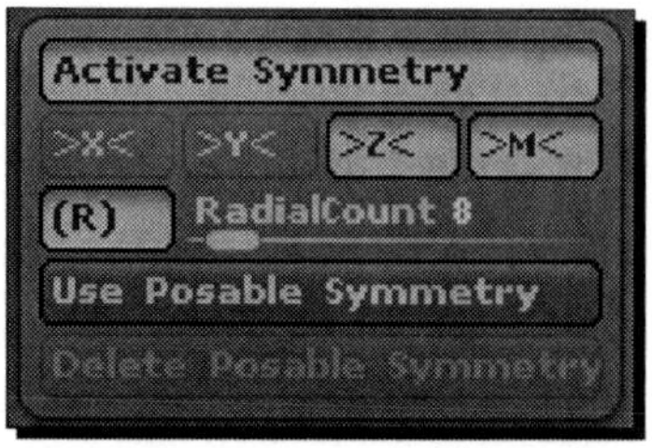


3. Sculpt the mushroom with radial symmetry. Use the **RadialCount** slider to adjust how many times your stroke is repeated around the object. If the radial count or the draw size is so high that the repeated strokes overlap, it will displace the surface evenly on all sides. Use this in combination with the **Standard, Move** or **Inflat** brush to shape the overall form in no time, as shown in the following screenshot:

4. Set the **draw size** to **50**, increase the **radial count** to **40** and choose the **Slash2 Brush**. With this setup, we can create the bottom side with one single stroke, as shown in the next screenshot, which is really fun. A slightly shaky stroke will add some nice variation:

5. Don't forget to turn off symmetry, when finishing the mushroom, nothing in nature is exactly symmetrical.

## What just happened?

We've just explored the amazing possibilities of radial symmetry. With this feature, objects with radial symmetry can be finished incredibly quickly. Think of tires, rockets, turbines, bucklers or pillars, which can be done in a matter of minutes, not hours anymore with radial symmetry.

When activating symmetry on more than one axis, we can also sculpt interesting patterns on a sphere, like a detail of a crown, for example.

As we've seen, the Slash2 Brush does not only carve in, but also raises parts of the surface at the same time.

When varying the stroke with radial symmetry, endless combinations of interesting ornaments can be created. Pick a new circle and give it a try.

## Have a go hero – creating a mushroom colony

Now that we've finished sculpting, let's create some sort of a mushroom colony and place it on the ground floor.

To duplicate the mushroom, we can just click **Tool | SubTool | Duplicate** and select the mushroom again. This will add a duplicate as a subtool. Note that radial symmetry considers all subtools and works from their common center.

Now let's use three more functions of Transpose to rotate and scale the duplicates.

1. To modify an existing Action Line, grab the **outer circles** of the end points to move them around, as shown in the next screenshot:

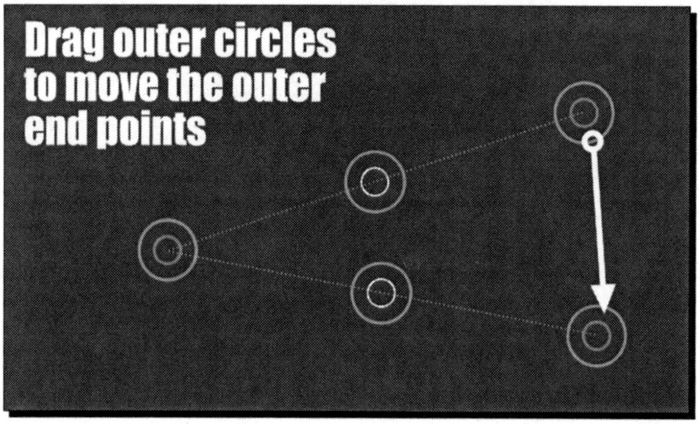


2. Grabbing the outer circle of the middle point will move the entire Action Line, as shown in the next screenshot:

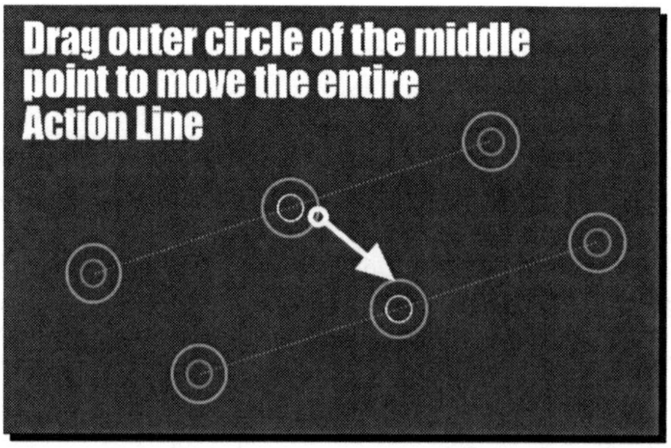

3. With rotate activated, grabbing the inner circle of an endpoint will rotate around the opposing endpoint, as shown in the following screenshot. By adjusting the Action Line, we can define our center of rotation, which is great:

The final mushroom colony could now look something like this:

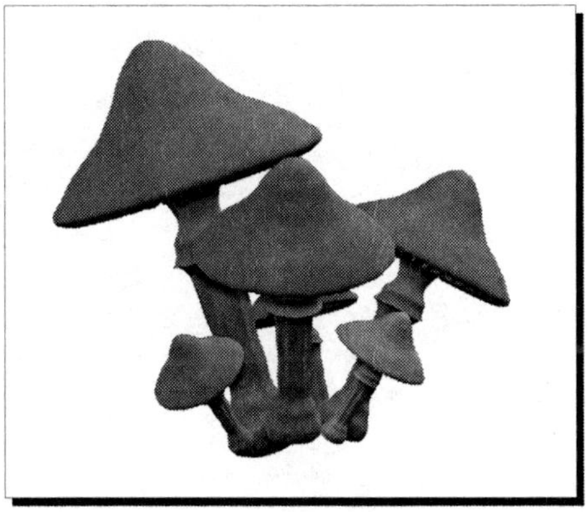

If you want to append all the mushrooms to the tree on the hill, you have to press **Tool | SubTool | Merge Down** a few times. If not clicked before, appending will only add the active subtool of the mushrooms to the hill, which is one mushroom only. By merging the mushrooms beforehand, they can be appended all at once.

> Merging down subtools keeps the Polygroups. This means we can still work on the mushrooms individually. Simply isolate them by their Polygroups like we did when sculpting the tree.

This is what our scene could now look like, if we press **Render | Best** with **Perspective** enabled and the MatCap White Cavity Material:

# Summary

We've finished our first environment scene by now, without any need to leave ZBrush. Quite easy, wasn't it?

We discussed in detail:

- How we can easily add additional meshes as subtools.
- How transpose helps us move, scale, and rotate our objects in the scene. The Action Line has various functions to accomplish that, like acting as a hinge when rotating around one endpoint. This is very useful, when rotating an arm for example, just place one endpoint on the shoulder joint and rotate the arm around it.
- How we can also start meshes from "primitives" like a Cone3D or even combine multiple ones with the **ReMesh All** function. We can use their initialize settings to control the initial shape before converting it to a Polymesh3D for sculpting.
- The Deformation subpalette provides us with another possibility to move or deform objects.
- How radial symmetry helps us to create ornaments or other objects, with radial symmetry in no time.

We've finished the whole environment of the tree in this chapter, which was the final step of our first model. It's now finished.

In the next chapter, we'll look into hard surface creation and how ZBrush exchanges models with other applications.

# 7

# Modeling a Sci-Fi Drone

*In this chapter, we'll talk about another workflow, starting a model in an external 3D application and finishing it in ZBrush afterwards. Starting from a concept of the drone, we'll then go ahead and talk about the most important modeling decisions. We'll also throw a quick glance at texture coordinates and finally learn how to bring the model from another 3D software into ZBrush.*

We'll cover in detail:

- How to exchange models between ZBrush and other 3D applications
- How to create optimized in-game meshes
- Creating the in-game mesh
- Unwrapping
- What UVs are and how to use them

# Using ZBrush with other 3D applications

In the **Tool Palette**, next to the **Load** and **Save** buttons, we can find another magical set of buttons that allow us to import and export meshes into and from ZBrush.

If we click on one of them, we can see that ZBrush is looking for `.obj` files, as shown in the subsequent screenshot. Since ZBrush version 4.0, the `GoZ` and `.ma` files are available to exchange models even faster. But, at the time of writing, **GoZ** only supports a limited number of applications, such as Maya, 3DSMax, Modo, and Cinema4D. So we'll concentrate on the `.obj` format, which can be read by almost any 3D application. If you use one of the applications named above, feel free to give it a try anyway.

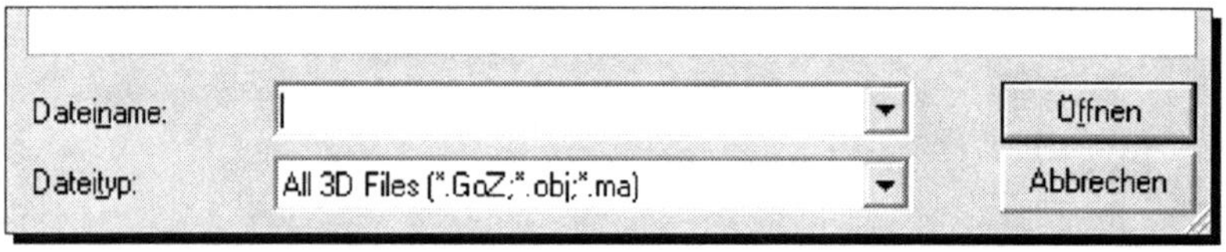


[ The `.obj` format is used for exchanging models between ZBrush and other 3D applications. `obj` files only store mesh information, no animations, cameras, lights, and so on. ]

In our case, this format allows us to start the optimized, in-game mesh of the drone in an external application and bring it over into ZBrush to detail it. But it works the other way around too.

But what does in-game mesh really mean?

# In-game meshes – less is more

Highly optimized meshes, to be used in games, are often called **low-poly**, or just **in-game meshes**. Since games are calculated in real-time, we try to preserve resources wherever possible to ensure it still runs smoothly, even on lower hardware setups. The most basic resource we try to optimize is the polygon count of our models. So we only use polygons where they add to the form.

Other important resources are textures, images that are applied to our mesh to add color, surface details, and so on. Game texture sizes are measured in pixels, like other digital images. Their dimensions are, most of the time, defined by power of 2. For example, 256 x 256, 512 x 512, or 1024 x 1024.

A 512 x 512 texture is four times the size of a 256 x 256 texture and will also take up four times the memory, so there are always questions about choosing the right texture size. As a rule of thumb, just think of how big the object will be seen in-game on your screen, to determine how many pixels of your monitor you'll have to cover.

# Workflows – where to start

In this chapter, we'll explore the workflow of working with a previously built in-game mesh. For this example, I used blender and GIMP Paint Studio. So our workflow looks like this:

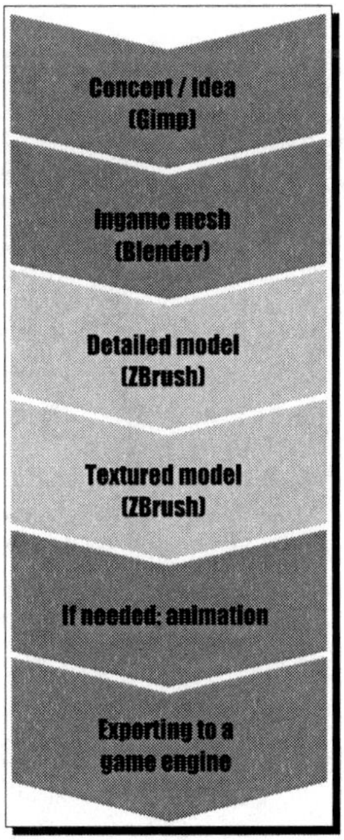

This workflow is a little bit faster and easier if we have some concept art and know exactly what we're going to do. But this limits us a bit in making massive changes to the concept while modeling, since we defined the in-game mesh in the beginning. For example, let's say we've built an in-game mesh of a horse, switched over into ZBrush for sculpting, but during the detailing we really wish it could be a unicorn with two heads. But our previously built mesh has only one head without horns, so at this point the fiddling begins. Sure, this is no dead end, and we can solve this too, but it all takes up time, which we can preserve if we plan ahead. So if you get a concept from the concept artist and your job is to rebuild it in 3D, creating the in-game mesh first is fine. If you're approaching this in a more creative way, having only a rough picture in mind, you may want to do it the other way around and build the in-game mesh at the very end.

Let's talk about the concept art to build the in-game mesh from.

# Concept art – the Pioneer Drone

Let's say we're currently developing a Sci-Fi-Shooter. One of the featured places is a dusty and rocky planet rich in resources, struck with poverty, and dominated by the mining companies.

This drone serves as a light scout, looking for raw material deposits. On success, it can be docked to a harvester and be used as a drill head to extract the resources, especially in the areas where bigger ships can't navigate freely anymore.

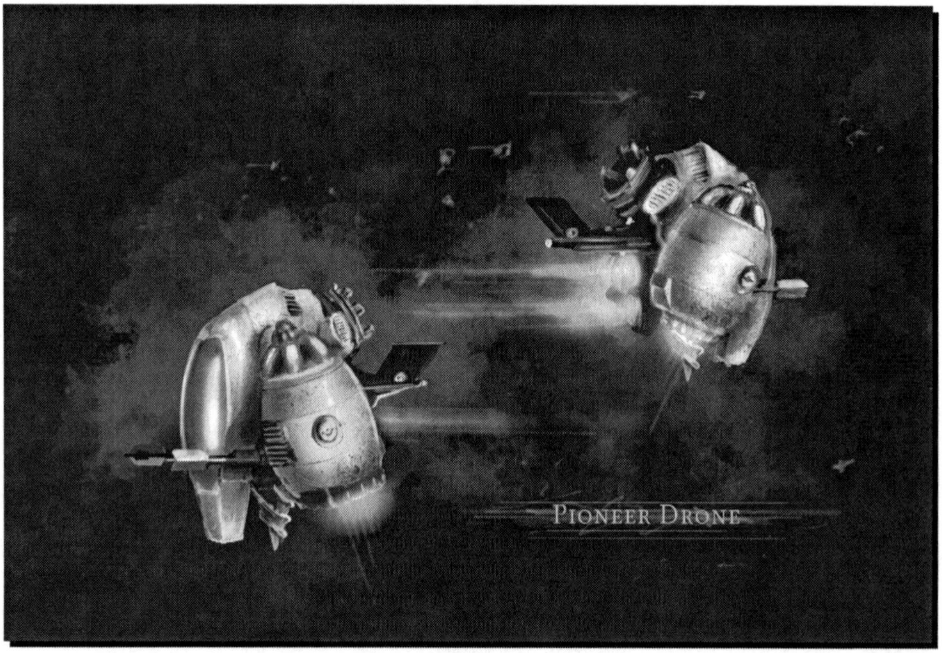

# The in-game mesh

Since this is a book about ZBrush, we'll keep this section of modeling in another 3D application rather short. There are plenty of tutorials out there that cover low-poly modeling, which also differs for each application. So we'll talk about more general decisions in the process. It is not assumed that you build this drone by yourself in the course of this short chapter, but rather understand some basic approaches for this. Feel free to give it a try anyway, but the in-game mesh will also be provided via a download link at the beginning of the next chapter.

Let's start with the statement that there's no rule where to start.

If building a continuous mesh, it's easier to start with large or central parts like a torso and develop the smaller parts from it.

It's useful to break down the model into smaller modeling tasks instead of building it all in one. This allows for more flexibility during the whole process, also making rearrangements easier. Thus, we split up the mesh into logical components, such as the engine, the hull, the drill, and so on.

In this case, I started with a very central part– the drill– which looks more complex than it actually is. If you use blender, a function called screw will create this for you out of a simple cross section. There are similar functions in other applications for this too.

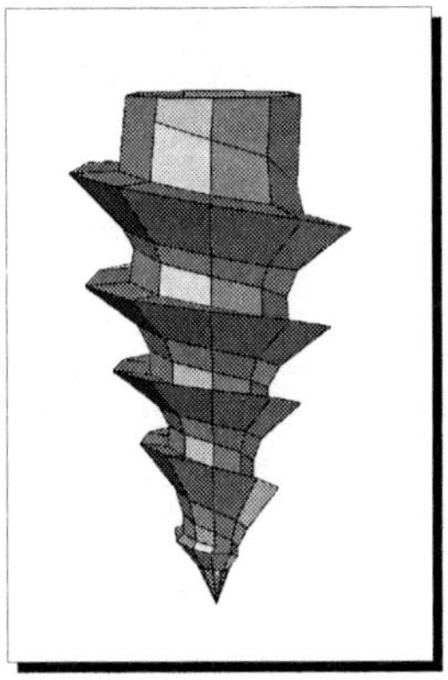

The hull and the windshield were modeled as two separate objects, allowing us to control their polygon count individually. This is also possible, since they bear different colors anyway, so we don't have to cover any line of intersection. Opposed to that, the two fans at the rear have to be connected to the hull, creating a nice continuous surface, which is a distinctive feature of hulls.

Also note that most of the mesh is composed out of quads. In the end, game engines will convert every polygon to triangles anyway, but it's much easier for us to work with quads. Especially in ZBrush, quads produce the cleanest results when subdivided.

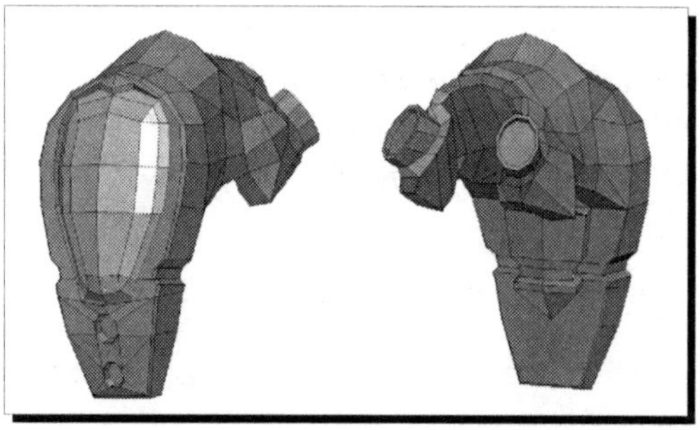

The engine, the hull is placed onto, is constructed out of nested cylinders and cubes. Underlying, partly visible components create the illusion of a highly complex object, the hull occludes, which adds to its believability.

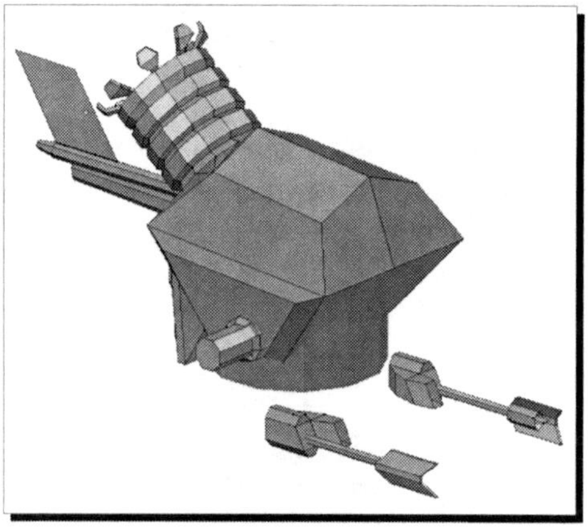

The subsequent screenshot shows the construction of the mesh as an exploded assembly drawing, which outlines how simple the model really is, when broken down into smaller parts:

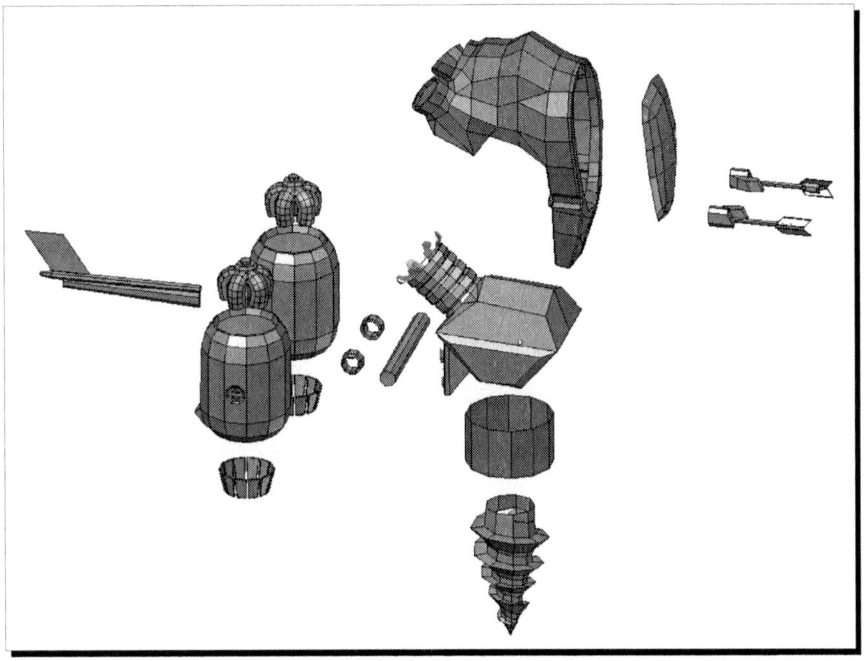

A technical model like this also works with hints to details, like a character illustration. If there's a detailed main part, the rest of the drawing can be rather loose and you'll still get the message across.

To further optimize the polygon count of our mesh, we deleted any polygons that aren't visible in the end, for the reason that there's no need for closed shapes in an in-game mesh.

Our final mesh now looks like the next screenshot. At this final stage, it's a good idea to check and tweak the silhouette of our model, so we can concentrate on the details from now on:

# Texture coordinates

After finishing the in-game mesh, the next step is to unwrap the mesh to prepare it for texturing.

You've probably heard of images applied to models being referred to as **textures** before. To map these textures onto our mesh, we have to tell the game engine which pixel of the texture shall be mapped onto which polygon. This process is called **unwrapping** and produces flat representations of our 3D geometry. A texture can then be applied to the model according to this map.

The following screenshot shows the result of the unwrapping process of a human head. In this example, we can easily recognize a face since it's all made out of one piece:

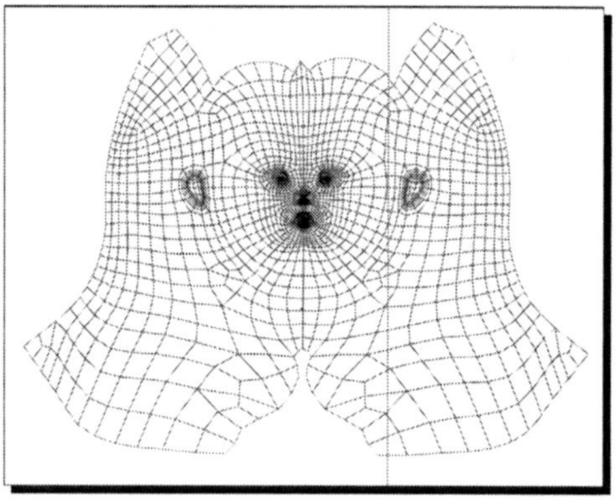

This laid out mesh structure is also referred to as texture coordinates, **UV-coordinates** or just **UVs**.

Technical objects, like our Pioneer Drone don't offer that much of a continuous surface, so breaking it up into little pieces is unavoidable. As you can see, this also comes at the cost of clarity, as the following screenshot shows:

> The `.obj` format stores UV-coordinates, so we can easily exchange models with texture coordinates between applications.

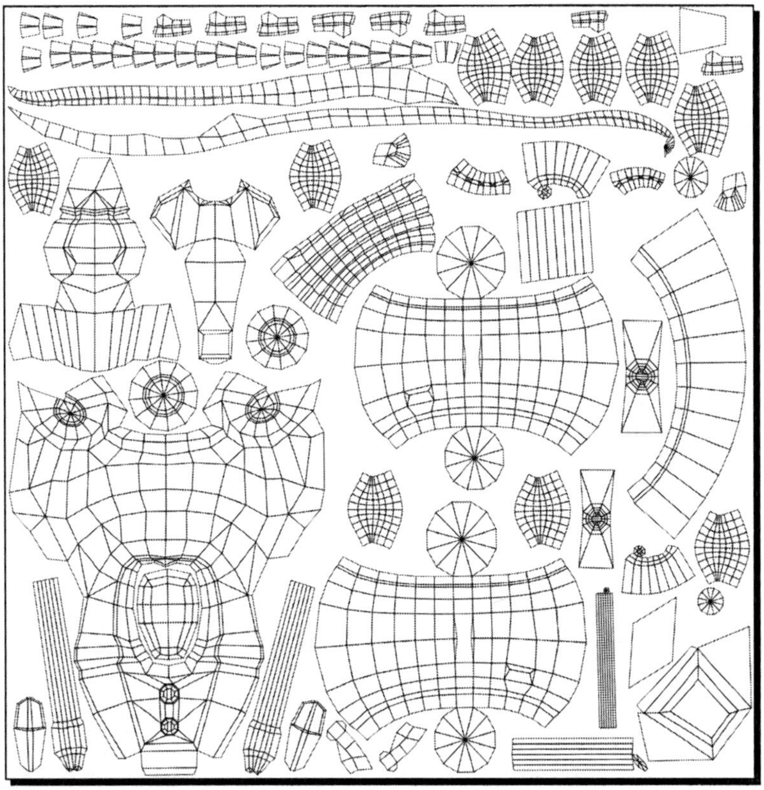

So, for displaying textures in games, we usually need to set up texture coordinates. The main challenge about unwrapping is to maximize the coverage of the texture, while keeping it still organized and clear.

The reason why we do the unwrapping at this early stage is that we will create Polygroups from our UV-coordinates in the next chapter. With well laid out Polygroups, sculpting is much more convenient. We'll talk a bit more in depth about creating UV-coordinates in the later chapters, but for now that's all we need to start off with the sculpting of the Pioneer Drone.

## Pop quiz – in-game meshes

1. What kind of information can be stored within the `.obj` format?
    a. Mesh information and UV-Coordinates
    b. Cameras and lights
    c. Animations

2. Why do we try to use as few polygons as possible for in-game meshes?
    a. To do less work on the models
    b. To preserve performance
    c. Because low polygon models look better

# Summary

In this chapter, we've learned a lot about texture coordinates and modeling in-game meshes. We've covered in detail:

- How to use the `.obj` format to exchange models, including texture coordinates between ZBrush and other applications
- How to to keep the polygon count and the texture size at a minimum to increase performance
- How to break down complex objects into smaller tasks
- How to handle in-game meshes by keeping as many quads as possible because quads are easier to work with and lead to much cleaner results in ZBrush than triangles
- How Unwrapping creates UV coordinates we can use to apply textures to our object

After completing the low-poly mesh, let's start sculpting our second game model right away, in the next chapter.

# 8

# Sci-Fi-Drone: Hard Surface Sculpting

*In this chapter, we'll sculpt our first hard surface model, the Pioneer Drone. After preparing the in-game mesh in the previous chapter, we'll now import and detail it in ZBrush.*

*We've already talked about organic sculpting techniques in the prior chapters. Since our drone is a technical object, we will now advance to hard surface sculpting techniques and brushes to achieve the desired technical look.*

We'll have a closer look at:

- Preparing our mesh with Polygroups
- Masking
- Hard surface brushes, especially Polish, Trim, and Planar brushes
- Working with Alphas and Strokes
- Sculpting a hard surface model from start to finish

## Preparing the mesh for sculpting

Before we start, let's prepare our drone so we can work carefree.

# Time for action – preparing the mesh

1. Import the downloaded mesh by pressing **Tool | Import** and navigate to the respective download folder.
2. As we saw in the previous chapter, the mesh is composed of several primitive objects. We can use that to create **Polygroups** by clicking on **Tool | Polygroups | Autogroups with UV**.
3. Enable **Polyframe**, either via **Transform | PolyF(rame)** or by pressing *Shift + F*. With Polyframe enabled, we should now see that ZBrush automatically created Polygroups for us.

4. Objects with many overlapping parts tend to be overly influenced by the shadows. You can disable shadows under **Render | Shadows** if you like.
5. Disable Subdivide smoothing by disabling the **Smt** button found under **Tool | Geometry | Smt**.
6. **Divide** the mesh **two times** so the slider shows a subdivision level of three.
7. Enable **Tool | Geometry | Smt** and divide three more times, up to subdivision level six, so that the mesh has around 2.6 million polygons.

## *What just happened?*

We've just finished some quick preparatory steps for the hard surface sculpting.

Let's have a closer look at what we've done:

# Autogroups

We started to make use of our object structure by using the **Autogroups with UV** button. Autogroups analyzes the mesh topology and creates a polygroup for every continuous surface part of the mesh. The Autogroups with UV function also considers how the mesh was unwrapped and where it was "cut".

The engine for instance, does have a continuous mesh topology, but is also unwrapped in two parts, one for the overall hull and one for the side detail. So, using the Autogroups button only analyzes mesh topology and creates one Polygroup for the engines, whereas the Autogroups with UV also considers the UV coordinates, creating two groups, as shown in the next screenshot:

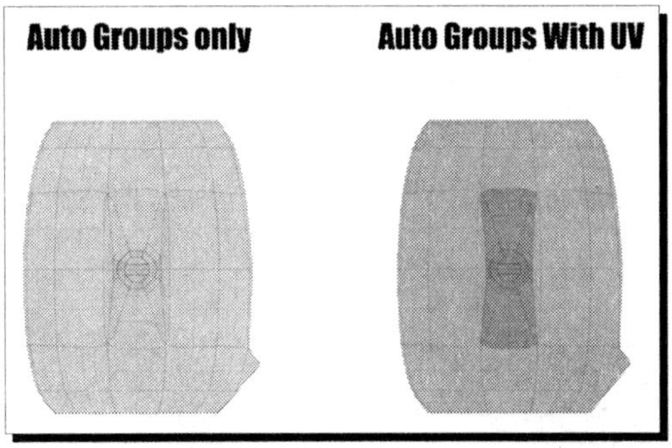


We can also split our mesh apart by its topology by clicking on **Tool | SubTool | GroupsSplit**. Like Autogroups, this will create a separate subtool for each continuous surface of our mesh. With the mesh split into several subtools, ZBrush can handle a higher polygon count than it could with one single mesh. But this would also make things more complicated, so for the sake of simplicity we will keep it as one.

We also talked about toggling shadows on and off in ZBrush. As you saw, shadows enhance the 3-dimensional effect, showing which parts of the object overlap others. But on the other hand, this may also keep us from spotting problematic surface parts that need further refinement when covered in shadow. This is like turning Perspective on and off, both are valuable options in different situations.

## Subdividing for hard surface sculpting

But why did we divide our model six times, starting from high to low, not vice versa?

The point about this is that we have our basic shape already defined and need to add some surface detail now. As we will see in the next example, the hard surface tools create nice sharp edges, but only if our mesh features enough polygons. So the hard surface sculpting part is really something that is done at higher levels of subdivision. If we want to change larger shapes, we can always step down as much as needed.

Also note that we turned off the **Smt** button when adding the first two levels of subdivision to preserve the shape of the model. The amount of smoothing depends on the density of the polygons. Since our in-game mesh is quite optimized, it has a very low polygon density and thus would be smoothed quite strongly. To better illustrate this process, the next screenshot shows the mesh of the drone divided six times, with and without smoothing enabled. As you can see, when turning **Smt** off, it preserves the entire shape and all its edges from being smoothed. Also note that low density areas like the tail fin that consists only of one quad, lose quite a lot of their shape when smoothed:

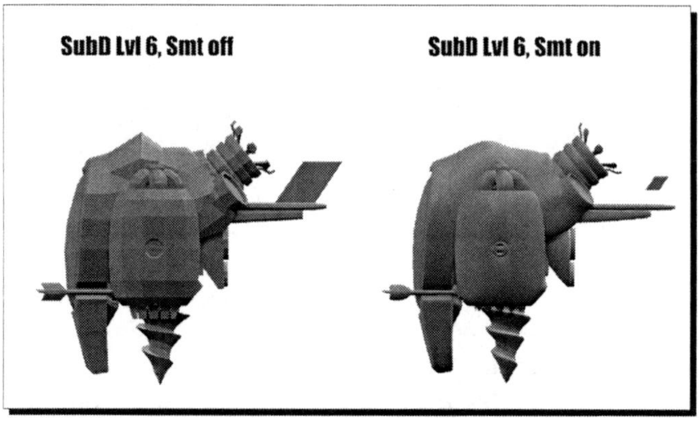


# Hard surface brushes

As we already saw, ZBrush 4.0 comes with a vast amount of brushes. But, if we take a closer look we'll see that there are, for example, 10 variations of the planar brush, so we can categorize them easily. Our three main brushes for hard surface sculpting, in this chapter, will be the **Planar-**, **Polish,** and the **Trim** brushes. Let's get an overview of what defines these brushes and how to use them.

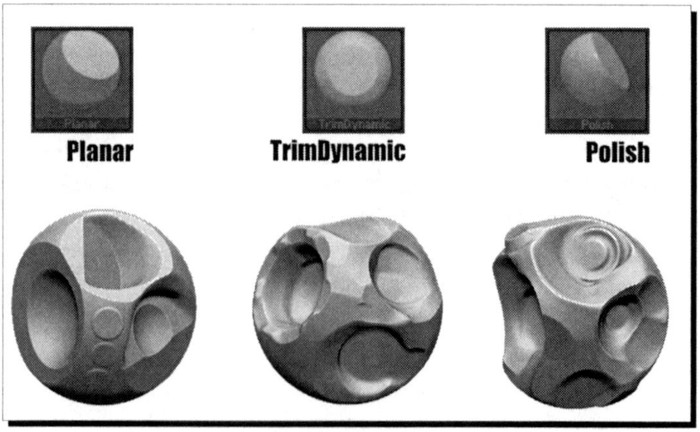

The **Planar** brushes work like cutting off some part of the mesh, or making it planar, hence the name. This will give us plain surfaces with sharp edges, like goggles, for example.

The **Trim Dynamic** also creates planar surfaces, but changes its orientation while drawing across the surface. The Trim brushes allow for a more sketchy way of establishing hard surface areas.

The **Polish** brushes can create smooth surface transitions with low pressure and sharp creases with high pressure. This is somehow an all-rounder, used quite often.

With that said, let's see what we can make of this.

## Time for action – sculpting the upper air outlets

1. Let's isolate the hull we'll work on now. Since we created polygroups with Autogroups UV, this only takes us one click. Pressing *Ctrl + Shift* and left-clicking on the hull will isolate this polygroup, as shown in the following screenshot:

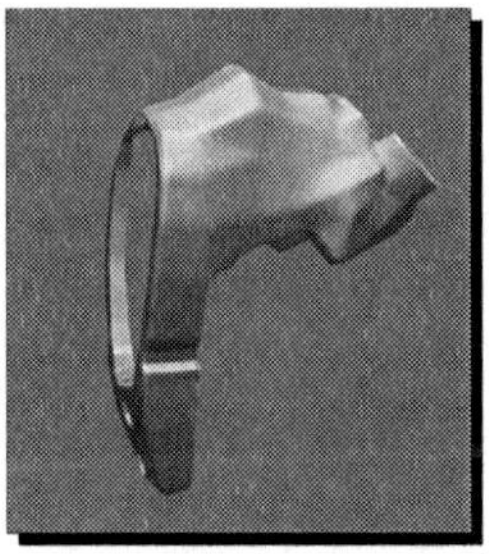

2. As we divided two times in the beginning without smoothing activated, we'll now have to smooth certain parts that should be rounded in shape, like the air outlets. To do so, step down two subdivision levels, either by using the SDiv-slider under **Tool | Geometry | SDiv**, or by simply hitting *Shift + D*.

3. Smooth the upper air outlets with the Smooth brush by pressing *Shift*, as the next screenshot shows:

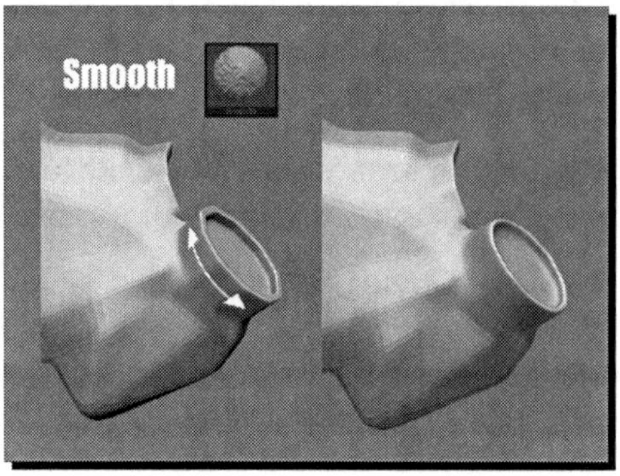


4. Step up to the highest level of subdivision again by pressing *D* several times.
5. Make sure that **Transform | Activate Symmetry** is active or just press *X*.

> If you're not sure which axis of symmetry should be activated, you can either go by trial and error or activate the **Floor Grid** to check the orientation by clicking the **Floor** button in the shelf or by hitting **Draw | Floor**.

6. We can paint masks with almost any brush we like, by pressing *Ctrl*. Switch to the **Standard** brush, set the **Rgb Intensity** to **100** and paint a mask on the inside of the air outlet as shown in the following image.
7. Switch to the **Flat Color Material** to check the masking.
8. To refine the mask, we can paint-erase it by holding *Ctrl + Alt*. Correct the masking on the inner rim and make sure there are no points masked accidentally on the outside.

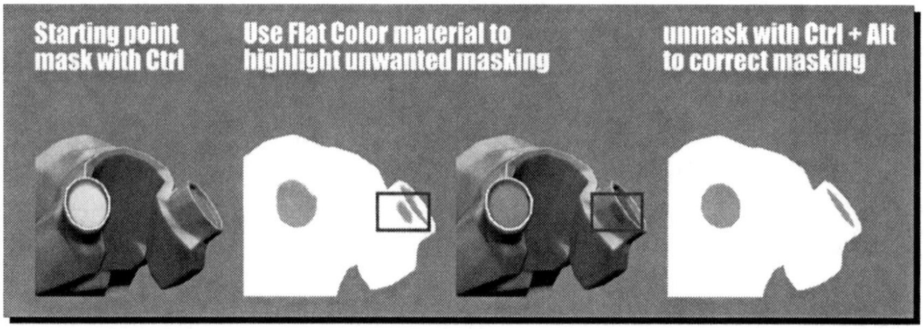

9. When finished with the mask, **invert** it by holding *Ctrl* and left-clicking on an empty part of the canvas or by clicking on **Tool | Masking | Inverse**.

10. Pick the **Planar** brush and flatten the inner part of the air outlet. Start in the middle and move the cursor outwards in one stroke, as shown in the next screenshot:

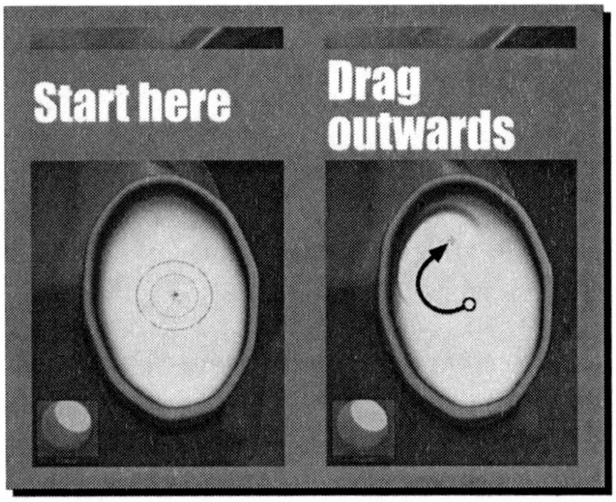


11. With the inner part flattened, let's keep the masking and create the grill. Rotate the model and snap the rotation with *Shift* to view your model exactly from behind as shown in the subsequent screenshot. Now rotate your model downwards a little to get a good view of one of the outlets.

12. To mask the grill, make sure perspective is turned off and you choose a brush without alpha, like the Standard brush.

13. After this, hold down *Ctrl* and drag a rectangular shaped mask on one outlet, starting on an empty part of the canvas. After letting go, symmetry will update the masking on the other half. Try masking the grill evenly as shown in the next image:

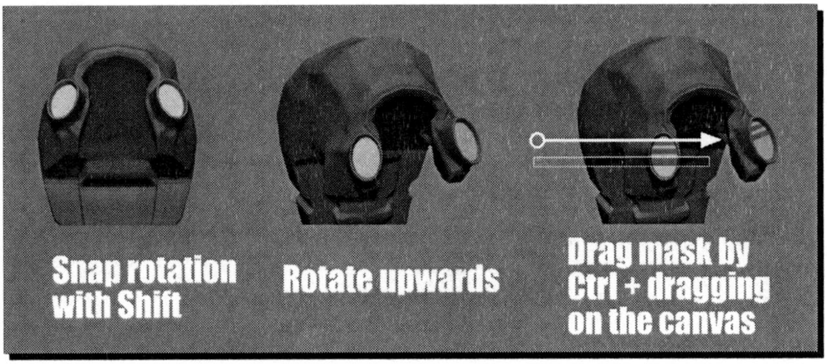

[ We can reposition the mask by pressing *Spacebar* while dragging the mask. ]

14. Now that our mask is finished, all we have to do is go to the **Tool | Deformation** Tab and **inflate** the unmasked area by **-20**, which will push it inwards. That's it; we've finished our air outlet grill.

## What just happened?

We've now finished the air outlet grills by using advanced masking and the Polish brush. Now, let's discuss some key topics:

Before using the **smoothing**, we stepped down two levels of subdivision. The Smooth brush, as well as subdividing with the Smt option have a stronger effect on areas with lower subdivision, so stepping down strengthens the smooth effect. This way we can better control if we want to smoothen fine details on higher subdivision levels or global forms on lower levels of subdivision.

Since it is used a lot, using hotkeys for stepping up and down in subdivision is quite a timesaver.

[ Press *D* to step up in subdivision
Press *Shift + D* to step down in subdivision.
Press *Ctrl + D* to add a new subdivision level. ]

## Masking

By now we've explored several ways we can create masks:

- We can create masks affecting the whole model, for example by masking all of its cavities like we did on the tree mesh.
- Custom masks can be painted and erased with virtually any brush by simply holding *Ctrl*. Erasing can be done by holding *Ctrl + Alt*.
- Additionally, we can drag a mask to get exact borders or to easily mask one half of the model.

Since masking works like polypaint, its resolution depends on the amount of vertices available. Therefore, we stepped up to the highest subdivision level to capture most of the detail. Another aspect masking and polypainting have in common is that the **opacity** of both is determined by the **Rgb Slider**. When working with masks, the Flat color material is a great way to check for errors.

As we saw and also will see, masking is a very powerful tool to complete all sorts of tasks.

What's new about the Planar brush is that its effect depends on where we start our stroke from. As we hover our cursor across the mesh, it orients itself to the surface and shows the plane the Planar brush will flatten more elevated points to.

## Pop quiz - masking

1. Which one of the following statements about masks is false?
    a. The resolution of masking depends on the amount of vertices available.
    b. The opacity of the masking depends on the Z Intensity.
    c. Symmetry will mirror any masking we do.

## Time for action – adding details to the rear exhausts

Let's explore some more hard surface sculpting:

1. First isolate one rear exhaust by *Ctrl + Shift clicking* on one of them.
2. Then *Ctrl + Shift and drag on the canvas* to invert the visibility.
3. Hide the second exhaust, as done previously in step 1, by *Ctrl + Shift-clicking*.
4. Invert the visibility again, like in step 2, with *Ctrl +Shift + drag*. You should now have isolated the two rear exhausts.
5. Smooth the outer hard edges of the upper exhaust like we did with the air outlets.

6. Pick the **TrimAdaptive** brush and lay in some dents, as shown in the subsequent image:

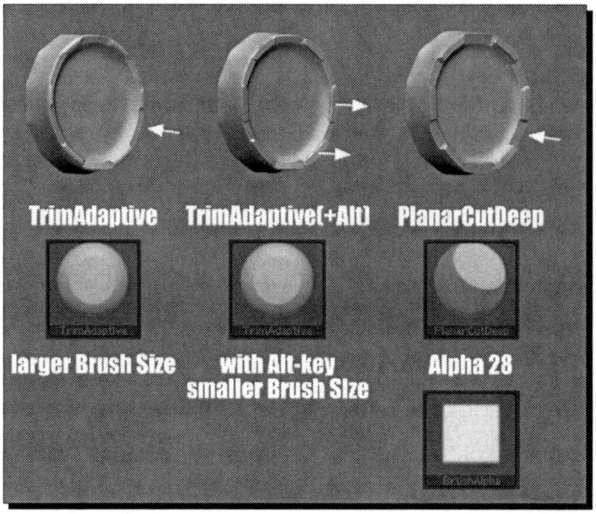


7. Lower your draw size, so that the cursor's diameter matches the rim's diameter. Refine the peaks while holding the *Alt*-key, as shown in the previous image.

8. Finally, pick the **PlanarCutDeep** brush from the **brushes tab** in **Lightbox.** We can navigate inside **Lightbox** by clicking and dragging.

9. Change the alpha of the PlanarCutDeep brush to **Alpha 28**. Changing the alpha can be done either in the shelf or by bringing up the quick menu with right-click or *Spacebar*, if we're working with the shelf hidden. The next screenshot shows both ways:

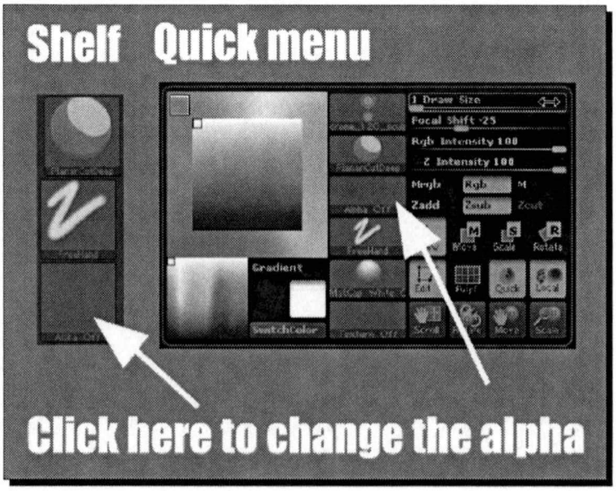

10. With the outer rim finished, let's work on the inner portion of the exhaust. Pick the **PlanarCutDeep** brush again and turn the **Alpha off**. With a larger draw size, push the inner portion inwards, as shown in the next image.

11. Lower the draw size a bit and hold down the *Alt-Key* to push a smaller portion of it outwards again.

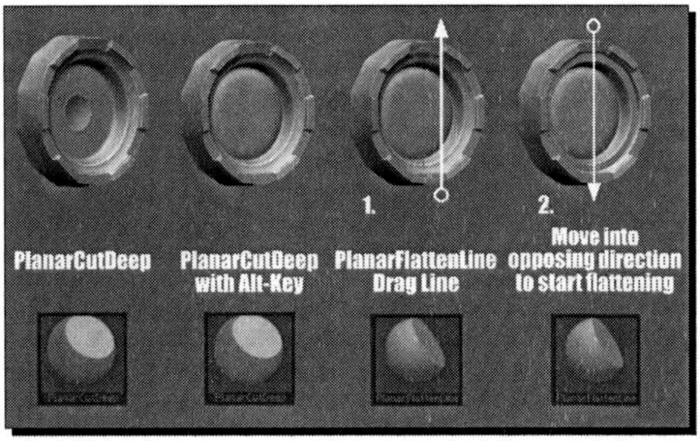


12. To add a second inner rim, as shown in the previous image, choose the **PlanarFlattenLine** brush. This allows us to drag a virtual plane we will flatten higher points to. Move your cursor on a lower part of where the inner rim should be and drag a line to a lower opposing point. To start flattening, move your cursor into the opposing direction of the drawn line, as shown in the previous image.

13. If nothing seems to happen, it's probably because your start and end points of the line are elevated too much. The next image better explains how the **Line** feature works. As we can see, it only flattens points that are lying "above" the plane. Just drag another line between two points lying directly at the inner rim, which are the least elevated to achieve the desired effect:

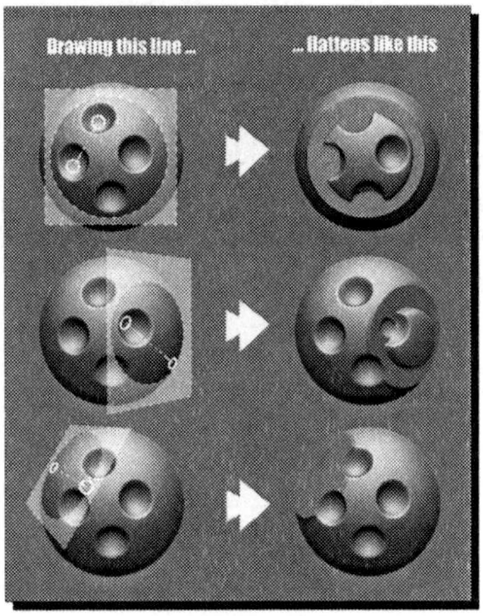

14. We're nearly done with the exhaust. For the final detail, choose the **Standard brush**, switch from dots as a **stroke type** to **DragRect** (-angle) and select **Alpha34**, as shown in the following image.

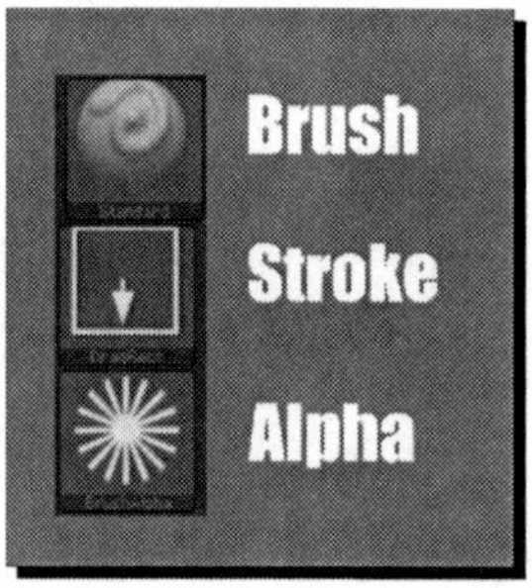


15. Make sure **symmetry** is turned **off** under **Transform | Activate Symmetry**.

> The hotkey for toggling symmetry is *X*. Note that this only toggles symmetry, but has no effect on which axis the symmetry works on. The axis of symmetry still has to be set in the Transform palette.

16. With the **Standard brush**, **DragRect,** and **Alpha 34** selected, start dragging outwards from the center of the exhaust, as the next image demonstrates. You can also rotate your brush while dragging:

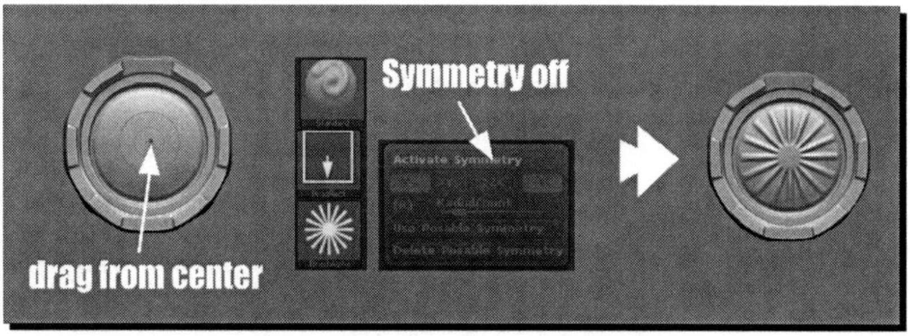


17. That was the final step; just make sure to turn on symmetry again for further sculpting.

## What just happened?

We've now accomplished our second hard surface modeling task. Let's quickly recap what we did.

The TrimAdaptive brush as well as many other brushes do have a direction that can be inverted by holding *Alt*. With this option, we only had to use four brushes for the exhaust, which is next to nothing.

Opposed to the more sketchy way of the TrimAdaptive brush, the PlanarCutDeep brush works more similarly to the Planar brush. It cuts vertices down to a plane. The PlanarCut brush additionally pushes vertices inwards; the **PlanarCutDeep** brush pushes them even more. As you can see, there are many presets originating from a few brushes.

## Alphas

Alphas are a kind of stencil for your brush. You may know how they work from other 2D image editors, which also provide an alpha channel. For us, this opens up a whole new level of sculpting, because we can add complex patterns to our brush and simply apply them to our mesh, like wrinkles, scratches, pores, and so on. We already worked with alphas in the previous chapters, as they come as a default preset with some brushes like the ClayTubes brush for example, which has a rectangular shaped alpha. By changing the alpha of the PlanarCutDeep brush to this rectangular one, we made sure that we got sharp angular edges, instead of rounded circular ones.

Alphas are basically only grayscale images, so we can easily create our own. We'll have a closer look at this in the later chapters.

But alphas are only one part of the equation. Together with the stroke types we can set, the possibilities are nearly endless. The Drag rectangle stroke we used for instance is very useful for placing exact details with accurate rotations, like ornaments, letters or the like. When using different brushes, have a closer look at their default alphas and stroke types to learn more about how to use them efficiently.

When we change the alpha or stroke type of a brush, ZBrush will remember its settings, even if we pick up another brush. On restart of ZBrush, all brush settings will be reset. If we like to do so without restarting, there's a button labeled **Reset All Brushes** in the Brush palette.

## Have a go hero – finishing the second exhaust

Now that we know how the land lies, finishing the smaller exhaust should be an easy task. As shown in the next screenshot, first the outer rim is flattened again, then the inner portion is defined with the **PlanarCutDeep** brush at different sizes, and finally finished with the addition of the **Alpha34** with the **Standard** brush.

Note that the design elements of both exhausts are the same, but arranged differently, to give it some variation.

If we unhide all other objects and the inner part of the exhaust isn't visible, we have to isolate it again and push it outwards with the **transpose tool**.

## Time for action – sculpting the hull

Now that we've completed the air outlets and the rear exhausts, let's go on with detailing the hull:

1. If not already the case, **turn on symmetry**.
2. Isolate the hull and smooth it as shown in the next screenshot. Try to preserve the hard edges by smoothing only sideways, which is how the hull pieces flow:

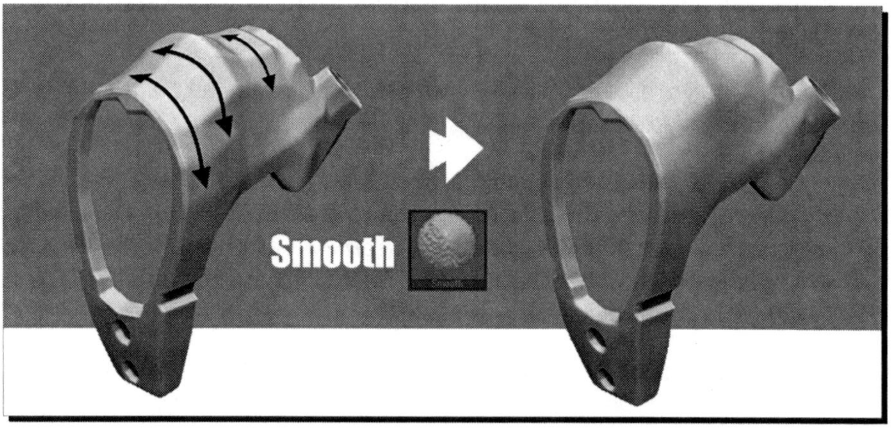


3. With that done, let's quickly shape the headlights. As the next image shows, this process is quite similar to what we've done with the rear exhausts.
4. First lower the subdivision level to smooth out the edges of the headlights better. Afterwards step up to the highest level.

5. Select the **PolishHard** brush from **Lightbox** and flatten the inner part with high pressure. Then hold down the *Alt*-key and raise the middle part of the headlights with medium pressure.

> With medium pressure the PolishHard brush will give us more rounded forms, opposed to high pressure which produces flat, sharp-edged surfaces. If you don't have access to a pen tablet with pressure sensitivity, pick the PlanarCut brush instead, which gives similar results to the PolishHard brush with high pressure.

6. Lower the draw size a bit and push a smaller area inwards with high pressure.
7. Finally, flatten the inner area with the **Planar** brush and you're done.

8. Let's continue on the upper part of the hull. First pick the **PolishHard-** or **PolishMed** brush and polish the hull surface as shown in step two in the following image. Similar to smoothing the surface, try to polish with the surface flow, preserving hard edges. To get smooth transitions with the Polish brushes, draw with very low pressure. The higher the pressure, the sharper the edges. Use higher pressure to establish a nice sharp edge at the top. I also lowered the topmost part a bit from step one to two:

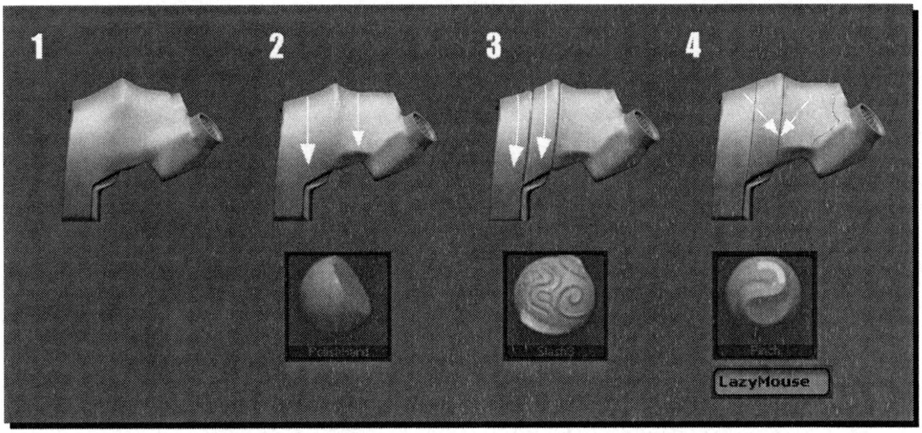

9. Following step three in the previous image, let's draw some creases that separate the hull parts. Switch to the **Slash3** brush. Set **Stroke | Lazy Radius** to **40** and lower the draw size, as usual, to carve in some fine creases. Since a hull like this would also cover the bottom, make sure the creases continue there. You may want to disable LazyMouse(*L*) for final corrections. For instance, the edges between the bottom and side are quite difficult to get right with LazyMouse on.

10. Finalize the creases with the **Pinch** brush. This will make the creases thinner and as a side effect also increases the vertex density in that area since it attracts the surrounding vertices. Therefore, the creases appear less angular. Because we try to follow the strokes of the Slash3 brush, which had **LazyMouse on**, let's turn it on for the Pinch brush too, by activating **Stroke | LazyMouse**.

11. Now comes the more freehand part. First, pick the good old **Claytubes** brush and lay in some basic forms as shown in the first step of the next image. Try not to push the surface too far in- or outwards, since we won't be able to capture points too far away for the in-game preview in the next chapter.

12. Following step two of the subsequent image, refine the rough forms with the **TrimDynamic** brush, which can flatten areas in a more freehand way than the Planar brushes do, while trying to maintain the underlying surface structure. I find this one of the fastest hard surface brushes to work with.

13. In the end, the Planar brushes are used to make some areas perfectly flat or to add some minor details. While working with those freehand strokes, you may want to protect the freshly drawn creases by quickly masking them.

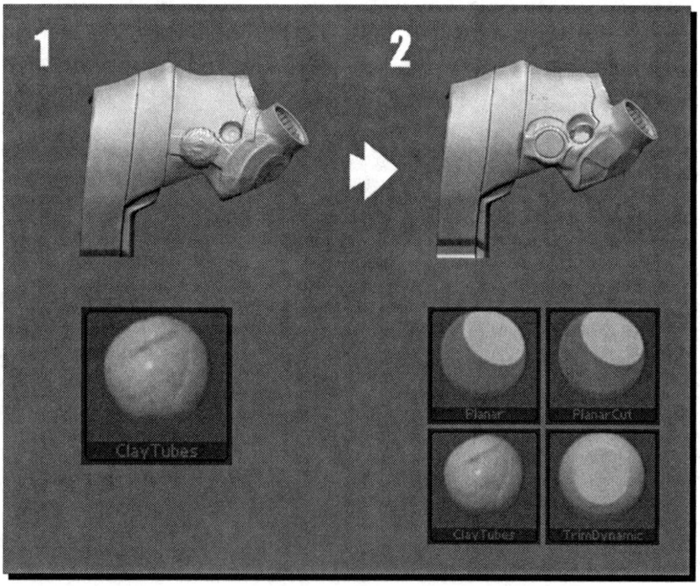

**14.** Let's proceed by adding additional air outlet details at the top of the hull. Rotate the model to view it from the top by snapping the rotation with *Shift*. Now switch to the **ClayTubes** brush and **mask** the **border** of the air outlet as shown in the next image. Make sure that the **Rgb Slider** is set to **100**:

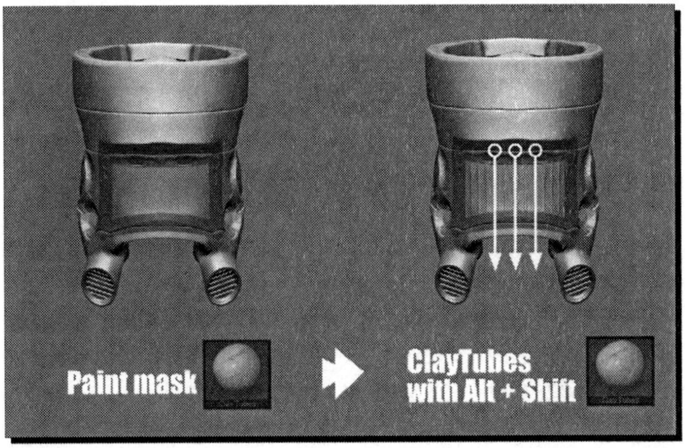


**15.** With that done, hold down the *Alt* key and start in the masked area, as shown in the previous screenshot. After left-clicking, hold down the *Shift Key* to draw a straight line. Note that the order of pressing *Shift* and *Alt* is crucial, because pressing *Shift* before clicking will switch to the Smooth brush. So we first have to hold down *Alt* and left-click and then press *Shift* to draw a straight line. Adjust the Z Intensity if you like to push it inwards even more. That's it for the hull.

## What just happened?

Now we've finished the hard surface sculpting of the hull. As we understand which brush can be used for which task, it all comes down to practice and familiarizing ourselves with the tools, which we did in this section.

As we saw, the Polish brushes behave differently depending on the amount of pressure. When we get used to this, it allows for quick polishing without having to change brushes all the time.

The point that we worked with the Pinch brush with LazyMouse on, underlines that virtually all brushes in ZBrush are simply well-thought-out presets. This does mean that we can also use functions inherent in one brush and use it in combination with another.

When holding the *Shift key* after left-clicking, we can draw straight lines at 45 degree angles, starting at the point we clicked. These straight strokes are always straight, relative to your view, not to the model. This allows for more freedom, if we want to draw a line in a certain way, we can simply rotate the model accordingly. Another possibility to draw straight lines is the **Line Feature** we already used with the Planar Flatten Line brush. We can find it under **Stroke | LazyMouse | Backtrack | SnapToTrack | Line.** Here, we have to activate **Lazymouse**, then **Backtrack** and then **SnapToTrack** and **Line**, to get the desired effect on any brush we like. We can also use *Shift* in combination with the Line feature to draw lines at 45 degree angles.

# SmartReSym—lifesavers if something goes wrong

Now we're in the middle of finishing a complete model, and chances are that something goes wrong. For example, we may accidentally have pressed the *X*-key and deactivated symmetry. We didn't take notice of it and continued working, but all of a sudden, we rotate the model and see that our work hasn't been mirrored over to the other side. No need to panic, a feature called **SmartReSym**, located in the **Deformations subpalette** will help us out here.

As shown in the next screenshot, we can easily mask good-looking areas that we want to preserve and simply leave the area, to be corrected, unmasked. After determining which axis we want to mirror on, it just takes us one click of a button to mirror the details over.

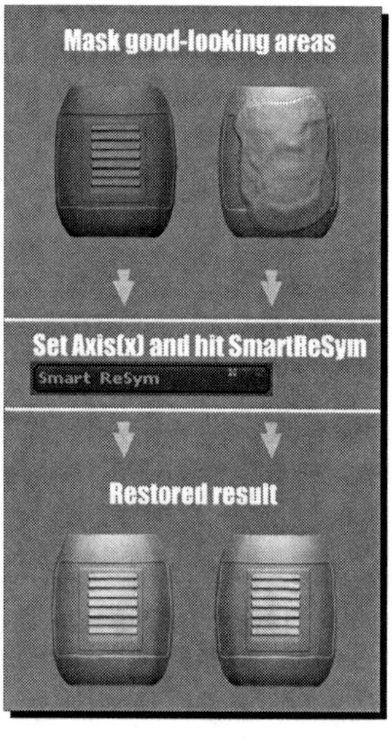

We don't even have to mask one half; we can also mask everything except for one air outlet and have it mirrored from the other side. After mirroring, make sure you check the mesh where the borders of the masking have been, there may be some little distortions that need some touchup.

Ideally, you never have to use SmartResym.

Knowing that, we're now prepared to create the engines, as shown in the previous example screenshot.

## Time for action – detailing the engines

Let's use masking again for quickly adding some nice details to the engines:

1. Step down two levels of subdivision and smooth the engines a bit to get rid of that hard-edged look while still keeping the hard edges at the caps.
2. Make sure **symmetry** is **on, perspective** is **turned off**, and your model is back at its highest subdivision level again to get the best masking possible. Also make sure **Alpha** is **set** to **off** and **RGB** is at **100.**
3. Isolate the engines and snap the rotation with *Shift* to view them exactly from the front.
4. Now drag a rectangular mask while holding *Ctrl* as usual, as shown in the next screenshot.

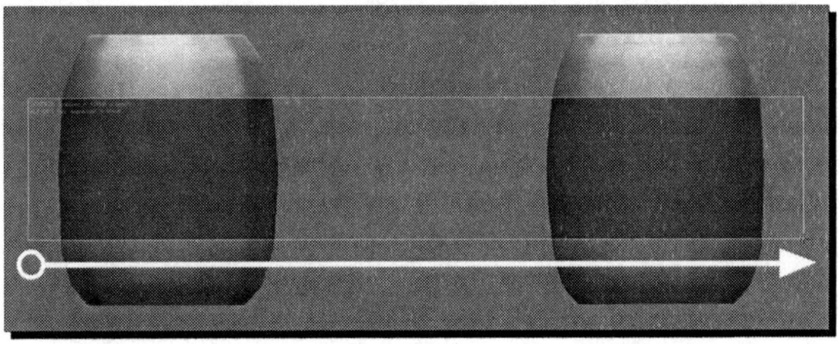

5. Snap the rotation again with *Shift* to view the engines from the side.
6. Now unmask a vertical stripe in the middle by holding *Ctrl + Alt* while dragging, as the next screenshot shows.

7. Invert that mask by *Ctrl* + left-clicking on an empty part of the canvas, as the following screenshot shows:

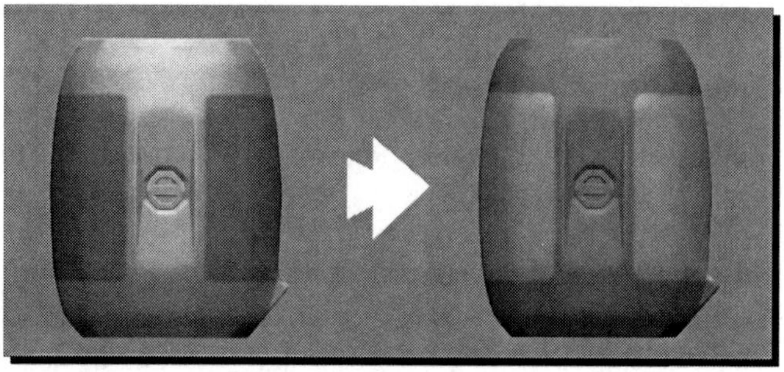

8. Blur the mask once by clicking on **Tool | Masking | BlurMask**.

9. Finally, in the **Tool | Deformation** Subpalette, **inflat** the unmasked area by **-15**, as shown in the next screenshot:

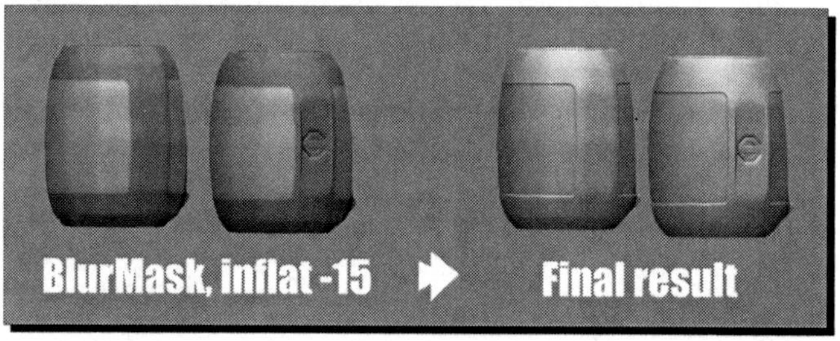


10. With that done, let's finish some minor details, as shown in the next image. The left part shows the bottom of the engines, which was inset by using the **PlanarCut** brush. The right part shows the flattened little detail, done with the **PlanarFlattenLine** brush with **Alpha28** selected:

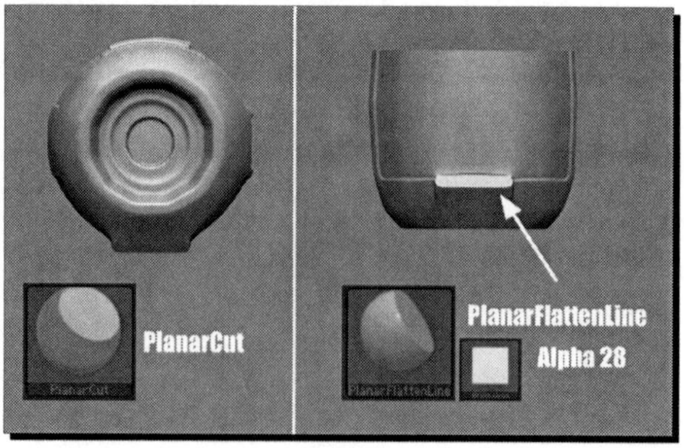

11. Let's finish the engines by doing what we're best at, adding air outlets. At first, snap the rotation of the engines to view them from the front.

12. Create a mask as shown in the next screenshot, using the techniques discussed previously. Make sure **symmetry** is **turned on**, so the masking gets mirrored over.

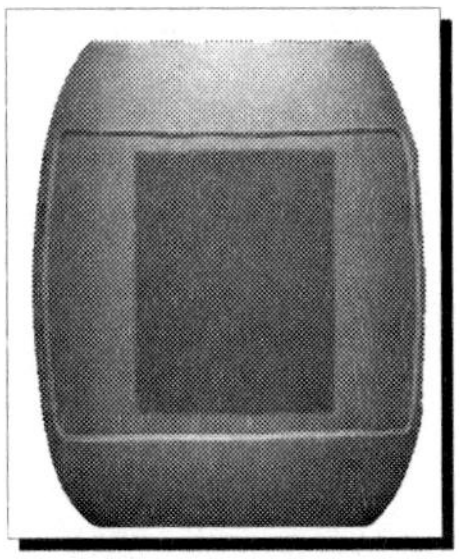

13. Invert the mask and **inflat by +10** in the **Tool | Deformation** subpalette, so it looks like a nice thin plate attached to the engines.

14. With that done, let's shrink the unmasked area. Hold *Ctrl* and drag to add to the existing mask, like shown in the next image. I tried to offset the unmasked area slightly away from the center, so it contrasts with the symmetrical look of the engines.

15. Switch to the **Slash2** brush and draw the outlets in straight horizontal lines by holding *Shift*.

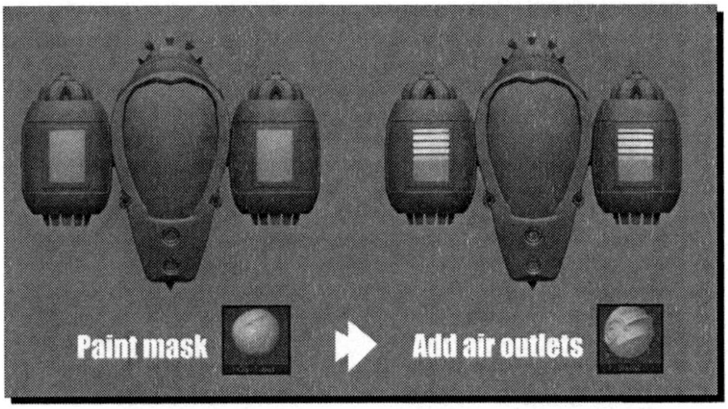


16. To add some final polish, you may want to add some rivets to the air outlets with the **PlanarCut** brush.

17. Finally, you may want to smooth some details, like the pipes on top of the engines or the drill head.

18. The tail fin can quickly be made rectangular again by using the Move brush.

19. Now that we've discussed all the tools needed to complete this model, you may alter it to your own wishes now.

## What just happened?

Actually, we didn't do anything new in this exercise, but we got a lot of practice.

In ZBrush, we only need a few tools to achieve quite a lot.

Here's what our final model would now look like:

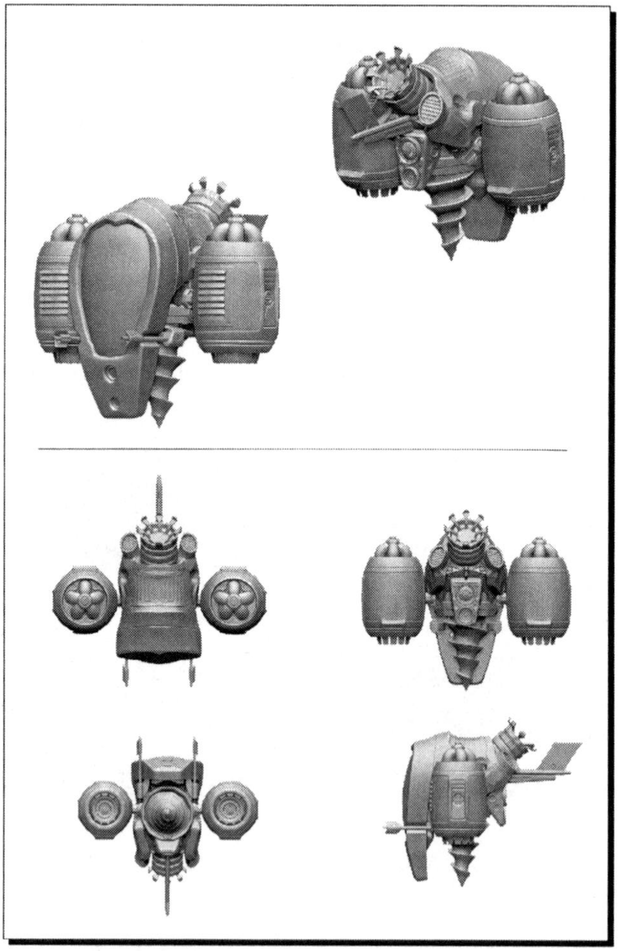

## Have a go hero – shoot it, strike it, cut it

What we can do now, is the most fun. Adding damages to make it look less clean and more used.

Especially as this is a resource harvester and scout, its hull should bear quite a lot of damages, scratches, bulges, and be covered in dirt.

As a technical object, it is very likely to be absolutely symmetrical, but not the scratches and the dirt. At this final stage, turning off symmetry will add the icing on the cake

Try adding some holes and bulges where they are most likely to appear. As a scout, it may have been shot from the front in a fight. On collisions with rocks, the outmost parts, like the engines, will take the most damages. When used as a drill head, dirt and rocks most likely will damage the drone from the bottom. The same counts for the takeoff with its massive engines blasting on the ground.

# Layers

Before starting to take the mesh apart, let's create a layer, so we can jump back to our original work easily. Layers are also very useful if we have to do an object in several states, like for example intact, damaged, and wrecked. We can add a layer for each and quickly switch between them. Also if we want to try out something, we can do it on a layer without losing the original work.

Layers are located under **Tool | Layers**. We can add a new layer by clicking on **Tool | Layers | New** with our model at its highest level of subdivision. So to add damages and finest details, make sure to step up to the highest level of subdivision before adding a new layer.

If we create a new layer, it automatically switches to record mode. This will record everything we do from now on, to that layer. If we click next to the record icon, we can toggle recording off. Out of recording mode, layers work very similar to Subtools, having an eye icon to toggle the visibility. Only one layer can be in recording mode at a time. If none of the layers are in recording mode, changes will affect the model directly. That said, we can now go crazy with adding nice irregularities.

We can use the Mallet- and Fracture brushes to quickly add damages like shooting holes, for example. For the scratches, the Slash1 and Slash3 brushes are very useful.

To achieve even more believability, vary the size regularly. There would only be similar looking scratches if it was attacked with claws.

Aside from the brushes, try out some Alphas in combination with different strokes. The Spray stroke can be used to quickly add some dirt, especially with alphas like 23 and 8.

Also the **DragRect Stroke** is very useful for exact damage placement.

You may also want to add another level of subdivision if your machine can handle it. Consider that this may slow down your working speed and may limit the number of undos available to a minimum, which are four by default.

Have fun detailing the mesh.

# Summary

That's it, we've finished our second model, the Pioneer Drone. While creating the drone, we learned a lot about hard surface sculpting. Your future modeling tasks will either be organic like the tree, technical like the drone, or a combination of both.

In detail, we've covered:

- When importing meshes, we can organize them in Polygroups by surface continuity, UV coordinates, or both.
- We can divide models with or without smoothing on, depending on our needs.
- Masking is very powerful in ZBrush. We can drag, paint, or erase Masks, even by using brushes.
- Polish brushes behave differently depending on the pressure we apply with our pen tablet.
- Trim brushes allow for a more freehand way of sculpting hard surfaces.
- Planar brushes easily flatten parts of our model.
- We can combine brushes with useful features like Line or LazyMouse.
- Alphas and Stroke types open up huge possibilities for sculpting with brushes.
- If something goes wrong on a symmetrical model, we can use SmartReSym to fix that.
- Finalizing the mesh with symmetry off will add to its believability.

Now that we've learned about how to create high polygon models, let's see how we can prepare these detailed meshes to be displayed in a game engine in the next chapter.

# 9

# Sci-Fi-Drone: Creating a Normal Map

*By now, we've finished sculpting our drone with all the fine details, vents, and bolts. But how can we bring this million polygon model into a game engine? We can't just load it because the polygon count is way too high. But what we can do is transfer the high polygon detail into a texture called a* **normal map***, which will simulate the details on a low resolution mesh.*

*By building the in-game mesh with UV coordinates in the beginning, we've already finished all the preliminary steps to create a normal map.*

*So in this chapter, we'll talk about textures in games, especially normal maps, to visually enhance our low-polygon drone inside a game engine.*

We'll have a closer look at:

- Textures in games
- Different types of textures
- Normal maps
- Generating normal maps out of ZBrush

# Textures in games

**Textures** are images applied to 3D objects. In games, most of the texture sizes are a "power of two", so typical sizes are 256 x 256, 512 x 512, or 1024 x 1024 pixels.

In modern games, there are several types of textures that affect the look of the model in the engine. The idea behind having that many textures in games is, like always, the need for saving performance. The following three are the most commonly used types:

- **Color/diffuse maps** are the most basic textures determining the base color of the object, most of the time ignoring any lighting direction. This is what we did by polypainting the tree at the beginning of the book.
- **Normal maps** are used to simulate high polygon details on a low polygon model by dynamically simulating light and shadow on the surface. You've probably seen them before because they can easily be spotted by the dominance of purple colors. Most of the time, normal maps are generated by software, opposed to handmade color and specular maps.
- **Specular maps** define the amount of specularity of the surface, where white means shiny and black means dull. Color in a specular map will tint the highlights.

However, this list isn't complete at all. There are many more types of textures but these are the most common ones used in games.

The types of textures that you'll use on your model will always depend on your engine, and more importantly, on the platform you're developing for. If you're developing for the modern PC market, you'll probably use the three texture types mentioned earlier, or even more, to get the most detail out of your game engine.

For example, when developing 3D games for the iPhone or other mobile platforms, there may be only one diffuse map with all the details, specularity, and lighting painted in, to save performance. The platform also affects the available texture sizes and polygon count of the models.

For this book, we'll assume that we are developing content for the modern PC or console market.

# Simulating details with normal maps

Because we can't smoothly display our high-poly models with millions of polygons in games, we can make use of normal maps; they will *mimic* the high-polygon details on the low-polygon surface by simulating the lighting of the high-polygon surface. We can think of normal maps like painting light and shadow on paper. The paper resembling the polygon remains flat, but by looking at it, we think that it has elevated parts that cast shadows onto it. This effect is calculated by the engine on the fly, so it can react to changes in the lighting direction. Like with a sheet of paper, the polygons will still remain flat, so if viewed from the side, there won't be any elevated details visible. By looking closely, you can spot the difference between normal-mapped low-poly and high-poly meshes at the edges of the model.

The following screenshot shows the normal map of the drone applied to a simple plane under different lighting conditions:

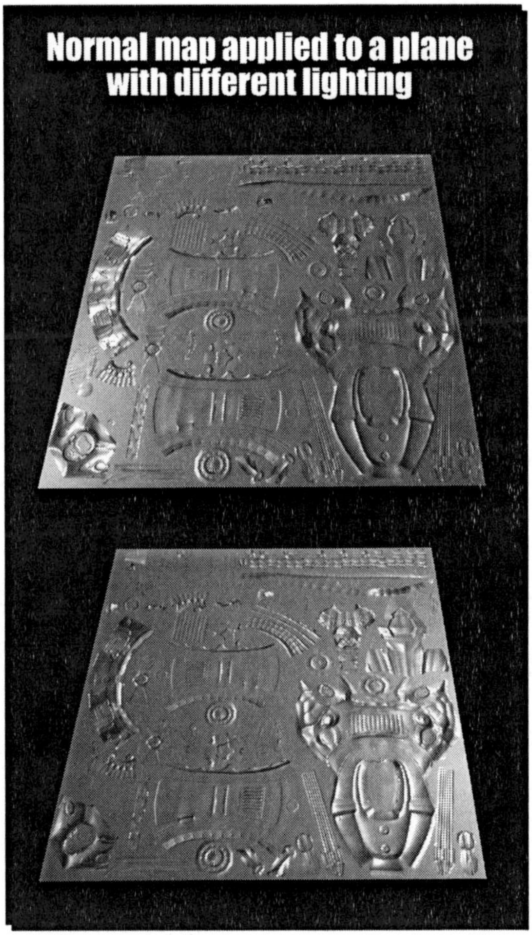

We can see in the previous screenshot how the high-polygon details are simulated on a plane surface by faking highlights and shadows. It is mapped onto a plane just for the sake of illustrating the process. If the normal map would be a brick pattern, this plane would instantly turn into a wall.

## Time for action – creating a normal map for our drone

Okay, we have our high-polygon object and our low-polygon object with UV coordinates ready, and we would like to view it in real-time in a game engine. Let's see how we can transfer fine details onto our low-poly drone with normal maps in ZBrush.

So, what we want to do is create a normal map and export it so that we can use it in our engine:

1. Open the latest version of the drone.
2. Step down to the lowest level of subdivision.
3. Make sure that **Tool | UV Map | UV Map Size** is set to **1024**, which are the dimensions of the texture in pixels in width and height.
4. Expand the **Tool | Normal Map** subpalette.
5. Enable **Tangent**, **Adaptive**, and **SmoothUV**, as the next screenshot shows:

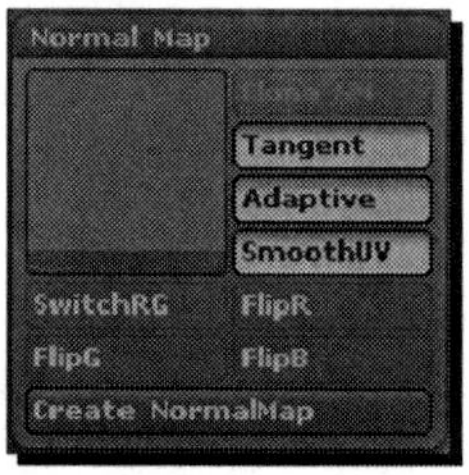


6. Click on the **Create NormalMap** button—this will incorporate only the visible layers. Check the **Notebar** to see the generation progressing, as the subsequent screenshot shows:

7. If this takes too long, you can cancel the process by pressing the *Esc* key. Turning off **Adaptive** will speed the calculation up but also decrease the quality of the normal map.

8. Before exporting that normal map, we first have to clone it by clicking on **Clone NM**. This will put a cloned copy into the texture palette where we can export it from.

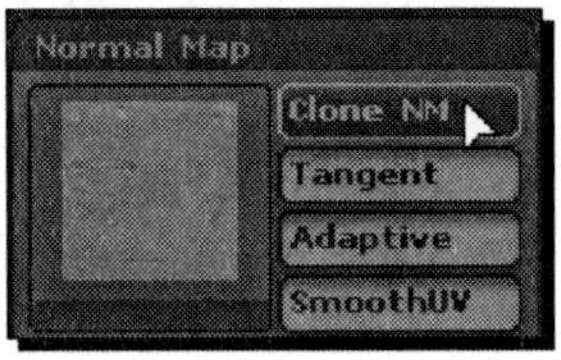


9. Open the texture palette in one of the trays. Here we can mouse over the little thumbnail of our normal map to get a bigger preview, as shown in the next screenshot. This will also display the dimensions of the texture at the bottom:

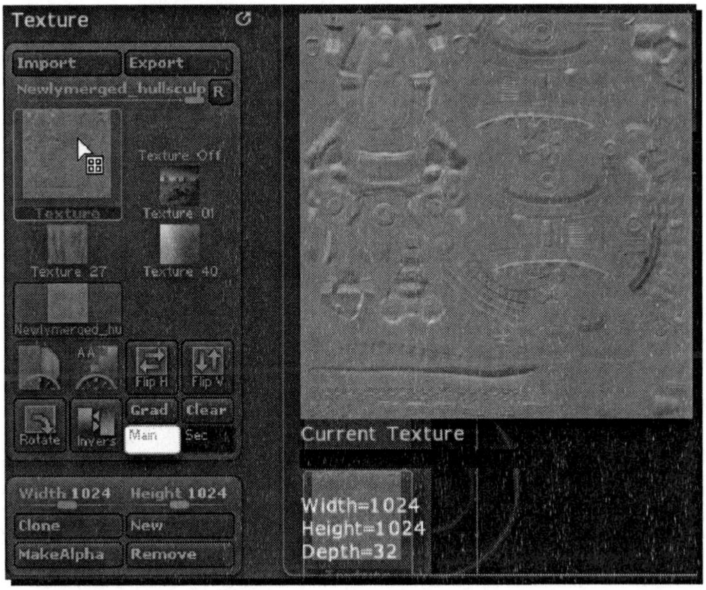

10. In this way, we can spot potential errors from early on, for example, the orientation. Remember what the UV coordinates of the drone looked like? If we compare the UV layout in the following screenshot with the previous one of the normal map, we can see that our generated normal map is flipped vertically:

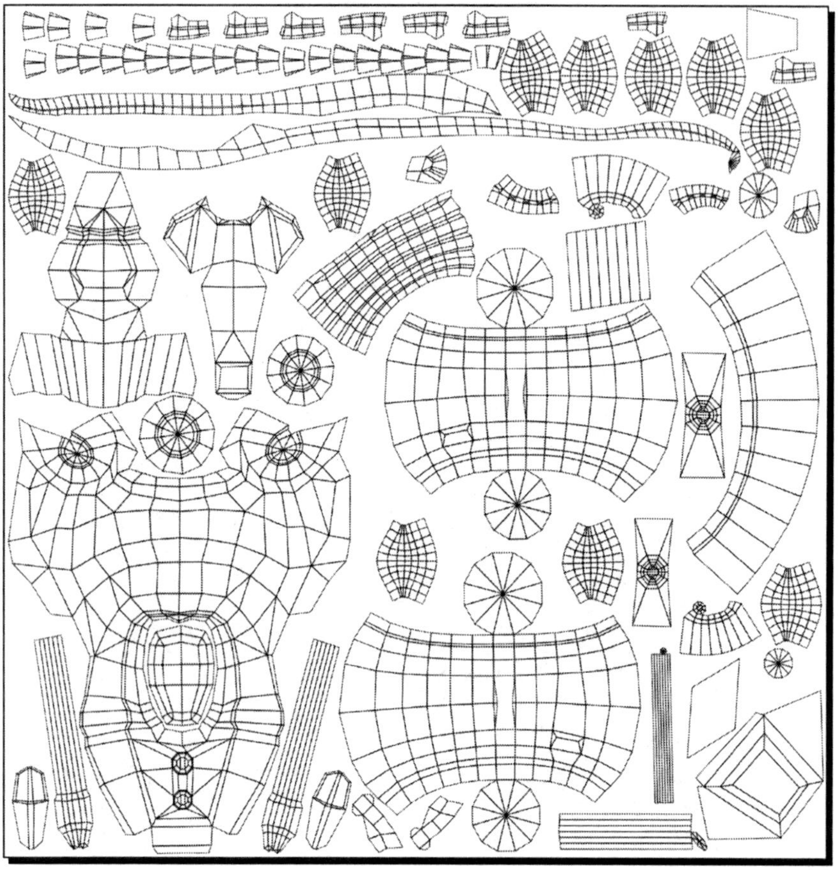

11. To fix that, simply press **Texture | Flip Vertically**.

12. With that done, we can export it as a `.tif` by clicking on **Texture | Export**. If opened in the Explorer or an image editor, our created normal map should look similar to this:

## What just happened?

We just created a normal map from our high-polygon mesh for our in-game mesh with just a click of a button. Let's have an in-depth look at this quick process.

To create a normal map, we stepped down in subdivision because ZBrush creates a normal map from the highest level for the currently active one. Because our lowest level represents the mesh we will use in the engine, we had to step down respectively.

In the UV Map subpalette, we can set the dimensions of our normal map. Here we can also find preset buttons for common sizes, such as 512 x 512 or 1024 x 1024 pixels, which is handy. If we set this slider to 512, our normal map would not only cover four times less the detail of a 1024 map, but would also take four times less the memory.

## Tangent and object space normal maps

When pressing **Tangent**, we chose to create a normal map in **tangent space**, opposed to **object space**, if unpressed. Tangent space normal maps are the ones to go for, as they allow for greater freedom. For instance, repeating textures over a model, also called **tiling**, is possible only with tangent space normal maps as well as animating the mesh. Object space could only be useful for immovable static meshes such as buildings. In most cases, tangent space normal maps are used. For example, our drone will be animated, so tangent space will be our method of choice.

You can easily spot the difference in the colors of the map. A tangent space normal map will mainly look bluish or purple, whereas an object space normal map will look much more colorful with higher contrasts, as shown in the next image:

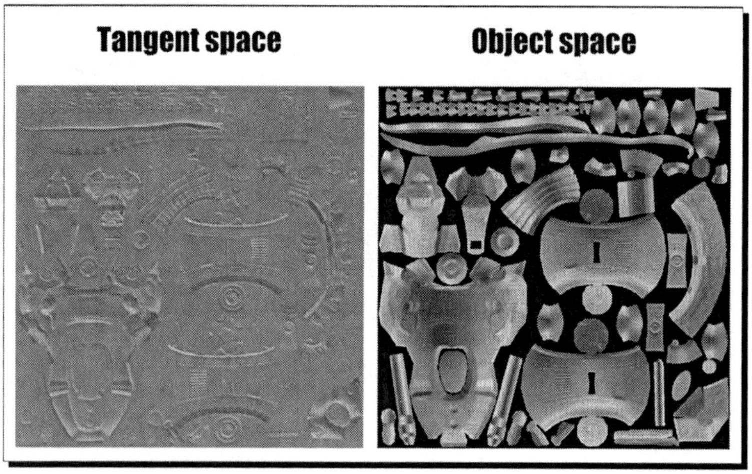


## Exporting the normal map

The need for flipping the texture before exporting depends on the engine or the 3D program you work with. Most of the time, the texture has to be flipped vertically when exported from ZBrush. This can also be done in any 2D image editor of your choice.

Finally, we can export the normal map in three different file formats; `.psd`, `.tiff`, and `.bmp`. If you would like to further work on the texture in Photoshop, you can choose `.psd`, but many game engines won't support this format natively. The `.bmp` Windows bitmap format comes along with weak to no compression and thus wastes too much space to be used in games. The TIFF format would be the format of choice, if you want to load it into a game engine directly.

## Pop quiz – textures and normal maps

1. What's the most basic texture that even mobile 3D games use to add color to their models?
    a. Specular maps
    b. Color/diffuse maps
    c. Normal maps
2. If a fellow game artist asks you how much bigger is a 1024 x 1024 map compared to a 256 x 256 texture to know how much more memory it would consume, what would be your answer?
    a. Two times
    b. Four times
    c. Sixteen times
3. Let's say you would have to bake a normal map for our spooky tree, which is a static environmental model. Could you use an object space normal map?
    a. Yes
    b. No

## Have a go hero – showing off the details with a normal map

Let's view the low-poly drone with a normal map in real-time. If you already have a game engine at hand, load the low-poly `.obj` model of the drone and apply the created normal map to it. Depending on your engine, you may have to load it into another 3D package first and then export it to the native format of your game engine.

If this is not the case, you can use the 3D program of your choice or try **Xnormal**, which is a free tool focused on creating maps from high-polygon meshes onto the low-polygon ones, like we just did. Along with these features comes a neat 3D viewer that can quickly display your model with several textures.

As stated earlier, this is meant only for a quick preview. If you have an engine at hand, use it because your model won't look the same in different model viewers and you probably want it to be as close as possible to the result.

Here's a screenshot of what the low-poly model could look like—viewed in Xnormal with only the normal map applied:

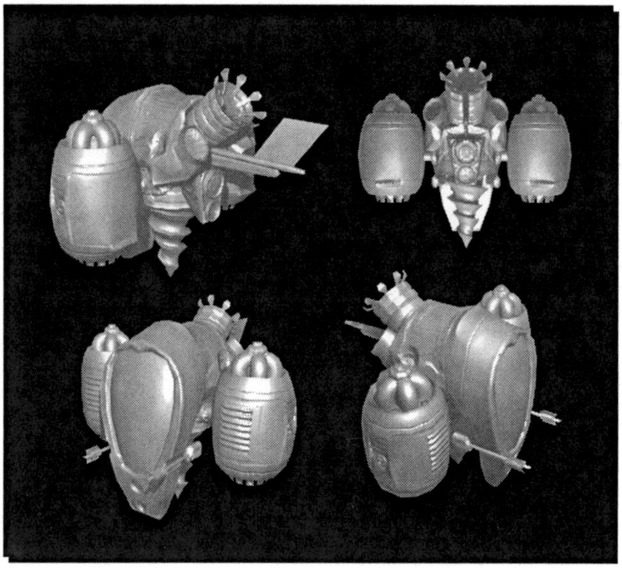

# Summary

We just did the final step to store all the detail of our sculpting in a normal map to view the results in any game engine, and simultaneously saving a lot of performance. We've also learned a lot about textures in games in general, especially about normal maps.

In this chapter, we saw that:

- Texture sizes are determined by a power of two, that is, 256 x 256 pixels or even 256 x 512, depending on the game engine.
- Games use several types of textures to save performance. The most common ones are diffuse, normal, and specular maps
- Normal maps can simulate highly detailed areas on flat polygonal objects with highlights and shadows.
- We can easily create normal maps from our high-poly object onto our low-poly object in ZBrush. Just set the texture dimensions, the quality, and the space and you're done.
- We mainly use tangent space normal maps, so we can tile the textures and animate the models.

That's it; we've finished our second modeling task, from modeling a high-poly model to baking a normal map for real-time viewing.

Now we're ready to dive into character production in the next chapter, which can be done at an amazing speed in ZBrush.

# 10

# Modeling a Creature with ZSketch

*In this chapter, we'll start off with our third model—a fearsome forest inhabitant by ZSketching it.*

*When sculpting the tree, we already learned how to start a model from ZSpheres. ZSketching takes this one step further by laying muscles and flesh on top of the ZSpheres. This is probably the fastest way to start organic characters. Let's see how this works.*

Specifically, we'll cover:

- Organizing a complex mesh using armatures
- Freeform sculpting with ZSpheres/ZSketch
- Modeling for animation
- Mesh conversion with Unified Skinning

## What the creature looks like

Let's throw a quick glance at the concept art to see what we're going to create in the next chapters.

The Brute is a crossbreed between a harmless emu and a wild forest bear. It is a roaming rogue living in the deepest forests. Only a few people have seen it and survived, so it's said to be between three and eight meters high. Despite its size, it combines strength and agility in a dangerous way. It is said that it hides his rather cute-looking head with trophies of its victims.

# ZSketching a character

We already worked with ZSpheres in the previous chapters, quickly creating the model of a spooky tree. Now we'll use the same technique to build some sort of skeleton, and then progress with the amazing fast ZSketch to lay in the muscles and flesh structure on top.

In this workflow, we can think of our ZSpheres as a skeleton we can place our virtual clay onto. So we try to build the armature, not as thick as the whole arm, but as thick as the underlying bone would be. With that in mind, let's get started.

**Quick and useful ZSphere actions**

| Action | Result |
|---|---|
| *Q* | *Draw* mode for adding new **ZSpheres** |
| *W* | *Move* mode |
| *E* | *Scale* mode |
| *R* | *Rotate* mode |
| *Left-click* on a Link sphere in *draw* mode | *Inserts* another **ZSphere**, useful for inserting additional joints such as the elbow joint in the arm |
| *Alt + left-click* on an existing ZSphere in *draw* mode | *Removes* the ZSphere from the chain |
| Rotating a Link sphere | *Rotates* all subsidiary or **child spheres** around the parent sphere, that is, rotating the legs together with the feet around the hip joint |
| Scaling a Link sphere | Evenly *scales* the **child spheres**; useful for shrinking whole body parts, such as the arms with hands and fingers |
| Moving a Link sphere | *Moves* all **child spheres** |

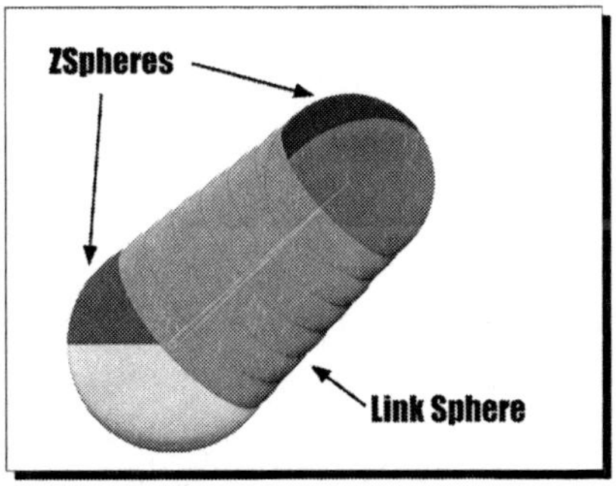


# Time for action – creating the basic armature with ZSpheres

Let's say the art director comes to your desk and shows you a concept of a monster to be created for the game project that you're working on. As always, there's little to no time for this task. Don't panic; just sketch it with ZSketch in no time. Let's see how this works:

1. Pick a new ZSphere and align its rotation by holding *Shift*.
2. Set your draw size down to 1.
3. Activate Symmetry on the X-axis.

4. The **root ZSphere** can't be deleted without deleting everything else, so the best place for this would be in the pelvis area.

> Placing the cursor on the line of symmetry will create a single ZSphere—this is indicated by the cursor turning green.

5. Start out to create the armature or skeleton from the root ZSphere, commencing from the pelvis to the head, as shown in the next screenshot. Similar to the human spine, it roughly follows an S-curve:

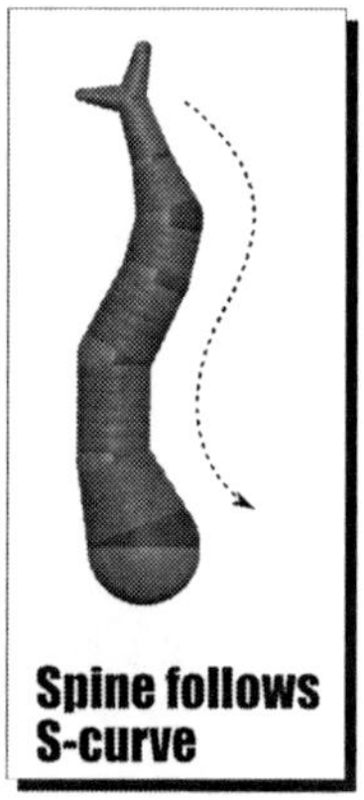


6. Continue by adding the shoulders. A little trick is to start the clavicle bone a bit lower at the spine, which gives a more natural motion in the shoulder area.

7. Add the arms with the fingers as one ZSphere plus the thumbs, we'll refine it later. The arms should be lowered and bent so that we're able to judge the overall proportions better, as the next image shows:

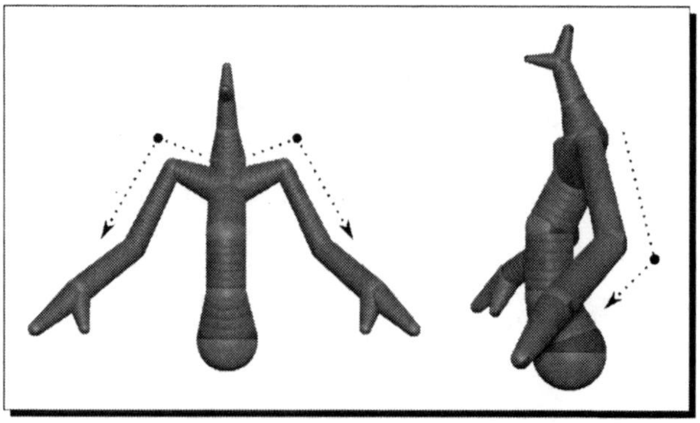

[ This "skeleton" will also be used for moving or posing our model, so we'll try to place ZSpheres where our virtual joints would be, for example, at the elbow joint. ]

8. Add the hips, stretching out from the pelvis and continue with the legs. Try to bend the legs a bit (which looks more natural) as shown in the next screenshot.

9. Finally, add the foot as one ZSphere for the creature to stand on:

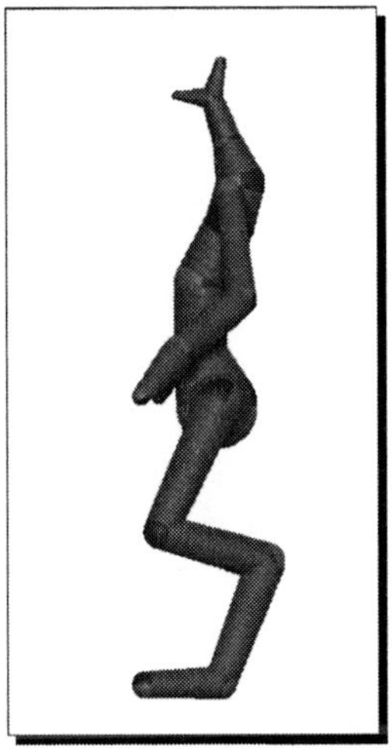

10. Now we have all the basic features of the armature ready. Let's check the concept again to get our character's proportions right. Because our character is more of a compact, bulky build, we have to shorten his legs and neck a bit.

[ Make sure to check the perspective view, too. Inside any game engine, characters will be viewed in perspective. We can also set the **focal angle** under **Draw | FocalAngle**. The **default value** is **50**. Switching perspective off helps comparing lengths. ]

11. Add another **ZSphere** in the belly area to better control its mass, even if it looks embarrassing.

*12.* To make him look less like Anubis, you may want to lower the top-most ZSphere a bit, so it will fit the horns. Our revised armature could now look like this with perspective enabled:

*13.* With the overall proportions done, let's move on with details, starting with the toes. Insert another ZSphere next to the heels and continue by adding the toes, including the tiny fourth toe, as shown in the next screenshot:

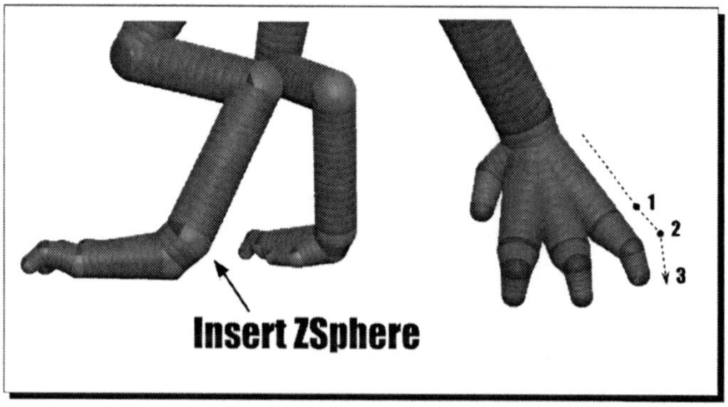


*14.* With larger ZSpheres, we can better judge the mass of the foot. But because we need a thinner bone-like structure, let's scale them down once we're done. Be careful to scale the **ZSpheres**, and not the Link spheres in-between them. This keeps them in place while scaling, as shown in the next image:

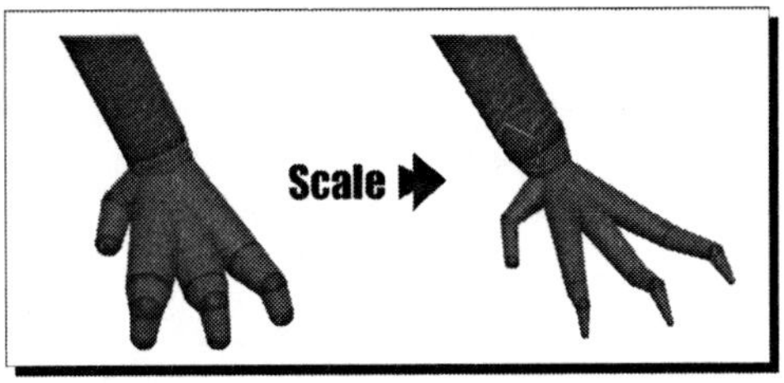


15. Let's continue with the hands. These can be tricky, even at this rough stage, so it may be useful to look at some reference images, either from anatomy books or the Internet. The next image shows some major lines that make up the hand. Starting the fingers in an outstretched pose is useful for getting the lengths correct:

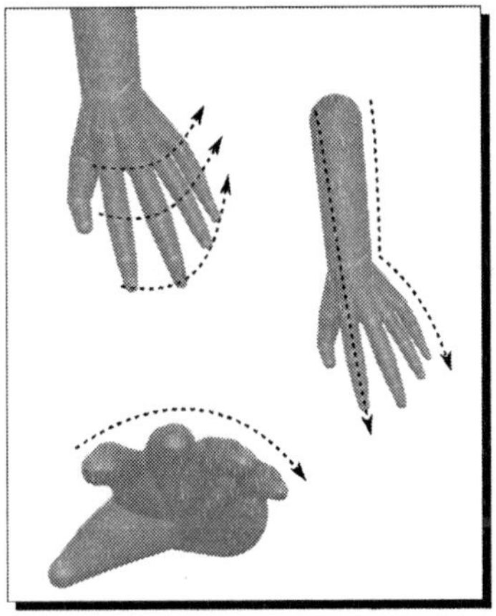

16. Add ZSpheres to the hand, following its bone structure, as shown in the next screenshot. It's easier to work out the length of the fingers first and then insert the joints afterward, as shown in the next image:

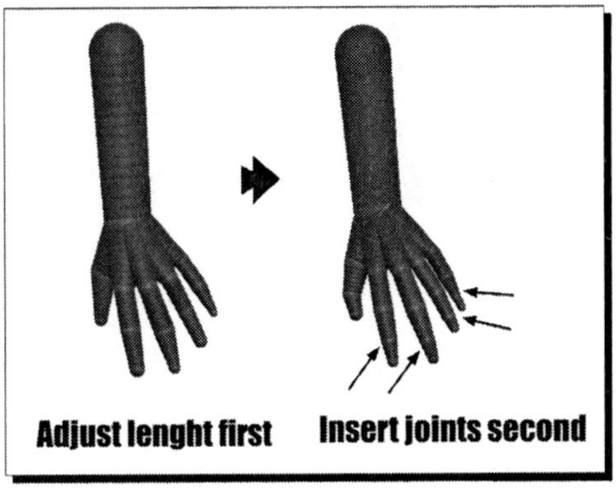

**15.** Let's relax the expression of the hand by quickly rotating the Link spheres of the fingers, which is a better pose for animation. If you look at your own relaxed hand, you'll see that the main bending takes place between the first and second bone of your fingers. Also note that smaller fingers are bent more when relaxed, as shown in the next image:

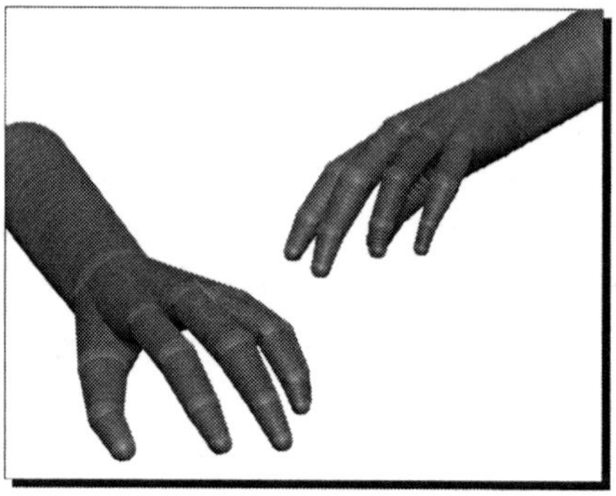

> Rotating the Link spheres is done relative to the camera view, so make sure to adjust the view accordingly.

**16.** Finally, we may want to scale down the wrist a bit so there's still room left to add muscles on top.

**17.** Save the armature, as usual as a `.ZTL`.

**18.** Our final armature could now look like this:

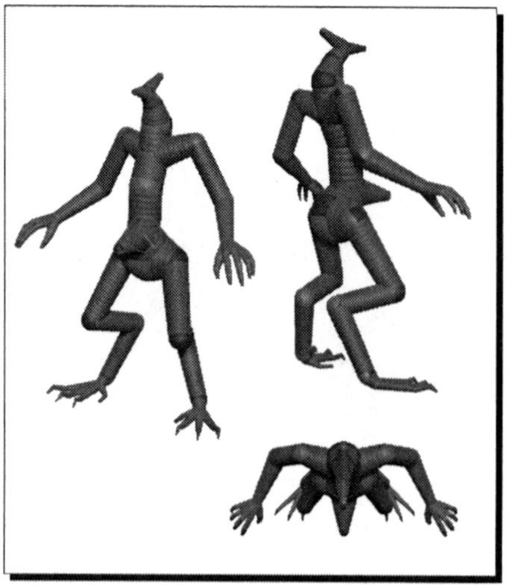

## What just happened?

We've just finished the armature of our creature. We can now use it to freely sketch muscles on top of it with ZSketch.

We also covered some basic anatomy, such as the form of the spine or the lines of the hand. If you're interested in anatomy, there are plenty of good books available, for example, *Die Gestalt des Menschen* by Gottfried Bammes, which is available only in German but the numerous illustrations speak for themselves. Also searching through the Internet can be a good starting point. Personally, I would choose artistic anatomy illustrations over medical ones because they also deal with the visual appeal, which applies to sculpture, too.

As we'll see on the next pages, the armature we built will now be used to sketch muscles on top. So when using ZSpheres, we can choose if we want to build volumes directly from them, like we did with the tree, or use them as a skeleton for sketching volumes on top.

# The character pose for animation

For characters in games, we always have to consider the next steps, which will be rigging and animation. **Rigging** is about placing bones and joints, determining how the character can move, whereas **animation** will finally move the character. Most of the time, a relaxed pose is better for the rigging process than the T-pose, with arms stretched out horizontally. The reason for this is that the model will deform better when it is modeled in-between its motion extremes. For example, an outstretched arm is an extreme for the elbow joint, so bending or relaxing it (like we did), solves this. The same applies for the fingers and the legs. Also lowering the arms makes sense, as most of the time, characters do have their arms lowered, not above their heads.

From an artistic point of view, the relaxed pose is also well-suited for judging the overall expression and proportions of the character.

Enough of that theory, let's move on with the most enjoyable part—ZSketching the creature.

**ZSketch hotkey reference**

To increase our working speed, let's get an overview of some hotkeys for ZSketching. Luckily, ZSketching is done with almost the same controls that we already know from ZSpheres and sculpting:

- *Press Shift + A* to enter sketch mode.
- *Left-click* to draw.
- Hold Shift to smooth.
- Hold Alt to inverse the direction of the brush. When using Sketch brushes, holding Alt deletes the drawn strokes.

Like with ZSpheres, we can preview a unified skin of our ZSketch by pressing *A*. Pressing *A* again will leave the preview mode.

Hold down *Ctrl + Shift + drag* to hide parts outside the rectangle.

Drag the rectangle, but before letting go, press the *Alt key* to hide all of the parts inside the rectangle.

*Ctrl + Shift + left-click on the canvas* will unhide everything.

When working on one part of the model, don't hide the mirrored part of it otherwise you may get errors on the mirrored side. So when working with symmetry on the left arm, have the right one visible, too. For that reason, with symmetry turned on, all hiding actions are symmetrical.

## Time for action – sketching the creature with ZSketch

Let's explore how easy it is to create characters with ZSketch. For me, this is one of the best features of ZBrush because it brings modeling closer to what sketching is—*quick and intuitive*. Let's see how this works by sketching out the creature's body. The hair will be added separately in the next chapter, so we'll now focus on the muscles:

1. Open or select the previously built armature.
2. Go to **Tool | ZSketch** and press the **EditSketch** button or hit *Shift + A*. Now we're in *Sketch* mode where we can sketch freely upon our armature.
3. Make sure that **Symmetry** is active.
4. Pick a material that starts with **Sketch**, which were especially designed to enhance the display of ZSketches. I'm using **SketchShaded4** here.
5. ZBrush automatically switches to the **Sketch1** brush when working with ZSpheres so we can start right away. The next image shows how we can lay strokes onto our armature and smoothen them afterwards to blend into the existing sketch or armature:

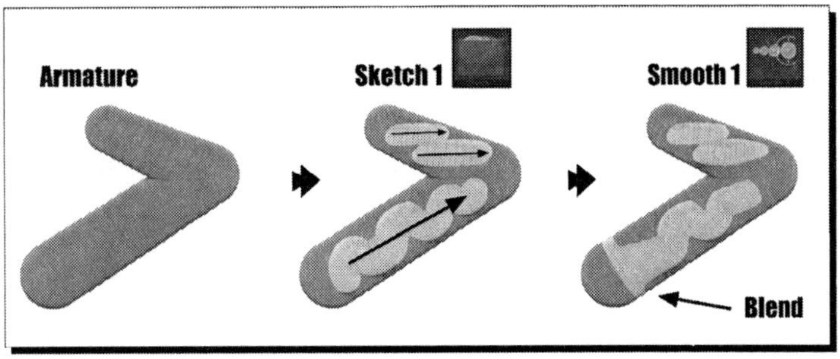


6. As shown in the third step of the previous screenshot, the **Smooth1** brush scales the strokes to blend into the underlying surface.

7. Begin laying strokes onto the model and smoothing them, starting with the form of the ribcage and the pectoral muscles, as shown in the following image:

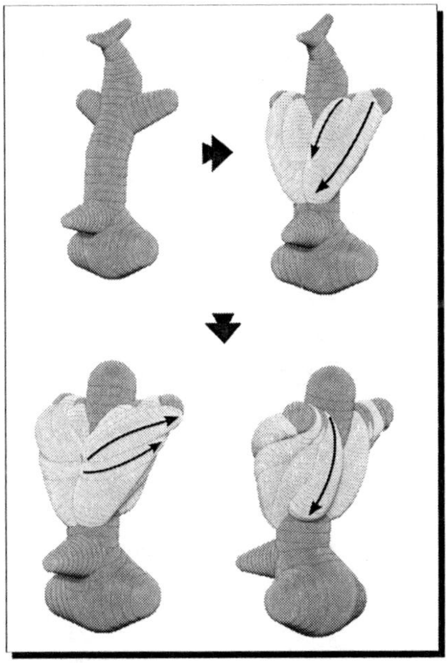

[ Have a look at the hotkey reference at the beginning of this section to speed up your workflow. ]

8. Add the belly by using a larger brush as shown in the following image:

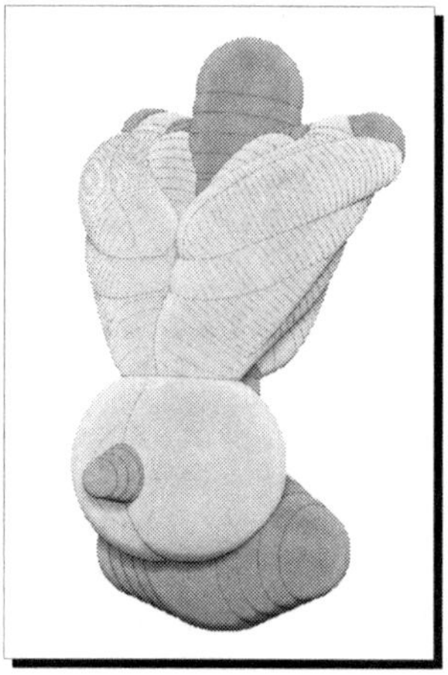

> **Visual aids for ZSketch**
>
> Like polygons, we can colorize our sketch by navigating to **Tool | Polypaint | Colorize** and picking a color. Turning off **Zadd** will colorize only—which is done in the next screenshot to better distinguish the sketch from the armature.

9. Continue with the sides and the back. For a living creature like this, the **ZSketch** follows the flow of the muscles. Larger muscles can be represented by larger strokes and smaller ones by smaller strokes. Unless you're absolutely familiar with anatomy, looking at reference images will improve your sketch.

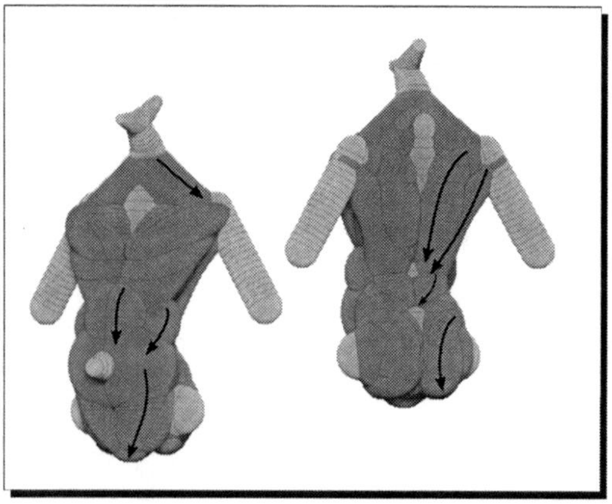

10. Now that we've established the mass of the body, let's continue with the neck. Start by adding a bigger sphere where the skull would be. Like real anatomy, we'll then draw the muscles that connect the bones at the neck.

11. Rough in the mass of the head with a few strokes.

12. For the horns on the head, pick the armature brush, which starts on the sketch and then freely extends into space. Like rotating, the direction it extends from the surface depends on the camera view. Because the horns are somewhat horizontal, drawing them from the top will be suited best for this.

13. Viewed from the side, the horns still need some correction. We can switch to the **Move tool**, by clicking on **Move** at the top of the shelf or by simply pressing *W*. Now we can push them into place as shown in the next image. With the **Scaling tool**, we can shrink the tips of the horns:

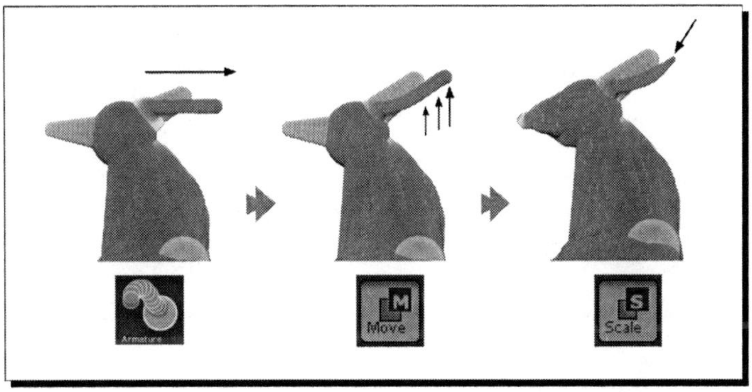


[ Although ZSketching relies on ZSpheres, they are not using hierarchies, so we can layer strokes in any order we want. ]

14. Adding some arms completes the torso area. Click on the icon of the **Sketch1** brush and select the Smooth 4 brush from the list. ZBrush will then display a message telling us that we have to press *Shift* to switch to the newly selected **Smooth 4** instead of **Smooth 1**, like before. The next image shows the difference between both:

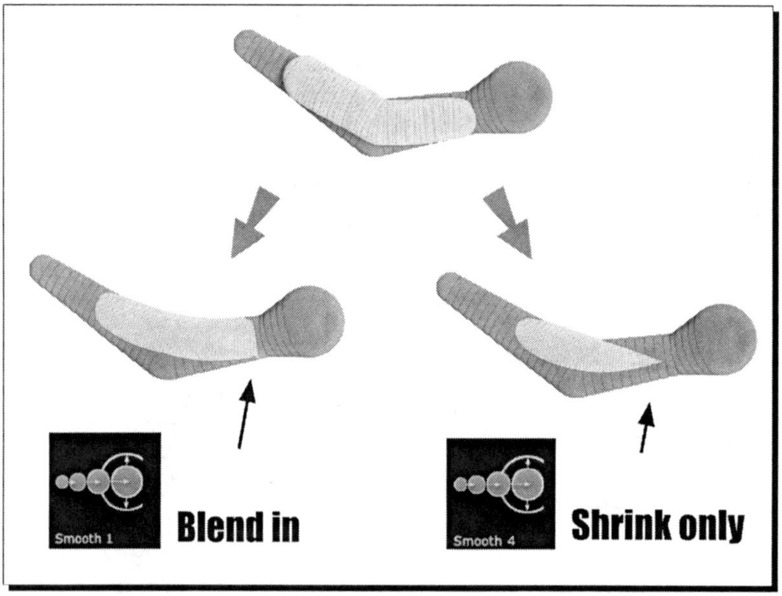


15. The **Smooth 4** brush is really useful for muscle structures because it shrinks both ends of the sketch stroke. Use it to quickly add the muscles of the upper- and lower- arm, as shown in the next image:

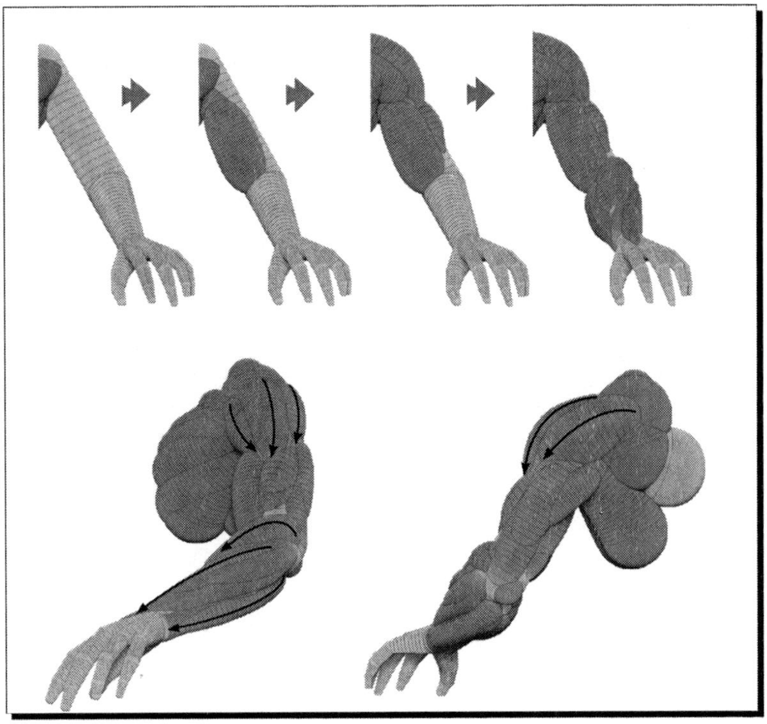

**16.** Now that the torso is done, let's step back again and check the proportions. At the moment he looks more like an athlete, but lacks the body mass the concept has. Let's correct the proportions with the **Move** tool, as shown in the next image. We'll come back later to finish the hands.

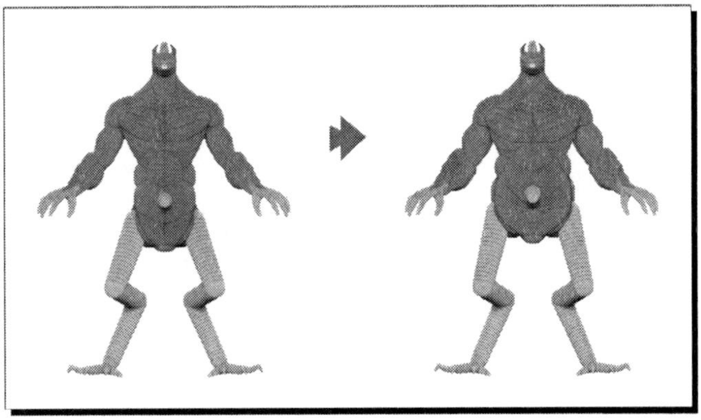

17. Let's continue with the legs. Its muscles are quite raised, so we'll switch over to the **Sketch 2** brush, which draws a more elevated stroke on the surface. We can think of muscles as fabric made of thick, intertwining threads. Looking closely at reference images helps to see which muscles overlap others. Work out the legs as shown in the next image:

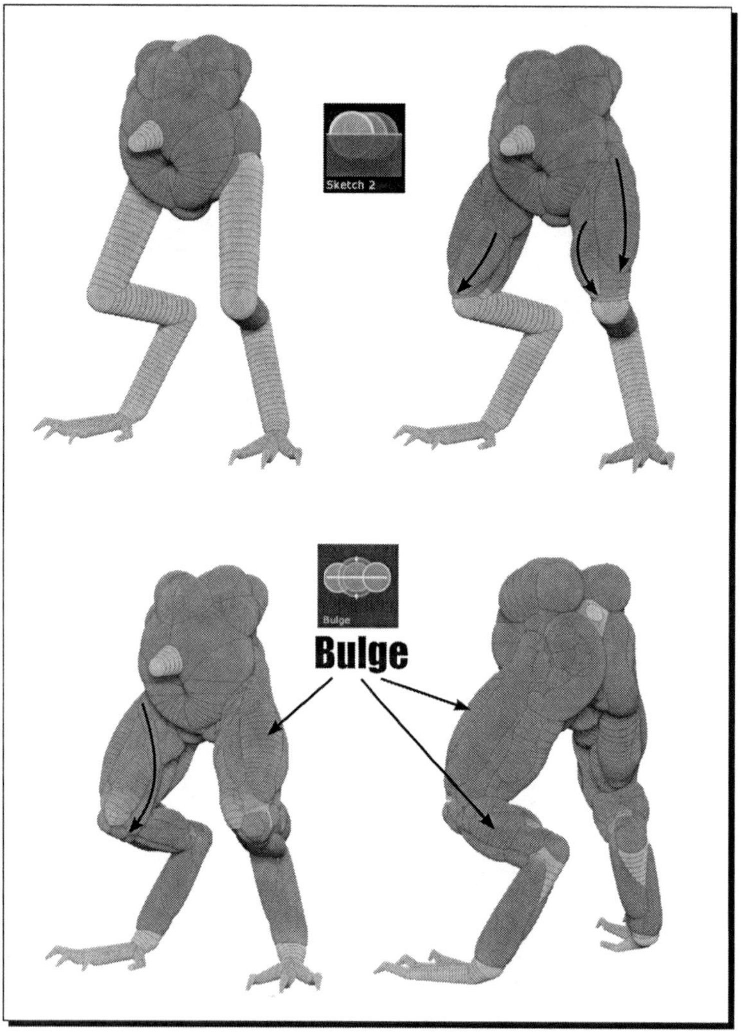

18. The **Bulge** brush bloats surfaces, which is very useful for the dominant muscles of the leg, as shown in the previous image. We can press *Alt* to shrink.

19. Save your work regularly with ascending numbers, so you can always go back if something goes wrong.

20. The last thing our creature needs for a fresh walk in the woods is some feet. They can be roughed in quite quickly with some thicker strokes on the main foot and thinner tendons on top of that, as the next image shows. For the toes, the **Smooth 1** brush is very useful because it adapts the stroke size to the small armature underneath:

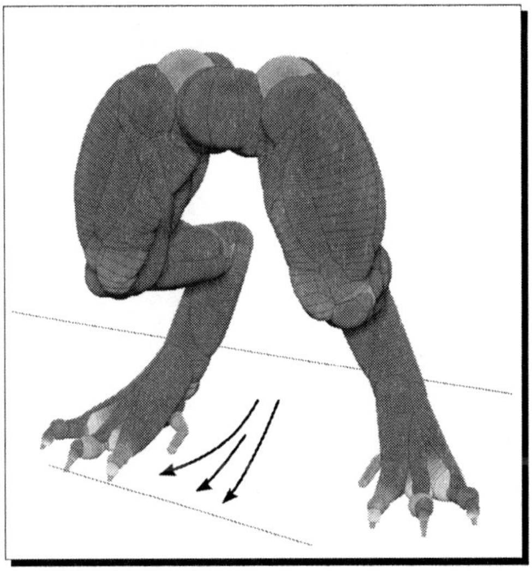

21. There's only one thing left to do now—the hands. Let's spread the fingers beforehand, so the ZSketch strokes won't jump over to the neighboring ones. Leave *sketch* mode by pressing *Shift + A*.

22. Spread the fingers by using Rotate and enter sketch mode again.

> To get a better overview, we can hide parts, for example, the feet when working on the hands. But we should always have the mirrored parts visible, too—for example, having both hands visible when working on them. Otherwise, we may get errors when ZBrush tries to mirror things over onto invisible parts.

23. For the **fingers**, start by adding some flesh onto the bones, followed by the joints and tendons, as shown in the next image. What looks like earthworms at the moment will be a good base to start sculpting from:

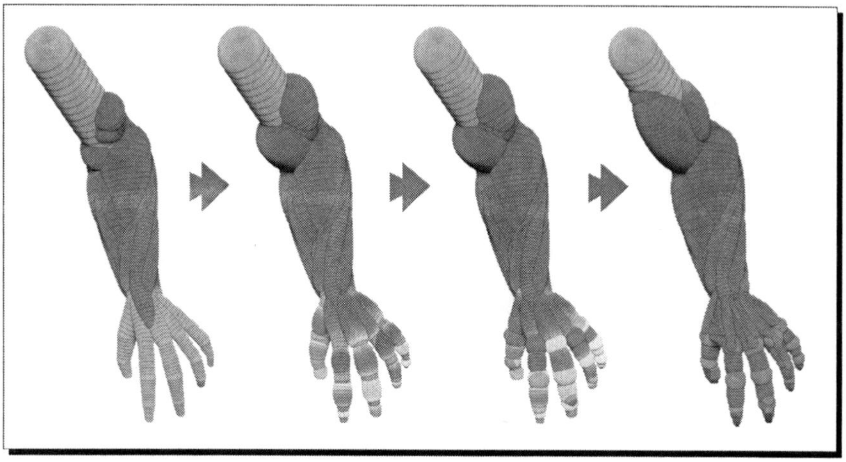

24. Now that we have laid in all the muscles, we can use our previously built armature to correct some of the proportions if we'd like to. Leave *sketch mode* with *Shift + A*.

25. Now go to **Tool | ZSketch** and press the **ShowSketch** button to **view** the transparent sketch and the armature at once.

26. Increase the **SoftBind** slider to **100** and go to **Tool | ZSketch | Bind;** this allows us to adjust the armature while the sketch smoothly follows, which is neat. Now we see what that embarrassing belly control was made for. Bound to the belly control, we can move or scale the belly without affecting the back.

> If we change the structure of the armature, we can simply go to **Tool | ZSketch** and press the **Reset Binding** button and let ZBrush update the connections between the armature and the sketch. Add, move, or scale ZSpheres as you wish to get the results you want.

27. Save your work.

28. If the character should be able to open and close his mouth in the game, we should add a jaw with the mouth slightly open.

**29.** After some reshaping with the help of our armature, the final sketch could look like this:

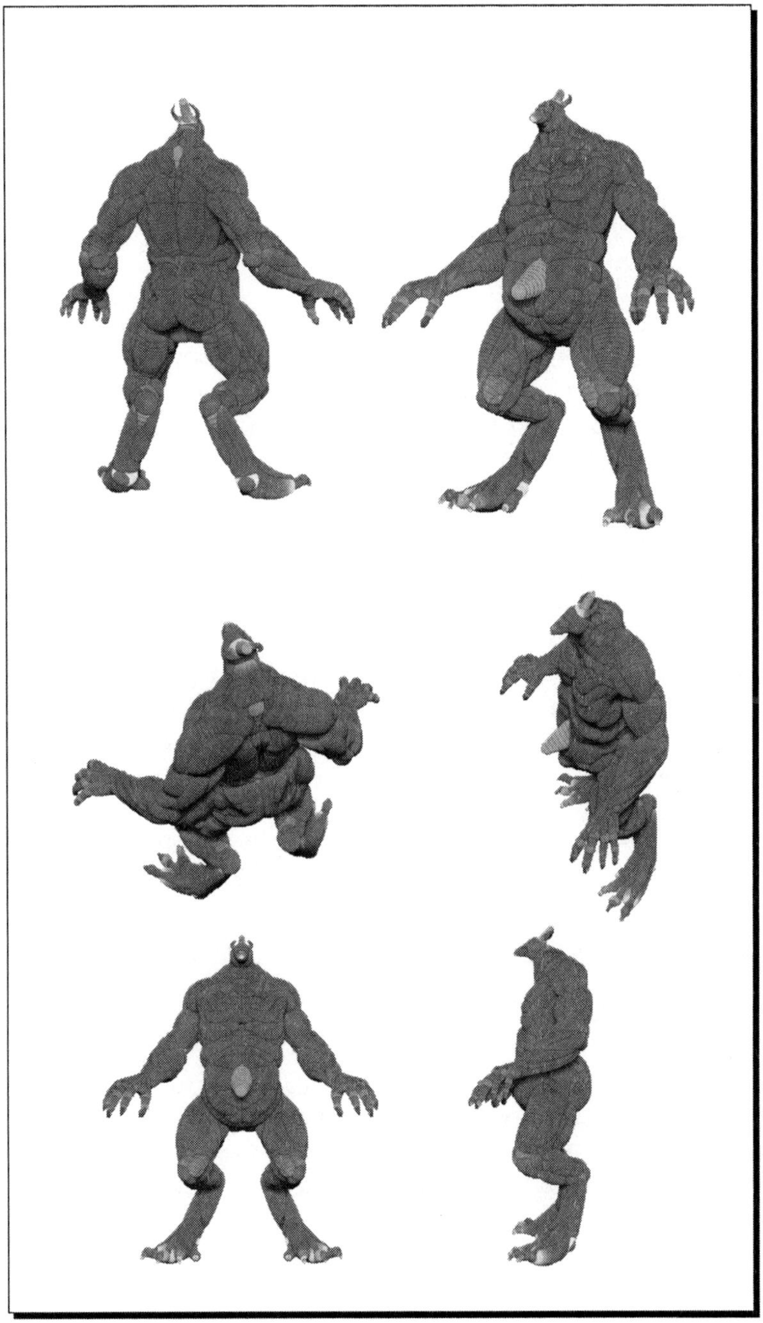

## *What just happened?*

With ZSketching, we just enjoyed the freedom of free-form sculpting a complete character without having to think about polygons, resolutions, or vertex densities.

# Brushes

We started out with the sketch brushes, layering strokes on the armature. As we saw, there are three different sketch brushes—Sketch 1, -2, and -3. Strokes with the **Sketch 1** brush stay close to the surface, whereas strokes with the **Sketch 3** brush will be elevated from the surface. The proximity of the stroke to the surface is controlled by the **Brush | Depth | Imbed** value, so all the three brushes are just presets.

The **Armature** brush does not follow the surface but rather starts off from it. Opposed to that, the sketch brushes will follow the surface as long as we paint on it. If we leave the surface at its borders, the sketch brushes will also lift from the surface, but they can join in again. So, use the armature brush for things such as tentacles or horns, and the sketch brushes for surfaces or for connecting those.

We get the best results if we combine our sketch brushes with the smooth brushes to blend into the surface.

# ZSketch and the armature

With an armature, we do have a good starting point for modeling our character. But ZSketching is also about modeling freely, right? All we have to do is pick a ZSphere and freely sketch away without any armature or predefined outcome. We can still build an armature afterward if we want to.

Opposed to normal ZSpheres, ZSketching is not hierarchy-based, so we can sketch freely without having to follow any structure. ZSketching is sometimes also called **ZSpheres 2** to emphasize that difference.

If the ZSketch becomes very complex and you get performance issues, you can go to **Tool | ZSketch** and press the **Optimize** button—this deletes unnecessary ZSpheres that are fully covered by others.

If we hit the *A* key, we'll get a preview of our ZSketch converted to polygons. The standard resolution for this is pretty low to avoid long computation times. But if we would like to see a more detailed preview, we can set the resolution under **Tool | Unified Skin | Resolution**. There's also a **Preview** button, which is what the hotkey *A* toggles.

Finally, we used our previously built armature to reshape our model. This is very useful for checking movement limits, too. This early stage is perfect to identify issues because they can be fixed so quickly. For example, a character may not lift his arms as he's supposed to because his head is too big. Changing this at a later stage will be much more difficult.

When entering *Sketch* mode, the brush selection will immediately switch to sketching brushes. If we want to edit our model with the sculpting brushes, we have to convert our sketch to polygons first, which will be the next step. Because this is not undoable, we use the ZSketch to lay in the main proportions and then sculpt in the fine detail.

## Pop Quiz – ZSketching a character

1. Imagine you would like to connect two shores by ZSketching a bridge; which brush would you choose?
    a. Sketch brush
    b. Armature brush
    c. Bulge brush
2. What do we have to take care of when hiding parts of the ZSketch that we're not working on?
    a. Be careful not to hide the root sphere
    b. Always have the mirrored parts visible too
    c. Be careful not to hide connecting ZSpheres
3. Let's say you sketched a beautiful horse, but your Art Director decided it should rather be a dumb rhino, what would you do?
    a. Redo all the work
    b. Convert it to polygons and try to change it with the sculpting tools
    c. Reshape the sketch with move, scale, and an armature
4. Why did we choose the "relaxed pose" for our character with his arms lowered and why not the "T-pose" with arms stretched out horizontally?
    a. Because our character is more of the relaxed type
    b. Because the character in relaxed pose will deform better when animated
    c. Because our character can't lift his arms that high

# Time for action – converting a ZSketch into sculptable polygons

Now we've got our sketch finished and would like to sculpt more details. So we have to convert it to polygons. Let's try that out:

1. Load the ZSketch of the creature.
2. Open the **Tool | Unified Skin** subpalette.
3. The following settings worked best for me. If your creature looks way different, experiment with the values to see what works best for you:

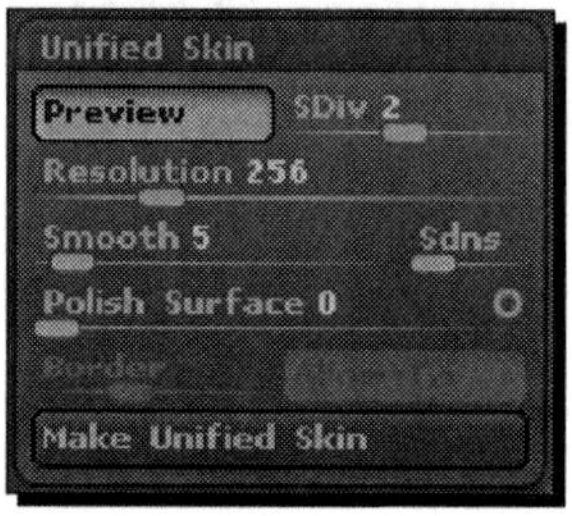


4. When testing which resolution will do best, **pay close attention to small details** such as fingers, toes, and horns, which tend to get lost on lower resolutions. Try to get the lowest resolution possible. Spreading the fingers even more may prevent them from being merged.
5. Deactivate **Symmetry**.
6. Press Make Unified Skin, which adds it as a new tool with the **Skin_ prefix** to the **Tool** list.
7. Save both the tools—the armature and the newly created skin.

## What just happened?

We just created a polygonal mesh from our ZSketch, we can now sculpt on.

The reason we tried to get the lowest resolution possible is that it's good to have lower subdivision levels for more global changes.

The preceding example will create a mesh with a resolution setting of 256. On top of that, it will generate two additional subdivision levels that capture the finer details. So when pressing **Make Unified Skin**, we should end up with a model with three levels of subdivision.

If we applied colored sketch strokes to our model, the **Unified Skin** will be colored, too. This can be a great base to start texturing from.

Disabling **Symmetry** before creating a **Unified Skin** creates more quads instead of triangles along the axis of symmetry. The difference may be marginal, but we should go for quads instead of triangles whenever we can.

# Summary

We learned a lot in this chapter about ZSketching models within ZBrush and how to tackle all sorts of tasks that arise while creating a complete character from scratch. Specifically, we've covered:

- A new way of creating models with ZSketch
- Building up volumes and muscles can be quickly achieved with the various sketch and smooth brushes
- For ZSketching, we can start off with a complete armature or a single ZSphere
- Building some sort of skeleton with an armature is useful if we know where we're heading with the character
- We can use that skeleton to control the ZSketch by binding it—like a skeleton with muscles on top
- If we make global changes to the model, such as adding a tail, we can edit or insert its skeleton later in the process, too
- Thinking ahead about the future movement of the character saves a lot of headaches when it comes to rigging and animation
- To create volumes, ZSketching is unmatched in speed and fun, but when it comes to fleshing out finer details, the sculpting tools are the way to go
- When switching from ZSketching to sculpting, we have to convert our sketch into polygons first

Now we can move on to sculpting and detailing our character in the next chapter.

# 11

# Sculpting the Creature's Body

*In this chapter, we will take our ZSketch from the previous chapter one step further by sculpting muscles and anatomical details, which are very important to make our character look real. We will also learn how to add props, such as a belt or fur, which define our character even more.*

So, this chapter will walk you through the complete sculpting of a full body character.

Specifically, we will cover:

- Adding detail to specific areas using local subdivisions
- Organizing our model with polygroups
- Sculpting the anatomy of the body
- Adding props, such as a belt and fur with subtools and mesh extract
- Working with layers to store and switch between poses

You can download the Unified Skin from the previous chapter by following the download link provided in the preface.

**Folder management tips**

On every restart, ZBrush forgets which folder we worked in before and looks for models in the `ZBrush\ZTools` directory. Instead of browsing for our models each time, there are two ways we can make this easier. The first option is placing all our models in the ZBrush default folder to access them faster. But you may have your own data structures, maybe even on another partition. So, the second and probably the superior method is to create a shortcut of our modeling folder and copy it into the `ZTools` folder. These shortcuts work, even if we browse our models with Lightbox.

# Adding local detail

When we created a Unified Skin from our ZSketch in the last chapter, our resulting mesh had quite evenly distributed polygons. Generally speaking, this is fine because even polygon distribution leads to cleaner subdivisions. But like in a drawing, we would like to add additional detail in important areas, such as the hands and the face—especially the face has a huge impact on the overall impression of the model. In this way, we can get away with a lower polygon-count, while still having some decent detail on the face and the hands.

## Time for action – adding local detail where we need it

So let's add some more detail to the face and the hands:

1. Load the model that we created using the Unified Skin method.
2. Make sure symmetry is active.
3. Paint a mask covering the hands and the head, as shown in the next image. Press and hold *Ctrl* to paint a mask with your mouse or switch the tablet pressure sensitivity off with **Preferences | Tablet | UseTablet**. In this way, the RGB intensity isn't affected by the pen pressure, so we get everything masked evenly. When holding *Ctrl*, the **RGB intensity** should be set to **100**. The **Flat Color** material helps to see the mask better:

4. Don't forget to switch the pressure sensitivity back on under **Preferences | Tablet | UseTablet**.

5. Invert the mask by *Ctrl + left-clicking* on the canvas.

6. Step down to the lowest level of subdivision by pressing *Shift + D* as often as needed.

7. With the face and the hands unmasked, press **Divide** or hit *Ctrl + D* once. When finished, ZBrush will switch back to the highest level of subdivision.

8. Go to the lowest subdivision level and activate polyframe to see the result, as shown in the next image:

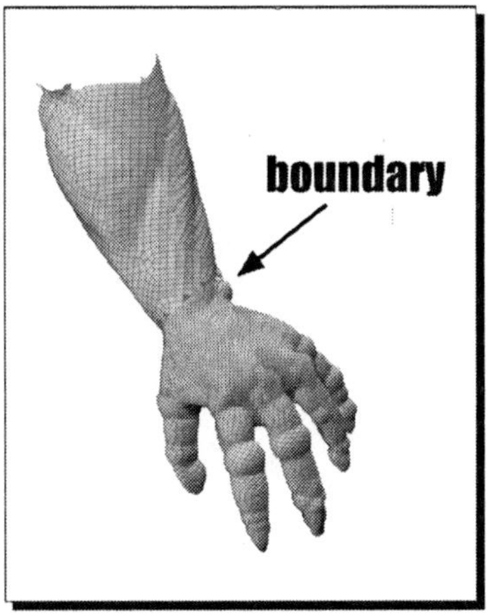

## *What just happened?*

We just added additional detail to the head and the hands, which are important to the perception of the model.

We added this detail especially because the head of our creature is very small, but still quite detailed around the eyes and the beak. But why not divide again? The reason is the difference of resolution across the model. If it differs too much, we would have to step up and down in subdivision levels, each time we would cross such a subdivision boundary to work on the same level of resolution.

ZBrush also creates a separate polygroup for the boundary-polygons, which is why they appear in a different color.

By painting a mask with symmetry, we add polygons symmetrically. If it wasn't, we would have to do a smart resym afterwards to restore the symmetry.

## Time for action – cleaning up the Unified Skin

Depending on the resolution you chose when creating the Unified Skin, you may have to fix some problematic areas, for example, the fingers. Let's do that quickly:

1. Step down to the lowest level of subdivision.
2. Correct the jaw and hands with the **Move brush**, as shown in the next image.
3. For the knees, use the **Slash3** or **Trim Hole brush** to carve a thin line into the surface, where the muscles overlap.
4. Look out for other problematic areas, such as the armpits, and fix them, if necessary.

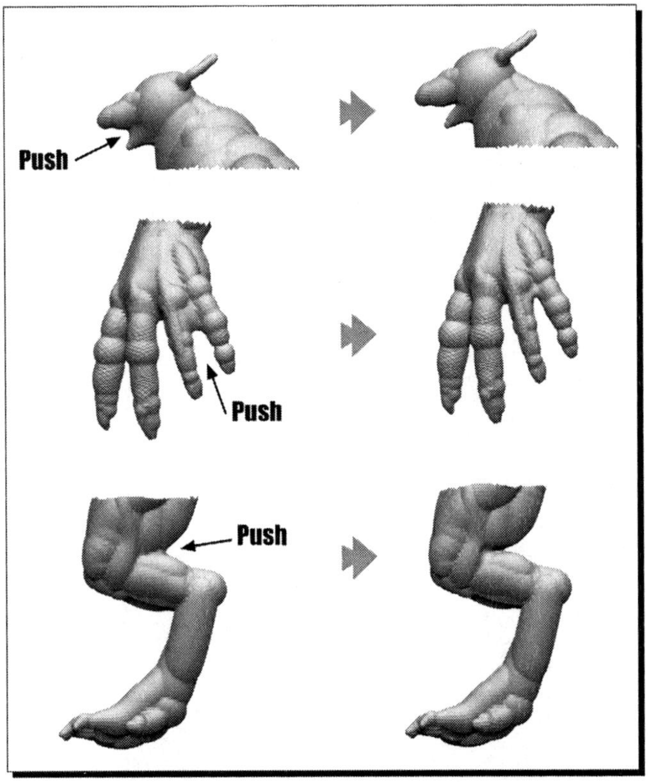


### *What just happened?*

We just did some quick corrections to our Unified Skin of the creature. We have to find a good balance between a reasonable low resolution and the preservation of smaller details such as fingers or other parts close to each other when creating a Unified Skin. Thus, some corrections are always necessary.

## Organizing our model with polygroups

As always, it is useful to prepare our model with polygroups before we start to sculpt.

When working on the Drone, we already used automatic polygroup creation based on UV-coordinates or separated objects. But both methods won't work here because the model is made out of one piece and has no UV-coordinates that we could use for creating polygroups.

Let's see how we can solve this by creating polygroups manually with Polypaint.

If you feel unfamiliar with polypainting, you may want to quickly flip through *Chapter 5, Texturing the tree with Polypaint* again.

# Time for action – adding polygroups manually

Let's quickly create some new polygroups for our model to ease the sculpting process:

1. Load the creature and enable symmetry.
2. Go to **Tool | Polygroups** and press the **Group Visible** button to create one polygroup for the entire mesh to get rid of the border polygroups we got by the local subdivision.
3. Pick the **Pen A brush**.
4. Enable polypainting, set the **RBG Slider** to **100**, and turn off Zadd. Fill the object with an intense color by going to **Color | FillObject**.
5. Now we can paint the mesh in different colors, where we would like the polygroups to appear. Choose strong, contrasting colors so that ZBrush can easily distinguish them. Paint in a region for the head, especially the jaw, the arms, and the legs, as shown in the next image:

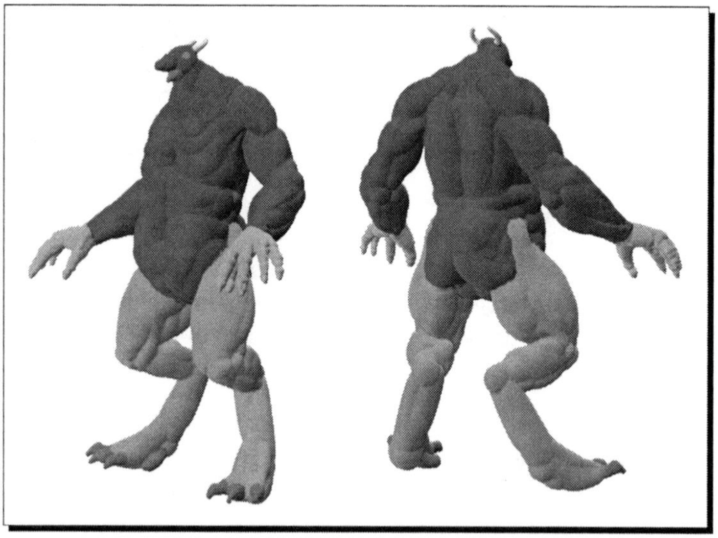

6. If we would like to continue polypainting a region with a certain color, we can pick its color by pressing *C*.
7. Make sure there are no holes or unpainted areas in your polypaint.
8. Apart from painting in the legs, arms, hands, and toes, add one more area for the eye sockets, as shown in the previous image.

9. When finished, go to **Tool | Polygroups | From Polypaint** with **PTolerance** set to **0.4**.
10. Deactivate polypaint and isolate the polygroup for the eye sockets.
11. Press **Tool | Geometry | Edge Loop** twice. Repeat this for the horns and the toes, but add only one loop for the toes.
12. If we smoothen the eye sockets now, we should see two edge loops surrounding it, as shown in the next image:

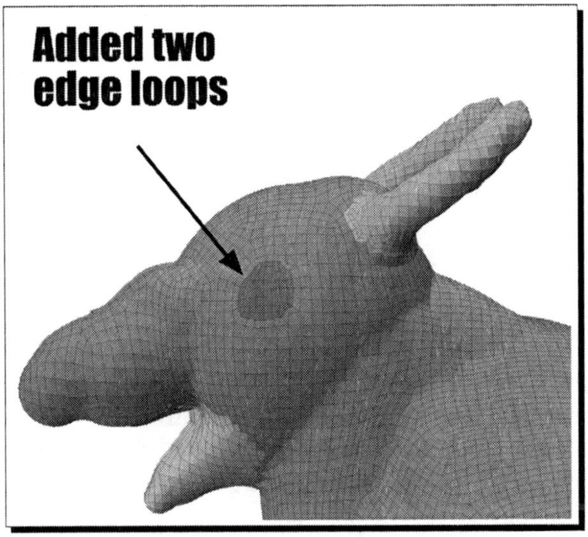


### What just happened?

To make sculpting easier, we just organized our mesh with polygroups manually. Finally, we used the painted polygroups to add additional edge loops that support the creature's anatomy. Let's have a closer look at what we did:

## Polygroups from polypaint

Polypainting gives us full control where polygroups appear. ZBrush evaluates the colors and creates polygroups based on that. This allows us to paint the toes in the same color, so all toes will be in the same polygroup. Manually placing the borders also helps with difficult areas, such as the armpits. These are hard to sculpt, if you have to mask the arm each time you would like to work on the torso. With our polygroups, this takes us just a single click.

By painting with the **Pen A** brush, we get sharp borders between the different colors with no blending. Blending two adjacent colors could lead to a separate polygroup, which is not what we want.

The **PTolerance** slider in the **Polygroups** submenu defines how many polygroups ZBrush will create.

But what if we would like to change how our mesh is separated into polygroups during the modeling process? No problem, because turning off **Polypaint,** by clicking on the **Colorize** button, will not delete the Polypaint information, it will only hide it. So we can simply alter the Polypaint and create new polygroups from it by following these quick steps:

1. Enable **Tool | Polypaint | Colorize**. The painted polygroups should appear.
2. Go to **Tool | Polygroups** and click on the **Group Visible** button to create a single polygroup for the whole mesh, overriding the old ones. The whole mesh should be visible for this operation.
3. Correct the polypainting to your liking. Don't forget to activate symmetry.
4. Go to **Tool | Polygroups | From Polypaint** again and deactivate **Colorize** to hide the painting.
5. Voilà! We have new polygroups.

## Edge loops

By adding an edge loop around the eyes, the topology supports our anatomy, which makes it easier to sculpt. We can also see that ZBrush creates a new polygroup for the edge loop, so we can select it separately. If you would like to get rid of it, isolate the eye sockets and the surrounding loop and click on the **Group Visible** button under **Tool | Polygroups**.

Now we're prepared to really start sculpting on our character.

# Sculpting the body

We're finally there, shaping our first character. As this is our second organic model, the techniques may be similar to the first one, while the topic is more complex and challenging.

Sculpting is a lot like drawing—there is no predefined order in which we have to draw. As we see something, we'll jump over to that point, continuing there. So feel free to work in a different order.

We'll now define the creature's body at its lowest level of subdivision, so we can add the belt and the fur in the next step.

## Time for action – let's sculpt the body

1. Let's sculpt the body of our creature. Start at the lowest level of subdivision.
2. Make sure symmetry is active.
3. With ZSketching, we added all the muscles, which are quite exaggerated at the moment. In some areas, they won't be that dominant, but rather hidden under the skin, leaving only subtle hints. This is especially true, with more corpulent characters such as our creature, where body fat smoothens out the muscular surface structure. Start smoothing areas that are meant to be rather even, such as the belly or the pectoral muscles.

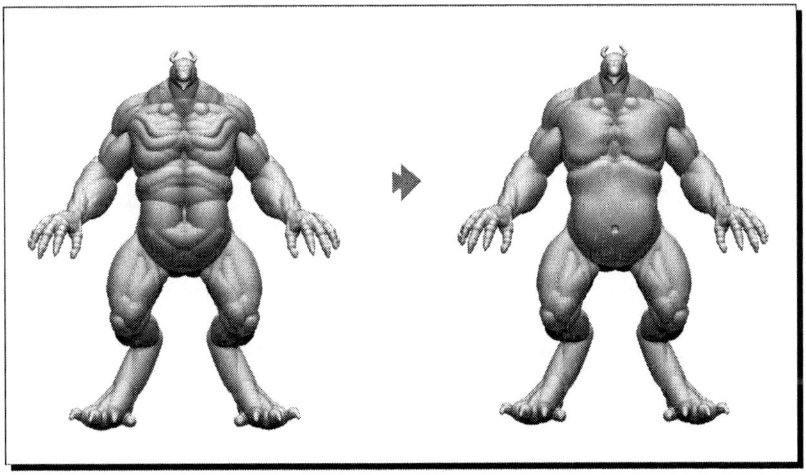

4. A great brush for "filling" some of the deep valleys between the muscles is the **Clay Tubes brush**. Use it in combination with the **Smooth brush** to add more subtle muscles' structures on the back.

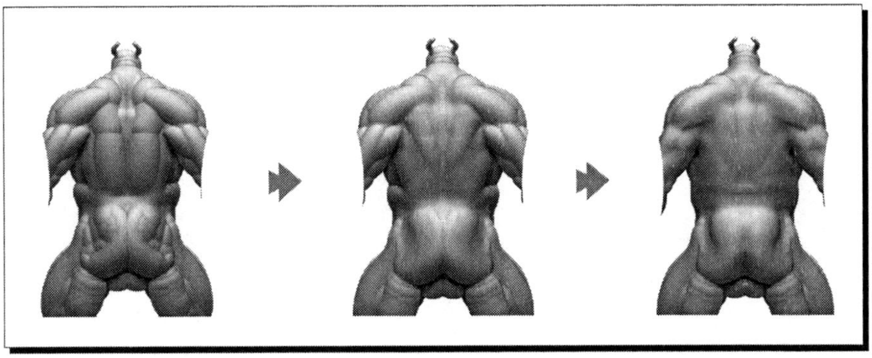

> **Speed up your workflow by using and assigning hotkeys**
>
> We can assign hotkeys to our favorite brushes by *Ctrl + Alt + Left-clicking* on them. ZBrush will then prompt for the hotkey that should be assigned to it. This works with other buttons in the interface too.
>
> Pressing *B* like "Brush" will open the list of brushes at our cursor.

5. Let's continue shaping the head from a snout into a beak. We can make use of our polygroups to hide the jaw while working on the oral cavity. Try to establish a clear boundary between the skull and the neck muscles, as shown in the following image:

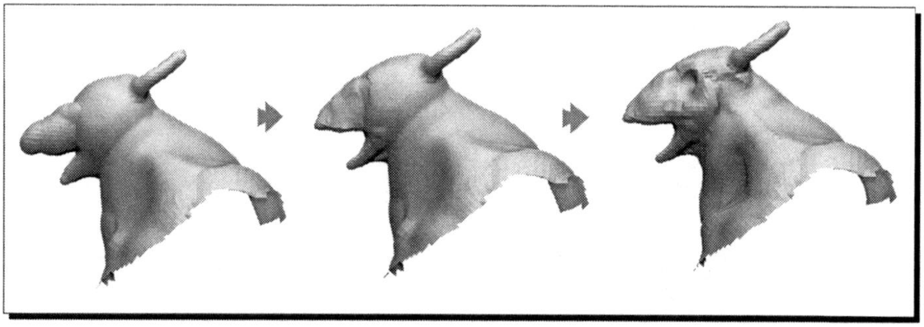

6. Use the **Move brush**, so the eye sockets are facing forward. Activating Polyframe helps moving the edge loops of the eye sockets into place.

7. Use **masking** and the **Move brush** to define the clavicle area more, as shown in the next image:

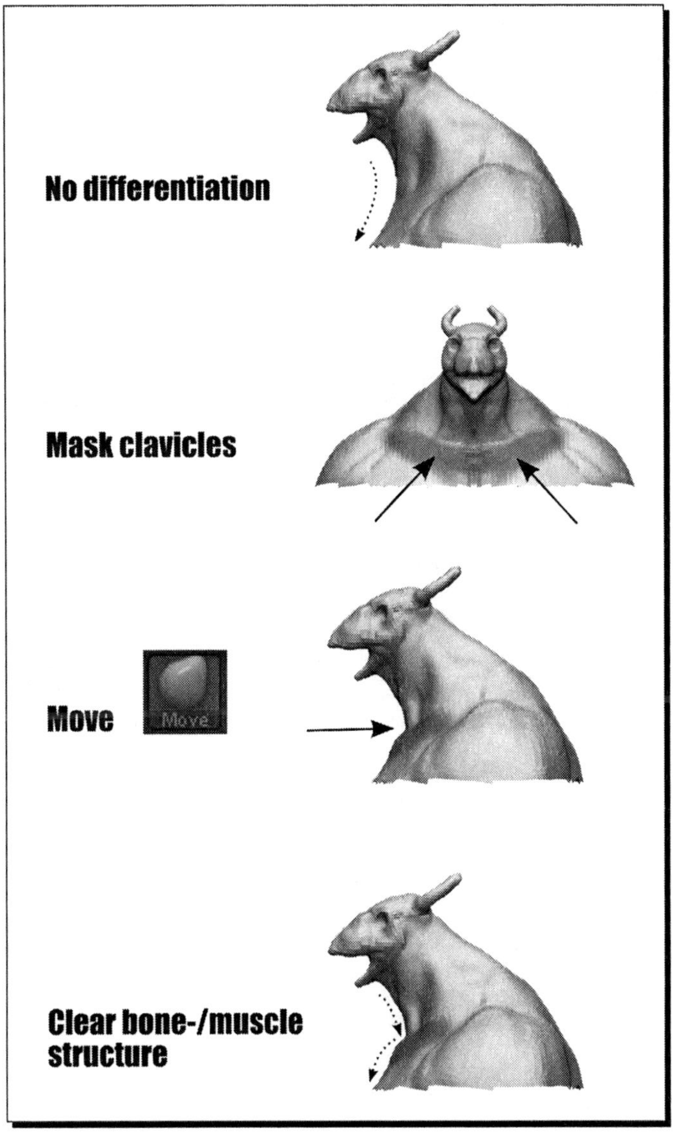

8. The following image provides some tips for building up muscles. As always, this can be done in various ways. We start with the **Clay Buildup brush**, which elevates the surface quicker than the **ClayTubes** brush. For smoothing muscles, the **Smooth Directional** brush is a good addition because it will only smooth along the stroke direction, without affecting the creases between the muscles too much. The **Clay Buildup** brush elevates the surface depending on its surface direction. So, painting on the sides of the strands will narrow the gaps between them, as shown in step three of the next image:

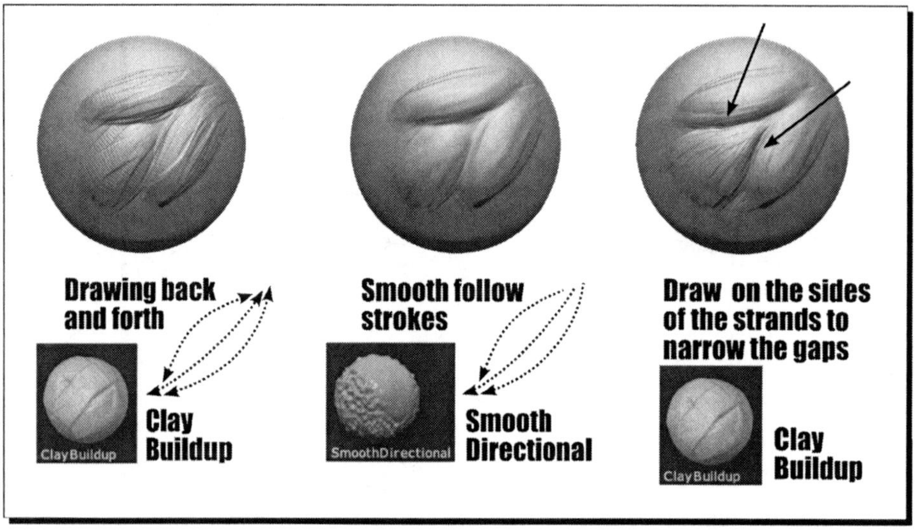


9. Using this technique, the following image shows the progress of the upper legs:

> Don't fear to start all over again in some areas. It's fairly quick at this stage and most of the time you will get a higher quality with a few fresh strokes instead of trying to correct something over and over again. Don't forget to carve into the surface before adding to it again.

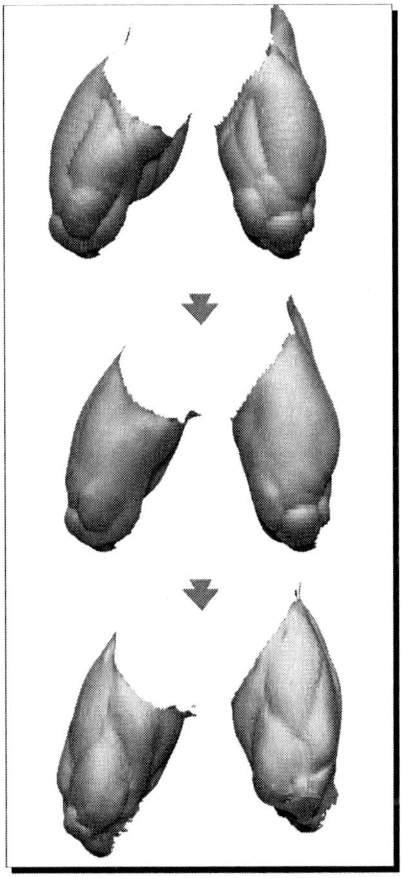

**10.** Add more mass to the torso. Our character will have a tight belt around his waist, so try to squeeze the belly in that area. Also narrow the shoulders more, to make his belly more dominant.

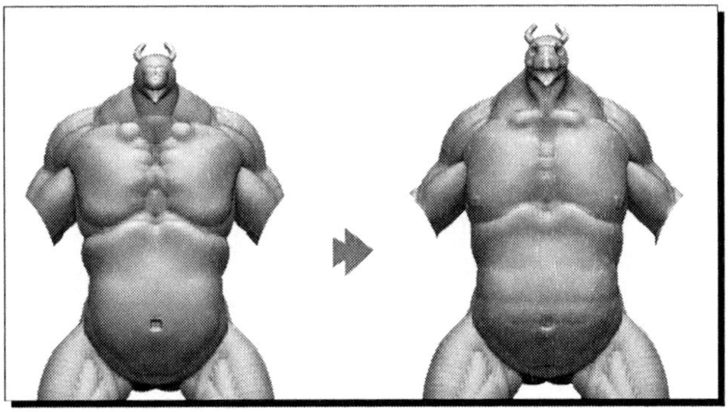

**11.** When we converted our sketch into a Unified Skin, we spread the fingers apart, so they wouldn't get merged. Now, let's bring them back together by using the transpose tool we already used for rotating the mushrooms in *Chapter 6, Adding an Environment to the Tree*. First isolate the hands.

**12.** Pick the **Rotate** tool from the top of the shelf or press *R*.

**13.** Hold down *Ctrl* and drag from the middle of the finger to its tip. This creates a mask based on the topology of the mesh, as shown in the next image. The masking changes depending on the start and the end point of the Action Line. ZBrush will automatically blur the mask once it is drawn:

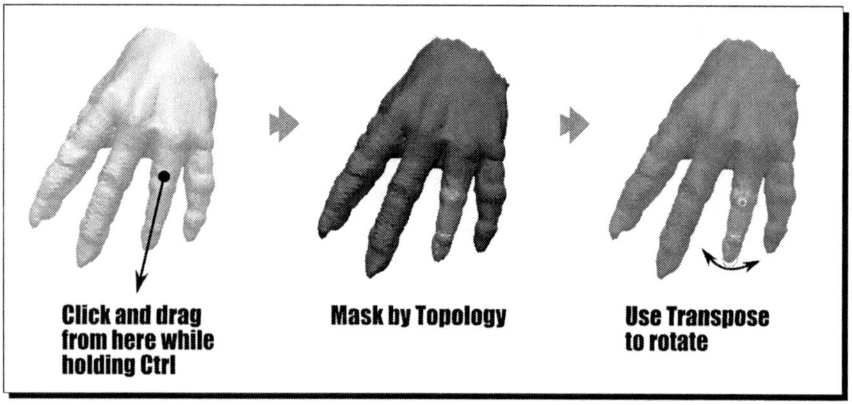


**14.** Clean up the mask by hand, if necessary, by switching back to **Draw mode** and holding *Ctrl* + *Alt* while painting. If we would like to blur our hand-drawn mask too, just *Ctrl* + *Left-click* on the masked area. This can be repeated several times.

**15.** Rotate the fingers by using the Action Line. It's the same process we used on the mushrooms in *Chapter 6, Adding an Environment to the Tree*—if you wish to look it up again.

**16.** If we rotate with the middle point of the Action Line, it will rotate around the line itself instead of around the end points.

**17.** Rotate the fingers as shown in the following image. When finished posing, refine the features of the hand:

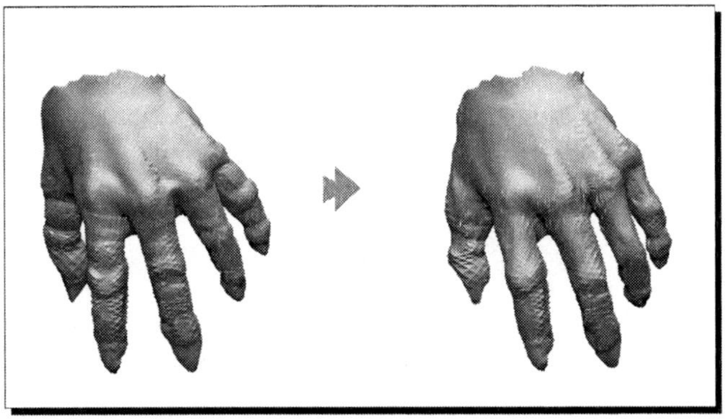

**18.** Continue sculpting the feet and the arms on the lowest level of subdivision until you get all the detail out of the available polygons.

**19.** At this point, I decided to delete the higher subdivision levels because there is no detail of the ZSketch in the higher subdivision levels that I would need anymore. Deleting can be done by clicking on the **Del Higher** button under **Tool | Geometry.** If your ZSketch had more fine detail, you may want to keep the higher levels to keep that detail too.

**20.** We can do a quick Best Preview Render with **Ambient Occlusion** and **Shadows** by opening the **Render palette** and pressing the respective buttons. Our creature would now look like this with the SoftPlastic material:

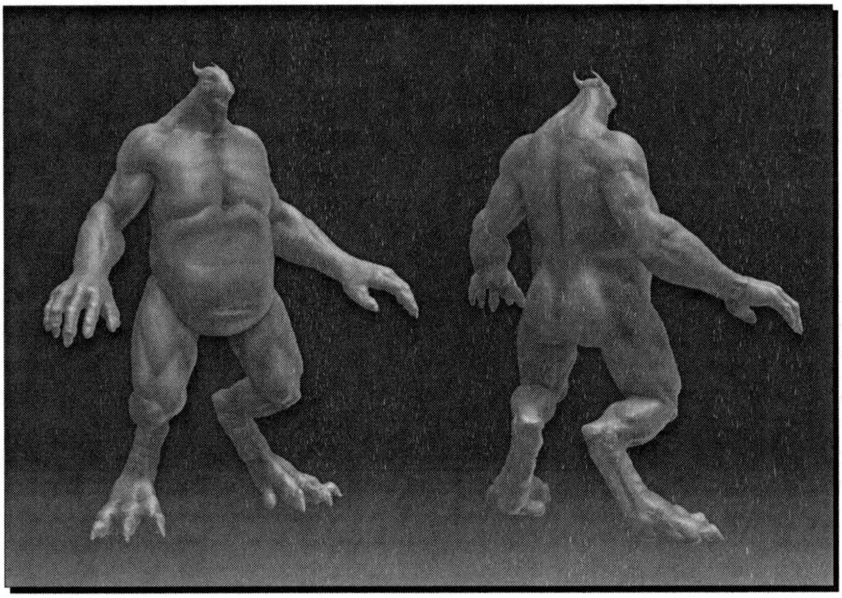

## *What just happened?*

We've now defined the major features of our creature and learned a lot about how to sculpt organic surfaces with underlying muscle and bone structures. Finally, we used the transpose tool with its topological masking to adjust the position and rotation of the fingers.

Let's talk about some more topics in depth:

## Surface contrast

We started out by smoothing some areas of the body, which are less muscular, such as the belly. Additionally, this helps us establish some rest areas for the eye. If a sculpture is covered all over in detail, it will look dull. But if there are cleaner and detailed areas side-by-side, it will look much more interesting.

## Hotkeys

Assigning custom hotkeys in ZBrush is fairly easy. Just *Ctrl + Alt + click* and assign a new hotkey to it. As we close ZBrush, it will ask if the new hotkeys should be saved. Clicking on **Yes** will store them; clicking on **No** will discard them. Another way of doing this is by going to **Preferences | Hotkeys | Store**. Here we can also save and load different hotkey layouts, for example, one layout for sculpting and one for ZSketching.

## Transpose and mask by topology

We continued by rotating the fingers into place with the **Transpose** tool. By *Ctrl + dragging*, we used the topological masks, which gives us a good starting point for masking the fingers. This topological masking depends on how the edges of the mesh are connected. A Unified Skin doesn't provide ideal topology, but it gives us a reasonable starting point. This can also be used to mask out things such as the arms or legs quickly, which is a lot faster than painting a mask by hand.

When using the **Transpose** tool for masking, ZBrush automatically blurs the mask for smoother transitions. This can be done manually, too, by pressing **Tool | Masking | BlurMask**. A quicker way for manually blurring a mask is *Ctrl + clicking* on a masked area. In the Masking menu, we can also do the opposite and sharpen the mask, if we need crisp transitions. On organic meshes, smooth transitions look more natural, but for mechanical parts, we should go for sharpened masks. Only masks created with the **Transpose** tool will be blurred automatically; hand-drawn masks stay as they are.

Let's step ahead by adding the belt and some fur to the character in the next step.

## Pop quiz – masking and polygroups

1. What would we have to do if we assigned a wrong hotkey to a brush and would like to discard that assignment?

    a) Delete the Brush

    b) Close ZBrush and discard the changes on exit

    c) Reload the model

2. Why did we organize our mesh by using polygroups?

    a) To create colors for texturing

    b) To be able to hide parts of the body with a single click

    c) Because the mesh is less boring to look at with polygroups

3. Why did we create symmetrical polygroups when polypainting them?

    a) Symmetrical polygroups prevent symmetry errors on hidden parts

    b) It is faster with symmetry and we're just lazy

    c) Polygroups only work symmetrically

4. What would be the fastest way to mask the three following areas: A leg, the navel, the upper half of the body?

    a) Topological masking (Transpose)

    b) Painting masks

    c) Dragging a mask

# Adding props to our character

Now that we've fleshed out our character in 3D, let's add the belt and rough in some fur, so we can judge the character as a whole. You may want to look up some of the basics of using subtools in *Chapter 6, Adding environment to the tree.*

# Time for action – adding the belt

1. Load the creature character and make sure symmetry is active.
2. Hold *Ctrl and drag on the canvas* to clear previous masking.
3. Divide the mesh one more time with **Smt active**.
4. Hold *Ctrl* and paint a mask around the hips, where the belt will be.
5. Clean up the mask, if necessary, by pressing *Ctrl + Alt*. With the **Flat Color** material applied, the mask would now look like this:

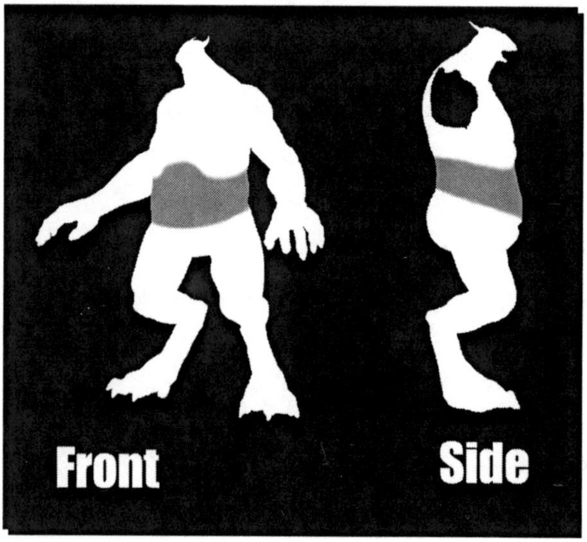


6. Open the **SubTool subpalette** and scroll down to the bottom. There we can find a big button labeled **Extract**, as shown in the next image:

7. Leave the Edge Smoothness (**E Smt**) at **5**, set the Surface Smoothness (**S Smt**) to **100**, and **Thick** to **0.8**. Depending on the size of your model, you may want to alter the thickness a bit.
8. Click on **Extract** and see the magic happen. This will extract the belt from the masking and add it as a new subtool to the list.

9. If the belt is too thin or too thick, just hide the belt, adjust the thickness, and click on **Extract** again.

10. When you're done, delete the unwanted subtools by making them the **active subtool** and pressing Delete. ZBrush will warn us that deleting a subtool can't be undone. Make sure you don't delete the creature accidentally.

11. When extracting a mesh with a mask, the extracted mesh will be masked, too. So we have to clear the masking on the character **and** the belt mesh. This is done by making them the active subtool and *Ctrl + dragging on the canvas.*

12. To keep track of our subtools, give it a meaningful name by navigating to **Tool | SubTool | Rename**.

13. Our extracted belt would now look like this:

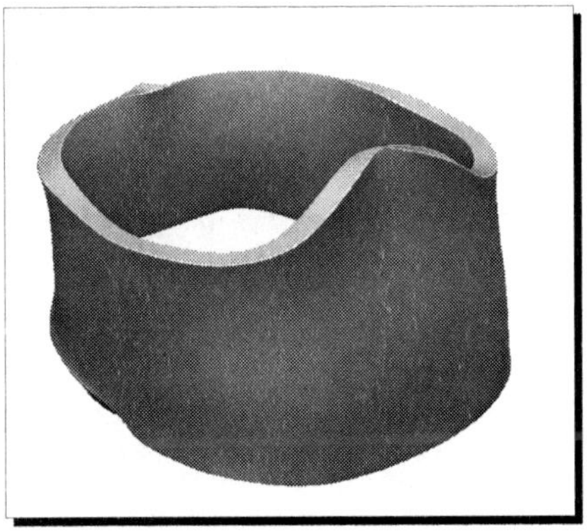

## What just happened?

We just created a belt for our character by simply painting a mask and extracting it. Imagine creating an armor, shoulder plates, hair, trousers, or a cap with this powerful tool. It takes just minutes to paint a mask and extract it.

Let's talk about it in more detail:

# Mesh extract

**Mesh Extract** extracts a new mesh from a mask, but it can also extract by visibility. For instance, isolating the head will do the same as masking it when pressing extract.

Next to the **Extract** button, we have three sliders to control the mesh extraction:

- **E Smt** stands for edge smoothness. This will produce meshes with more rounded corners. Because we wanted sharper corners, we kept it down at **5**.

- **S Smt** stands for surface smoothness. Lower values will represent the masked area more, whereas higher values will produce more smooth meshes. In our case, lower values produce a belt that still has some muscle surface structure on it, which is not what we want, so we put it at the maximum of **100**.
- The **thickness** is pretty self-explanatory.

On extraction, ZBrush will apply the extracted mask to the new subtool. So we have to clear it before we can further work on it. The masking on the mesh we extracted from is kept too, so we can extract with new settings, if we want to. If we're satisfied, we have to clear that original mask. This can easily be overlooked because the original masking is then hidden by the new mesh extract.

## If things go wrong

In step three, we subdivided the mesh before creating the mask. Because the detail of the mask depends on the amount of available polygons, this can be useful. Subdividing the mesh with **Smt** on will also smooth out overlapping polygons, which may cause errors when extracting.

If you get errors when extracting, you can check your masking with the **Flat Color** material to make sure you haven't accidentally masked any other parts.

If there are still unwanted areas that are extracted, you can do the following:

1. Press *B* and select the **SelectLasso** brush.
2. Make the **extract** the active subtool.
3. Hold *Ctrl + Shift* and drag a lasso selection around the unwanted areas. Before letting go, press *Alt* to hide everything inside the selection.
4. Go to **Tool | Geometry | DelHidden**.

## Have a go hero – ZSketching on top of our creature

If you would like to extract something and heavily modify its shape, you may want to try out the **Move Elastic** brush, which moves and relaxes the surface in one stroke. This is ideal for bigger changes in shape.

Let's take this even further. Imagine we would like to add some tentacles on his back. Mesh extract won't be much use here because it only produces meshes that lay close on the surface.

But there's another trick—using ZSketching on an existing mesh by following these simple steps:

1. Append a new ZSphere as a subtool.
2. Switch to the ZSphere tool, making it the active one.
3. Scale it down so that it is inside the mesh and completely hidden. Placing one object into another works best with transparency.
4. Enter Sketch mode by pressing *Shift + A*.
5. Our sketch strokes will now follow the surface of our mesh.
6. Have fun with it. Here's a quick doodle of what this would look like:

This technique allows us to add any form we want to our existing meshes. For clothing and things that are close to the surface, we can use **Mesh Extract**. For more complex forms originating from the mesh, we can use ZSketching instead.

# Time for action – roughing in the fur

Let's add the fur to our character. At this stage, it is important that we can see how the character looks with all its features, in order to improve the overall look from early on. Basically, this follows the same steps as creating the belt, so we'll keep this rather short:

1. Mask the area, where you want the fur to appear on the character, as shown in the next image. It also continues between his legs, like in the concept. Don't try to add finer details; they will be smoothed out on extraction anyway:

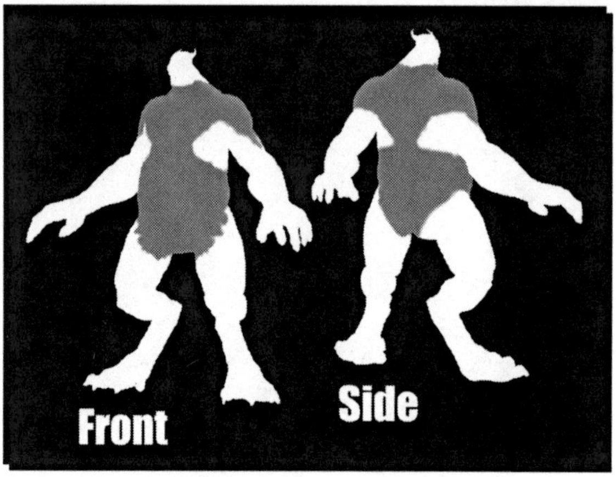


2. Extract the fur with **E Smt** and **S Smt** at **5**. Set the thickness to **0** because we don't need an inner surface.
3. Rename the extract.
4. Clear the mask on the body and the new fur extract.
5. Activate symmetry.

> The symmetry setting is always per subtool.

6. What will become the hair would now look like this:

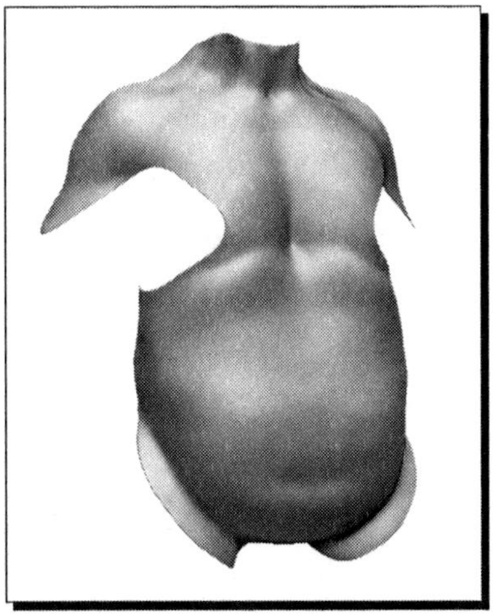

7. At the moment, the hair extract we did looks more like a copy of the body. Let's take care of that. Pick the **Clay Buildup brush** and sculpt the hair, as shown in the next image. Try to sculpt it like the belt would press the hair at the belly. Also, use the **Clay Buildup** brush to add some rough hair-like structure. But don't waste too much time on the details; we'll come in and refine it later:

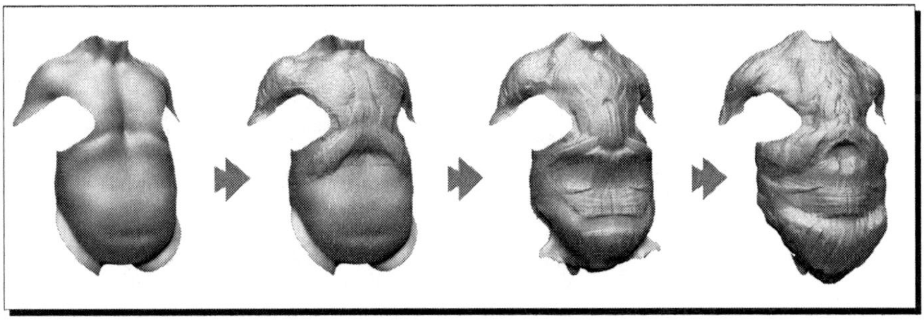

8. Try to imagine where the fur would stack up the most—for example, on the chest, and where it would hide parts of the surface. For example, the hollow clavicle area will probably be hidden by the fur. At this stage, we try to define the material only by volume. The flow of the hair, and how it gets pressed by the belt should tell the viewer that it is fur, without the help of any color. The next image shows two close-ups—what the hair would now look like:

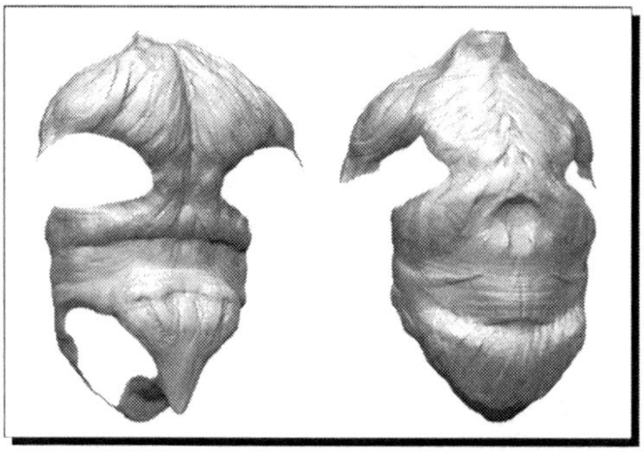

9. Now we have almost everything that makes up our character, in place. So we may want to work on the overall proportions now, as shown in the next image:

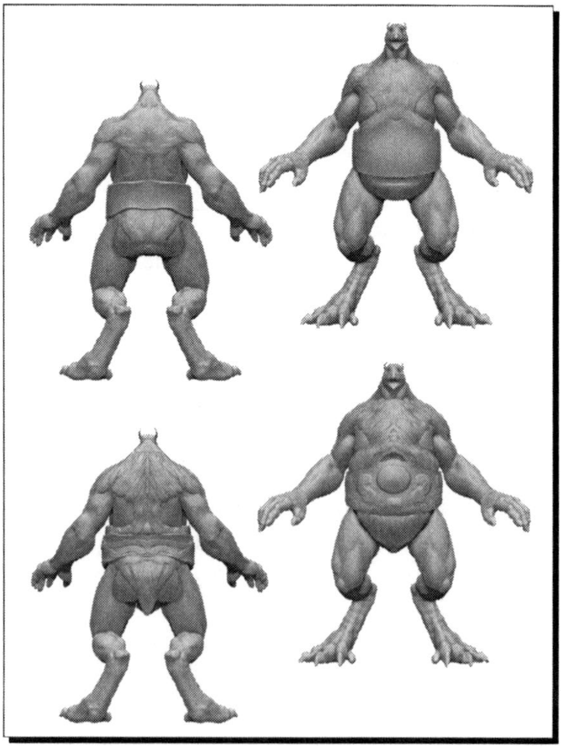

**10.** Use the **Scale Slider** in the **Deformation** subpalette to control the size of the belt, the **Move brush** for the proportions, and the **Clay Buildup** brush for the rough detail on the belt.

> **Tips for working with multiple subtools**
>
> With multiple subtools, we can press *N* to get a list of the available ones sorted alphabetically, like the brushes. This allows us to quickly select a specific one.
>
> Selecting visible subtools can be done even quicker: Pressing *Alt* and *left-clicking* on a subtool will automatically switch to this one.
>
> If we want to get rid of the darkening effect on inactive subtools to judge the overall look, we can append a dummy subtool, such as a ZSphere, and place it inside of our mesh. If we select it, everything else will then be of the same (darkened) color. We can also control the amount of darkening in the **Preferences | Edit | Inactive Subtool Dimming** menu.

## *What just happened?*

We just created the base for what will become the fur of our creature, the same way we did for the belt. We can now step ahead and finish the body of the creature.

When creating digital models, we should try to get the structures and materials across at every stage. So the modeling should point out changes in material or surface, as well as the texture and the animation. If we do so, it will then add up and create a believable 3D model.

When working with multiple subtools, we can switch between them by pressing *N*. If we have only two subtools, this will toggle between them.

As we saw, we can add a dummy object, such as a ZSphere, to get rid of the darkening effect on the inactive subtools. Another possibility is to fill each subtool with a white color, which will then override the darkening effect. The downside of this method is that we get no more indication of which subtool is active.

Because each subtool can have its own color, we can use this to, for example, darken the hair, or already add some overall tones to the subtools.

Let's continue by adding eyes and closing the mouth.

# Time for action – refining the head with eyes and mouth

Let's step ahead and add eyes and a closed mouth to the head:

1. Let's add some eyes for our character. Select the **Sphere3D** tool.
2. In the **Initialize** settings, set the **HDivide** and **VDivide** to **64**, and go to **Tool | MakePolymesh3D.**
3. Open the model of your creature and append the newly created **PM_Sphere3D**.
4. Open the **Draw palette**. Activate all three axes of the floor button and then press the button itself. You should now see three grids—one for each axis.
5. To align the three grids with the character, set the **Elv** (**Elevation**) slider in the **Draw** palette to **0**.
6. Position the sphere in the character's right-eye socket by using the **Transpose tool**. It's crucial to put it in the character's right-eye socket because ZBrush will mirror only from this side.
7. Go to **Tool | Geometry | Mirror And Weld** with only the **X-axis** selected, as shown in the next image:

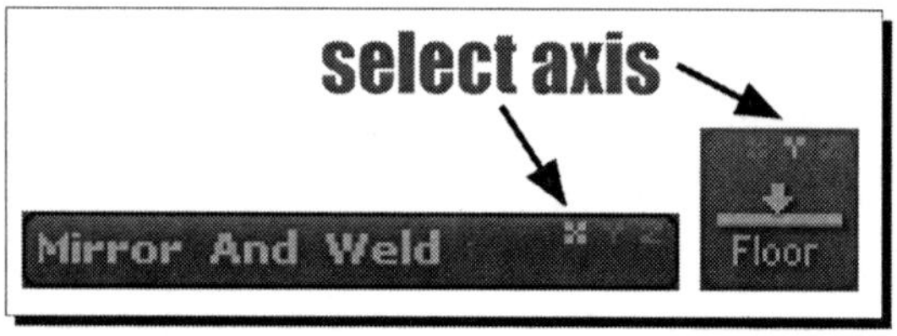


8. If we put the sphere on the wrong side, we'll get a message saying "**The resulting mesh contains no polygons**".
9. That's it; we just added eyes to our character. All there's left to do is to *rename* the subtool to something meaningful, such as "Eyes".
10. The head of our creature could now look like this:

**11.** Now let's add a layer to open and close the mouth, so we can judge the mouth in both positions. First, switch to the highest level of subdivision.

**12.** Open the **Layers subpalette** and add a new layer by pressing the button that looks like a new document with a little plus icon.

**13.** If you have **Colorize** activated and added a new layer, the model will go black. Just disable colorize to display it as usual.

**14.** In the **Layers** palette, the layer you just added should have switched automatically to **record mode**, which means, it will record everything we do from now on to this layer. If only the eye icon is visible, just click left from it to switch to *record mode*. The layer in *record mode* should look like this:

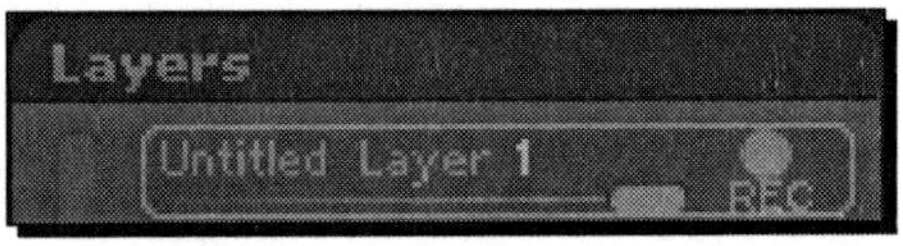


**15.** Now paint-mask the jaw, and invert the mask.

**16.** Turn off symmetry and make sure to view the model exactly from the side.

17. Close the mouth with the **Transpose** tool, as shown in the next image:

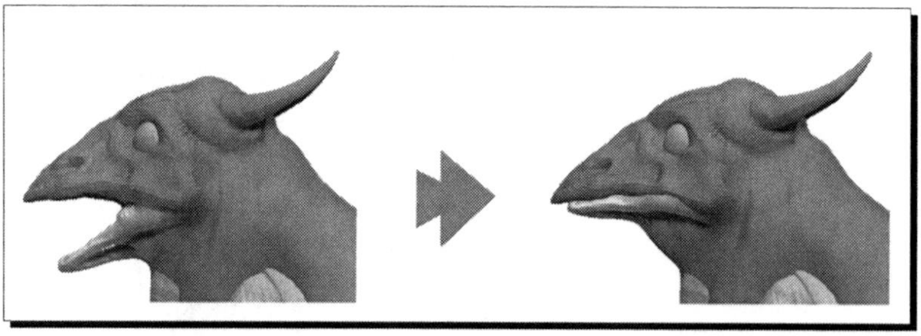

18. When done, activate symmetry again.

19. Exit record mode by clicking on the eye icon, next to the record icon of the layer.

20. Now we can use the slider below the layer to open and close the mouth as we like.

## *What just happened?*

We just added the eyes and a layer to open and close the mouth quickly. Now let's talk a bit more in-depth about the preceding steps.

# Adding the eyes with mirror and weld

Before adding the eyes, we used the initialize settings to control the resulting amount of polygons of our eyes. To better see what the mirror and weld operation will do, we activated the floor grid.

By pressing the respective axis on the floor button, we determined which axis to display. The same goes for the **Mirror And Weld** button, where we set the X-axis to mirror on. Because the floor grid was offset, we used the **Elv-Slider** to reset it. If we don't and try to mirror and weld, ZBrush will display a message, warning us that the floor grid doesn't display the real mirror axis. **Mirror And Weld** supports only meshes without subdivision levels or layers. We would have to clear all layers and delete all subdivision levels except for one to mirror such a mesh.

Because it is called mirror and weld, it will weld everything that crosses the axis of mirror. This could be useful for a cyclops, but our character should have two separate eyes.

## Closing the mouth with layers

Layers help us organizing things or establishing different poses without losing our original work. When we added the new layer, it automatically switched to record mode. In this way, everything we did was recorded to that layer. If we exit the record mode, it will then be stored in the model itself. We can think of layers as information that is added on top of the model. So with no layer in record mode, we can still work on the model itself.

Only one layer can be in record mode at a time. If we activate the record mode of another layer, the previous layer will exit record mode automatically. Layers can store changes in geometry, polypainting, and masks.

The intensity slider below the layer allows us to adjust the intensity of that layer. In this way, we can blend different poses or details very easily. The intensity slider below the layer can even be negative, ranging from 1 to -1. A negative value will invert the changes, hills will become valleys and vice versa. At the bottom of the list is another slider, also resembling the intensity of the layer. The only difference is that it ranges from -5 to 5, so if we applied some sculpting on a layer and would like to push it even more, we could use a value greater than 1.

If we would like to clear all layers, we can use the **Bake all** button, which will apply all visible layers to the model and delete all invisible ones.

On higher subdivision levels, where you may only have a limited number of undo's, layers come in handy to try things out.

# Finishing the sculpting on the body

With all this done, let's finish the sculpting of the body. When adding the belt, we already added another level of subdivision. Let's work it out step-by-step. As there are no new sculpting techniques involved at this stage, there are mainly images showing off the progress. The images also include the development over several subdivision levels, so now you should judge for yourself when to step up another level.

# Time for action – finishing the body

1. Let's start with the head, as shown in the following image. Start to define the rough forms at the lowest subdivision level and then work through the higher ones. As sculpting is always a creative process, the forms can change quite a bit. For the head, I decided to go for a more aggressive head, to make it conform with the rest of the body. Even at the final stage, the neck is kept smooth because we will add feathers in this area later on, which hides any muscular structures:

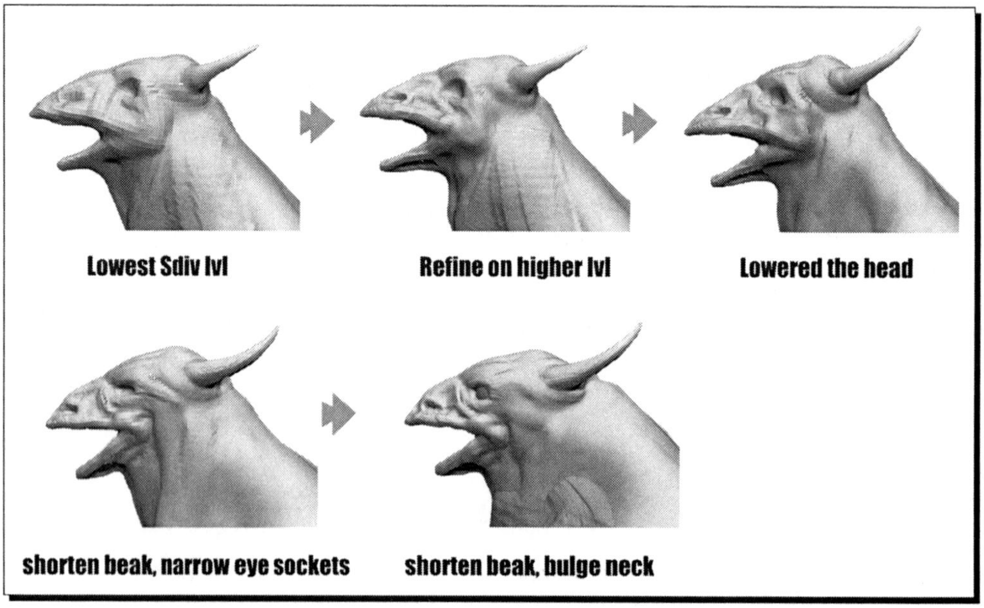


2. For the hands, the **Smooth Directional** is useful to better work out the wrinkles. In this way, we can smooth along a drawn wrinkle without smoothing the one next to it.

3. When working on the overall form, try to define where there are bones or muscles under the skin. Bones, like the knuckles, will produce forms with more contrast, whereas muscles form more bulged, smooth surfaces. The palms can be roughed in, but because they will rarely be seen, we don't need to waste too much time on detailing them.

   For isolating the fingers, we can use the **SelectLasso** brush. *Ctrl + Shift + Alt* will hide inside the selection.

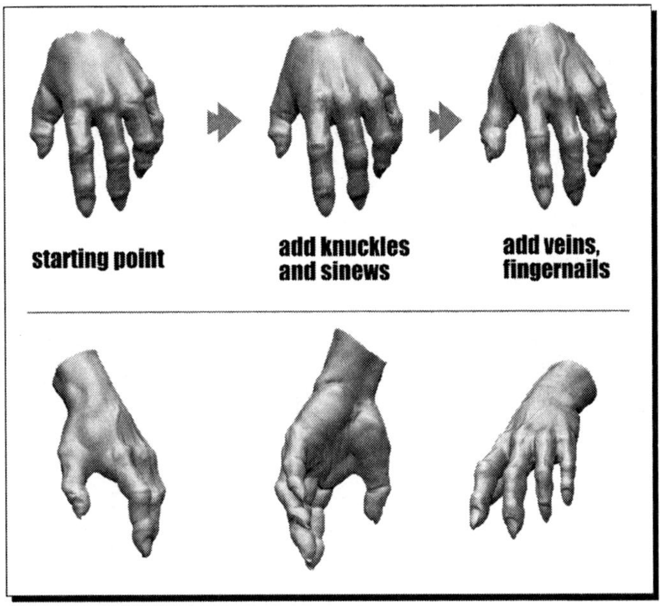


4. When doing the hands, also work out the arms accordingly, as shown in the next image. It's important that the muscles of the lower arm twist around the arm, when the hands are rotated like this:

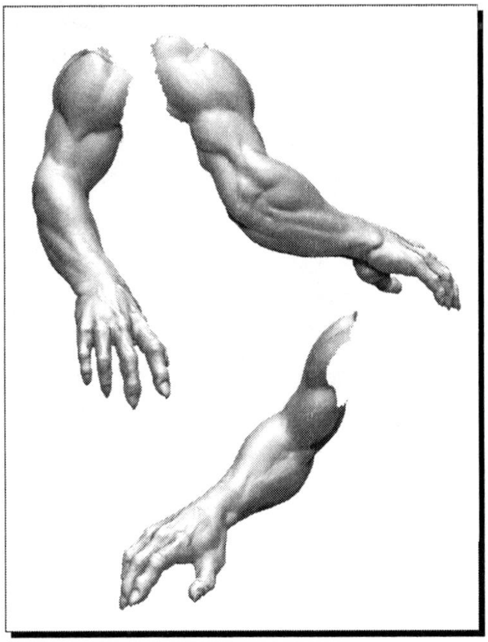

5. Detailing the feet follows the same principle as the hands. With feet like these, we have some artistic freedom of how the bones and muscles interact. It just has to look believable, not real. Opposed to hands, very few people know how birds' feet really look like. To get the soles of the feet flat, we can use the **Flatten** brush.

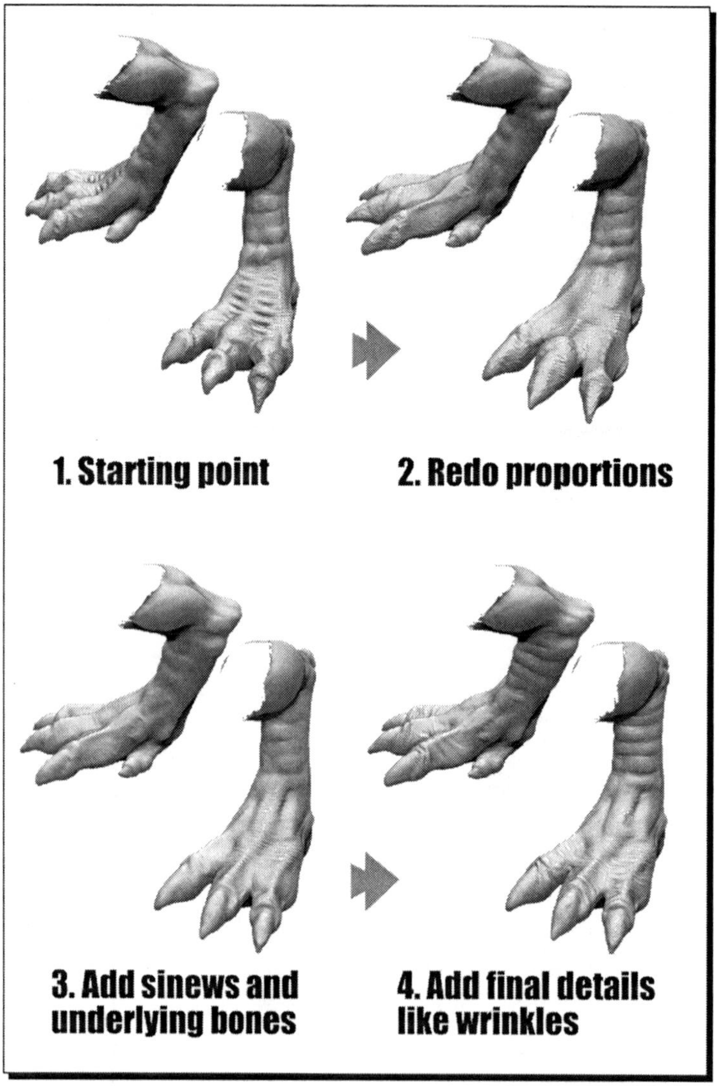


6. Continuing with the body, try to work out the back and the torso. Like the palms, don't waste too much time on areas that will definitely be hidden by fur. For the legs and the back, you can look for pictures of bodybuilders as well as anatomical ones for reference.

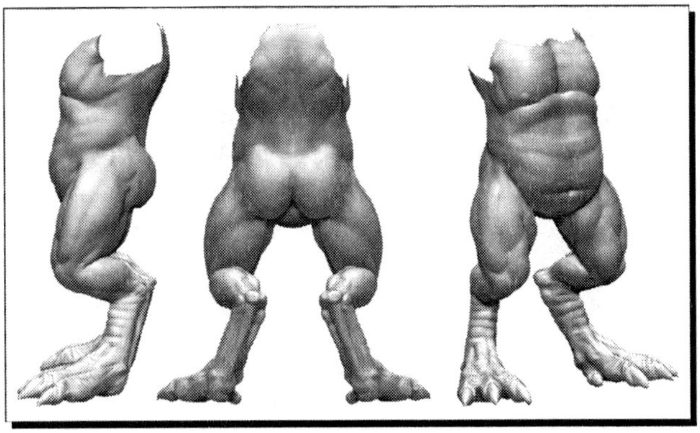

7. Our creature's body would now look like this:

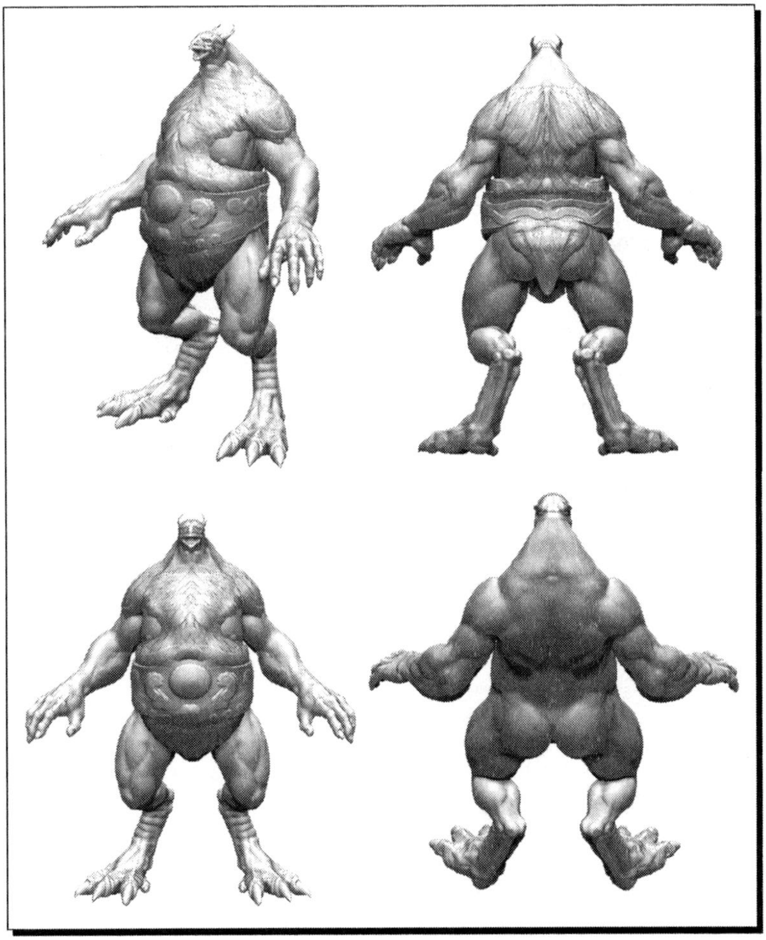

## *What just happened?*

We've now completed the body of the creature. By now, we're pretty familiar with the sculpting techniques involved in this. However, one new thing we crossed was the **SelectLasso** brush for isolating the fingers, for example. As we select it, ZBrush displays a message, telling us that this Brush is now our **Active Selection brush**. This means, every time we press *Ctrl + Shift* to hide parts, this brush will be the one that gets activated. This follows the same principle as the **Smooth** brush, which only gets activated when pressing the *Shift* key. If you want the default selection method back, just select the **SelectRect** brush.

The same set of brushes is available for masking, namely, the **MaskPen**, **MaskLasso**, and **MaskRect** brush. As their names indicate, the **MaskPen** brush is for painting masks, **Lasso** for lasso masking, and **Rect** for rectangular masking.

# Summary

In this chapter, we've learned quite a lot about how to bring a characters sculpt to finish. Let's draw the main points together again:

- Adding detail locally can be done using local subdivision
- We easily organized our model by creating polygroups from Polypaint
- Inserting edge loops help us to create topology that supports our modeling, for example, around the eye sockets
- The Transpose tool helped us rotate the fingers and can also be used to quickly create masks by topology
- By creating our own hotkeys, we can work even faster now
- We added additional props to our character with mesh extract
- For more elaborate props, we can use ZSketching on top of a mesh
- Symmetrical pieces, such as the eyes, can quickly be created using mirror and weld
- Layers help us keep things organized and to work non-destructively

With the body finished, let's go ahead detailing the fur and the belt in the next chapter.

# 12
# Sculpting Fur and Accessories

*With the body of our creature finished, we'll now focus on sculpting the fur and adding some accessories in this chapter. To create convincing fur, we will take a closer look at using alphas. This will not only cover how to use alphas but also how to create your own, which is a crucial step when dealing with fine details such as hair, ornaments, or scales.*

In this chapter, we will learn how to:

- Create custom alphas for fur
- Sculpt the fur with alphas and strokes
- Sculpt convincing materials, such as fur and cloth
- Add props to define the character more

> You can download the creature from the previous chapter by following the link provided in the preface.

# Creating alphas for feathers and fur

Following the concept, our character should have some fur as well as feathers. So, we'll try to get a smooth transition from a feathered head to a furry chest and back. To create convincing fur and feathers, we'll create custom alphas for each:

**Alphas** are just grayscale images, so we can easily create our own in any image editor. As this is not ZBrush-specific, here's only a short breakdown of how to create the alphas for the feathers and fur. This is not a step-by-step tutorial, but rather an explanation of how to build custom alphas to create more realistic sculptures. You are encouraged to create your own alpha, but you can also download both of them by following the link at the end of this section.

First, let's have a look at the existing alphas to better understand how they work. Here are two examples that come along with ZBrush. The first one is the alpha of the **Snake** brush, found in the brush list. The second one is the **ScalesFish** brush that can be found by opening **Lightbox**. After that, it will also be displayed in the brush list until the next restart of ZBrush:

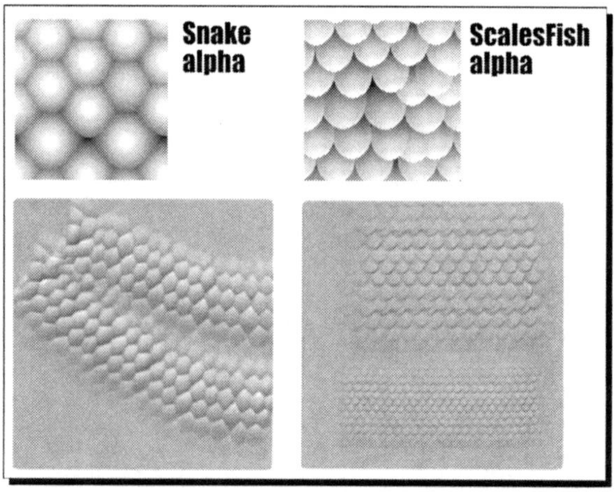

As we can see in the previous examples, both images are grayscale images, where black means no elevation and white means full elevation. The shades in-between can be used to create various forms. In the example of the ScalesFish alpha, each scale has a gradient on it. It starts with black at its origin and fades to white at its tip. This way, it will look as if the scales would be overlapping each other. We'll use the same trick to create some convincing feathers.

## Time for action – creating an alpha for the fur

As mentioned earlier, this example is only a short breakdown of the steps I used to create the alpha in GIMP. You'll have to apply these steps to the image editor of your choice:

1. First search for some references. The following image can be found on wikimedia if you look for "emu". (Source: `http://upload.wikimedia.org/wikipedia/commons/1/19/Emu_showing_feet.jpg` (Photo by Flickr user Aenneken, under Creative Commons Attribution License))

2. Pick an area that resembles the structure of the fur well. To do that, either crop the image, or create a new one from the selection.
3. Convert it to a grayscale image. You may also increase the contrast.
4. Check the size of the alpha you're going to create. Something between 100 and 300 pixels in width and height should be fine, depending on whether you plan to use it for smaller or larger details. In our case, the alpha is 168 x 300 pixels large. Since ZBrush version 4.0, non-square alphas are supported.
5. Paint over on another layer, starting with a dark gray, as shown in the next image.

6. Paint on a new layer on top of that with a brighter color, which will be the strands lying on top. Combine both of them, as shown in the following image:

7. Save it in a format that ZBrush can recognize, which is for example, `.psd`, `.tiff`, or `.png`.

8. That's it for creating a custom alpha. As this is quite a fast process, you can even create more than one alpha to add some more variation to the fur.

> You can download the finished alphas from the Packt website by following the link provided in the preface.

## What just happened?

We've just learned how to create our own alphas by quickly painting them.

When painting overlapping material, such as fur or feathers, it's important that there are brighter and darker areas in the alpha, so that some parts will be elevated more than others—this emphasizes the effect of overlapping.

The following image shows the same process for creating the alpha of the feathers. Simply duplicate and rotate one feather to get a nice-looking row. Then duplicate it and put it below. It's important to darken the origins of the lower row to increase the overlapping effect:

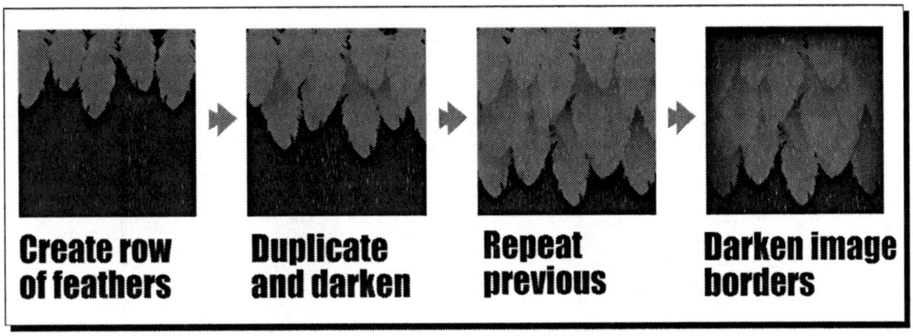


If your source image is of a high quality, you can even pick directly from it, without any overpainting. All you have to do is convert it to grayscale and adjust the contrast. As most images from the Web have plenty of compression artifacts in them, hand painting can be a quick and clean solution.

When done, you can also add a soft black border around the alpha to make it blend better with your sculpture. You can also skip this and set a radial fade in the **Alpha | Rf slider**. Setting it in ZBrush may give you more control and variation, but the downside is that you have to set it again every time you restart ZBrush. The choice is up to you.

There's already a good collection of alphas provided by pixologic where you can download alphas for your projects: `http://www.pixologic.com/zbrush/downloadcenter/alpha/`.

# Time for action – sculpting the fur

Equipped with the furry alphas, let's jump in directly and add the final detail to the fur:

1. Load the creature.
2. Switch to the fur as the active subtool.
3. Pick the **Move** brush and make sure that the fur forms a closed volume around the body, as shown in the next screenshot:

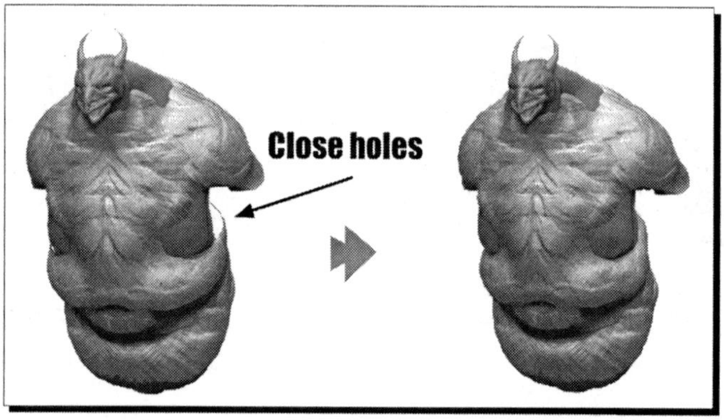


4. The alphas will be used only for final polish, so we have to get the global shapes right before advancing to the fine details. Pick the **ClayBuildup** or the **Clay Tubes** brush and sculpt the basic forms of the fur, as shown in the next screenshot. Start with laying in the main directions the fur should follow. Be careful when using the **ClayBuildup** brush. It builds up fast, quickly creating bloated surfaces that have to be corrected. Keep adding details when stepping up in subdivisions. When done with this, you should already be able to tell in which direction the fur flows and where it overlaps:

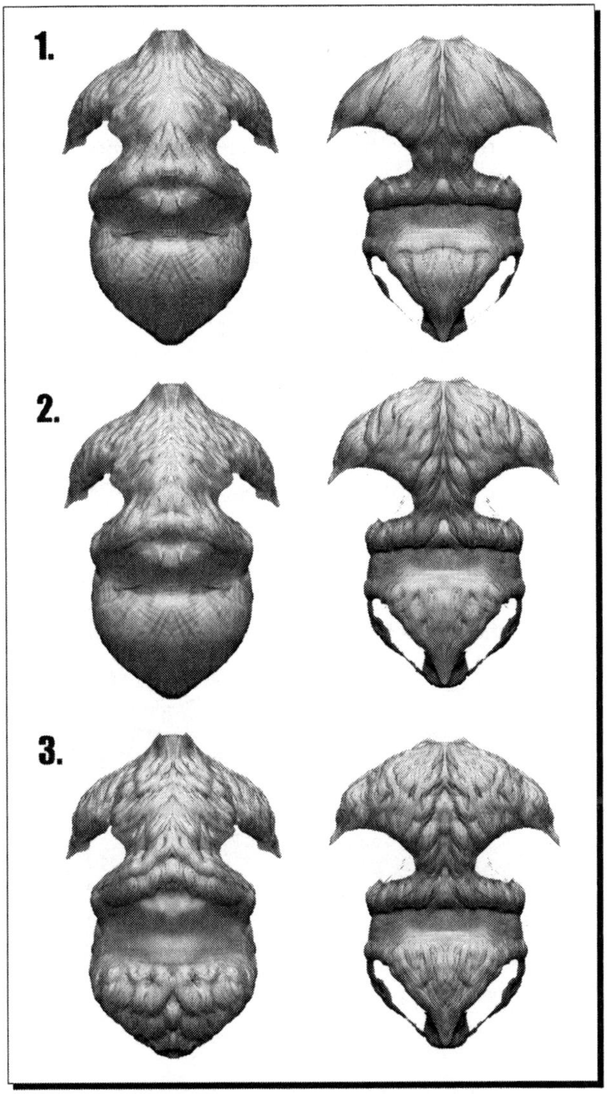


*5.* When the additional polygons of the fur slow down your computer, you may want to switch to the body subtool and lower its level of subdivision. This will free up system resources.

*6.* Divide the fur subtool to a few million polygons so that the alphas can be applied without a loss of detail due to a low polygon count.

*7.* Create a new layer for the details and name it appropriately.

*8.* Pick the **LayerConst** brush.

9. Activate **Brush | Auto Masking | Directional**. This will make the alpha follow the curve of the strokes better.

10. Click on the **BrushAlpha** icon to get a floating list of available alphas. At the bottom of that list, click on the **Import** button and load the alpha for the fur. You can also access this function via **Alpha | Import**.

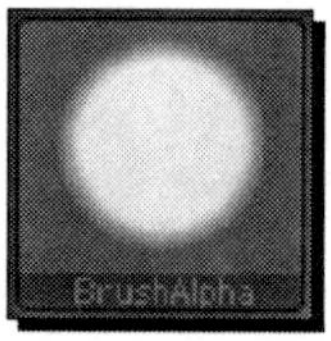


11. Open the **Alpha palette** and activate **Alpha | Aa** (anti-aliasing) and set the **Alpha | Rf** (radial fade) to **10**. With these settings, some test strokes should look like this:

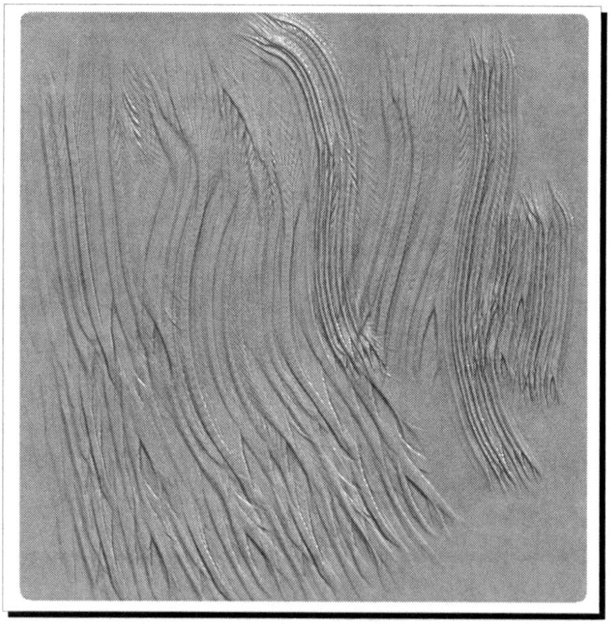

12. Check in which direction the alpha is pointing. If the tips of the alpha are facing upward, you can either draw all the strokes in the opposite direction or flip its orientation by pressing **Alpha | Flip V** (vertically).

13. Make sure that the layer is in record mode and start adding details with the **LayerConst** brush to the front of the fur without symmetry. When adding fine detail, try to follow along the directions of the strands we sculpted in earlier, as shown in the following screenshot:

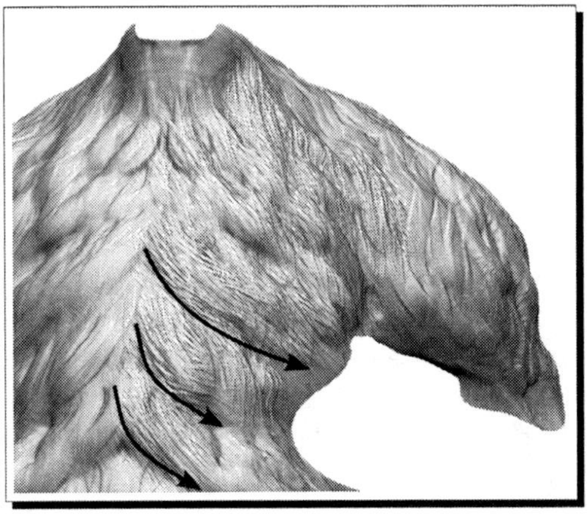

14. With the front finished, we can activate symmetry again to continue on the shoulders.

15. When detailing the back, turn off symmetry again.

16. If you're unsatisfied with any area, you can just smoothen it and do it again. The detailed fur would now look like this:

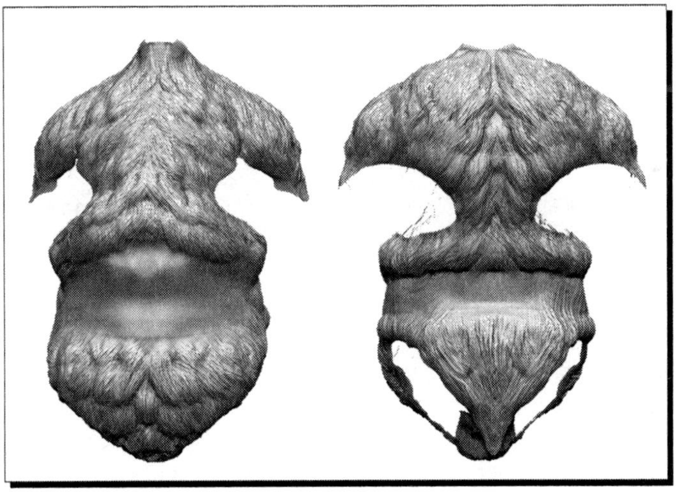

# *What just happened?*

We've just learned how to add the very fine details when sculpting with alphas. Let's have a closer look at the topics we covered.

## Sculpting with alphas

When we added the larger details and determined the flow of the fur, we had two options: Depending on the style of the game, we could have sculpted the fine detail by hand, or use alphas for that. With the tree, from the earlier chapters, we sculpted the fine detail without alphas, creating a more clear and unrealistic style. When sculpting fur by hand, we could have used the **Slash** and **Pinch** brushes to achieve a similar effect. But because our fur covers a large area of our character, it would also have taken up much more time.

When working with our fur alphas, we used the **Alpha | Rf** (radial fade) and the **Alpha | Aa** (anti-aliasing) buttons. **Radial fade** fades the alpha at the edges of the image, so it blends better in existing patterns. This has the same effect as painting a soft black border around the alpha in our image editor. The **anti-aliasing** button simply adds anti-aliasing to the alpha, producing smoother results with less stair-stepped edges.

Another useful set of buttons we used are the **Alpha | Flip V** and **Alpha | Flip H**. As their names say, they flip the alpha vertically and horizontally. Because our alphas are not symmetrical, flipping them horizontally can add more variation to the strokes while saving us the time to create another one.

## Sculpting with symmetry

As we sculpted the fur on the chest and the back, we disabled symmetry. But why did we do this? The reason is the UV map: When unwrapping the character model in the next chapter, we will create a unique UV map, which means each polygon of the model will get its own space on the texture. When modeling symmetrically, this will waste almost half of the texture space, as it will simply be the same on each side, but flipped. Sculpting without symmetry also enhances the impression of the character because the chest or the back will probably be viewed the most. Because we can't view both sides of the shoulders at once, sculpting with symmetry just saves us time here. Another, much more complicated possibility would be using a mirrored UV-map for the character. If you choose to do this, sculpting with symmetry absolutely makes sense. This will save up texture space at the cost of uniqueness in the look of the model. Although, doing a symmetrical UV-map or even a combination of both is out of the scope of this book, it's good to know the possibilities.

## Erasing layer contents

When sculpting on a layer, smoothing unsatisfying areas does not always give the best results. In this case, we can use this simple workflow to paint-erase parts of a layer:

1. First disable the layer visibility, so the unchanged model is visible.
2. Click on **Tool | Morph Target | StoreMT**. This stores a version of the mesh at the current visible state.
3. Put the layer back in record mode again.
4. Pick the **Morph** brush, adjust the **Z Intensity** to your liking, and start *paint-erasing*. The **Morph** brush will morph the mesh back to what was stored in the morph target beforehand, which was the unchanged model.

Now we'll step ahead and detail the head and the neck, so the fur can blend in nicely.

## Pop quiz – layers and alphas

1. If you're unsatisfied with some parts that are stored in a layer, how could you erase them?

   a) With the Smooth brush

   b) By deleting the layer

   c) By using a Morph target

2. What would a rectangular alpha with a white dot on a black background do?

   a) It would create an elevated rectangle with a hole

   b) It would create a rivet-like bulge

   c) It would create a hole

3. Why didn't we pick our fur-alpha directly from the photo reference?

   a) Because it is copyrighted

   b) Because we can't use colored alphas

   c) Because the `.jpeg` source image had too many artifacts

# Time for action – detailing the head

Let's continue adding fine detail to the head and blend it with the fur:

1. Select the subtool of the body, making it the active one.
2. Create a new layer and rename it.
3. Pick the **Standard** brush, turn off **Stroke | LazyMouse**, and select **DragRect** as stroke type.

4. Import the alphas for the fur and the feathers.
5. Activate anti-aliasing and set **Radial fade** to **3** for the alphas.
6. Make sure that the body subtool has a few million polygons, so we can apply the fine details. If the performance is too low, you can lower the subdivision level of the other subtools (*Shift + D*) or hide parts of the mesh (*Ctrl + Shift + drag*).
7. Pick the feathers alpha and start out from the eye, as shown in the next screenshot. Clicking-and-dragging away from the center will scale the alpha, while spinning around will rotate it. After a short time, you'll get used to the **DragRect** stroke type. With this stroke we can adjust the placement and rotation of the details very precisely. Take your time to not only place and scale it, but also to rotate the detail correctly, so that it blends perfectly with the neighboring ones:

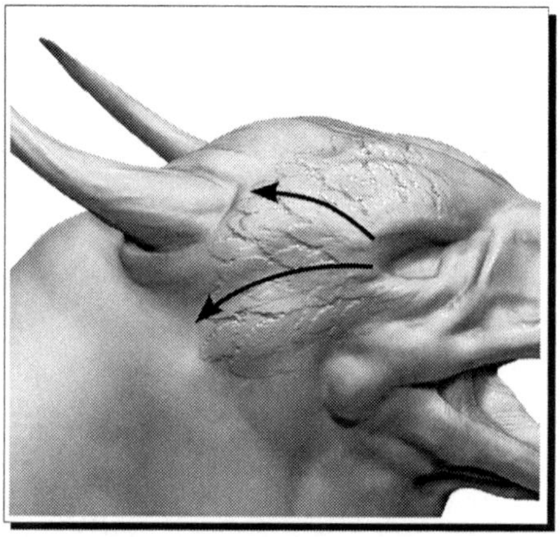

8. Continue with adding feathers on the head. On the neck, start mixing hair and feathers, as shown in the next screenshot. On the top part of the neck, some strands of hair show through, whereas at the bottom part only a few feathers are visible. This way it blends well into the existing fur. Also, try to make the feathers and strands larger as you get farther away from the eyes:

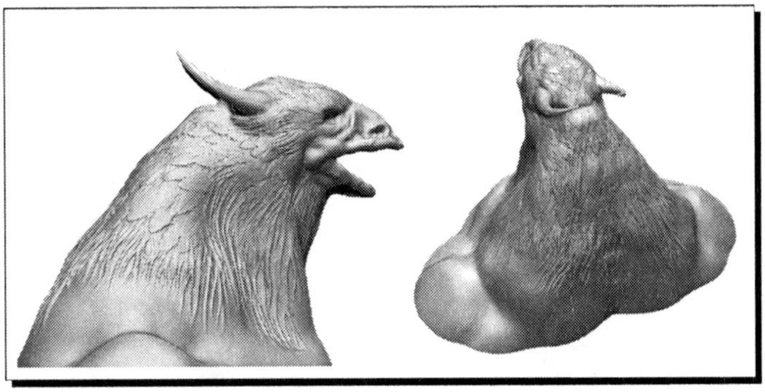

9. Near the axis of symmetry, you may want to deactivate symmetry again so that the alphas don't cross each other.
10. Switch back to the fur subtool and move it into place, so that it blends well with the fur on the neck.
11. Pick the **Slash 2** brush and add a few final cuts to the fur, so it looks even more unique.
12. Finally, use the **Slash 3** and **Slash 2** brush to make the border, where the fur merges with the chest, fuzzier. If you want to, you may also add some fur to the chest itself, so that it blends even better.

**13.** With all that done, our creature would look like this:

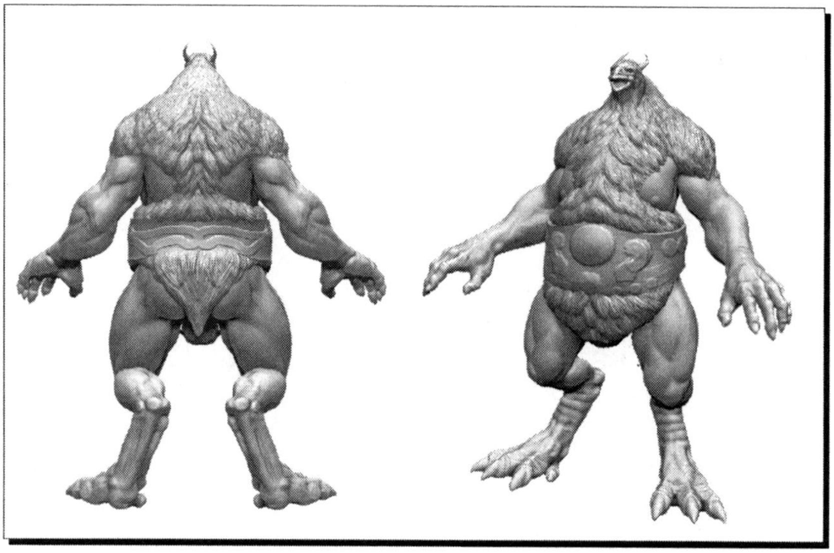

## What just happened?

We just added the fine detail to the neck, mixed two different alphas, and made everything blend. By now, we've learned that we can apply alphas with different techniques, like with **DragRect** or by drawing continuous strokes. As we saw, both are useful, depending on the task.

When sculpting accessories such as fur or cloth, it always comes down to the techniques that we used in this chapter. Lay in the global directions, then add secondary details, and finish it with some final touches. However, when sculpting cloth, one thing that can come in useful is the gravity modifier, located under **Brush | Depth | Gravity Strength**. This allows us to add gravity to our strokes, similar to cloth folds being drawn downwards by their own weight. Give it a try; it's fun.

Let's continue with finishing the last accessory we need for the creature—the belt.

## Time for action – sculpting the belt

Let's sculpt the final piece that's left—the belt. By now, you know all the techniques involved in sculpting an accessory like this. That's why this is kept short, so you don't get bored hearing the same things all over again:

**1.** Pick the **Smooth Crease** brush, which will maintain the creases of the belt when smoothing.

2. If you already roughed in some details, the inside of your belt may look like the one shown in the next screenshot. To correct that, pick a clay brush, activate **Brush | Auto Masking | BackfaceMask**, and fix it. **Backface masking** will prevent the brush from affecting the back side of thin objects. Don't forget to activate **backface masking** for the smooth brush too:

3. Add at least one subdivision level to the belt and establish the overall form by using the **PlanarFlatten** and **Clay** brushes. If no subdivisions are added, the sides that represent the thickness of the belt have no vertices to sculpt.

4. When working on the sides of the belt, the **PlanarFlatten** brush is not much use because it would only make a box out of our belt. Here we can use the **TrimDynamic** brush instead, to get smoother transitions, as shown in the next screenshot:

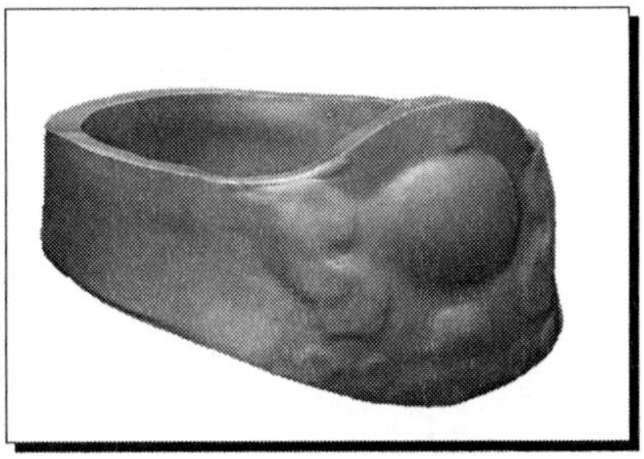

5. Pick the **ClayBuildup** brush and sculpt in all the finer details as you add more subdivisions. As this belt should be made of a harder material, such as metal, the ornaments are big in shape and rough on the surface texture. In the back, we can also add a belt buckle. When finished, the belt would look like this:

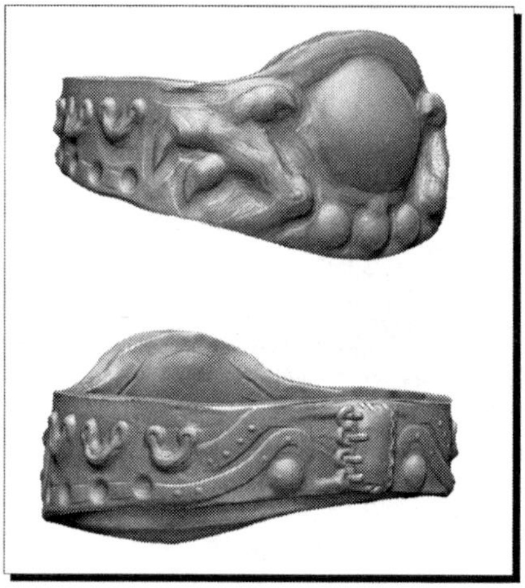

6. Finally add a new layer, deactivate symmetry, and add some scratches with the **Slash 1** or **Slash 3** brush. Our finished belt would now look like this:

## What just happened?

We've just completed the last piece that makes up our character—the belt. We didn't do anything new in this exercise, so let's just have a look at what could be the final result of all our work—a complete character with fur and accessories:

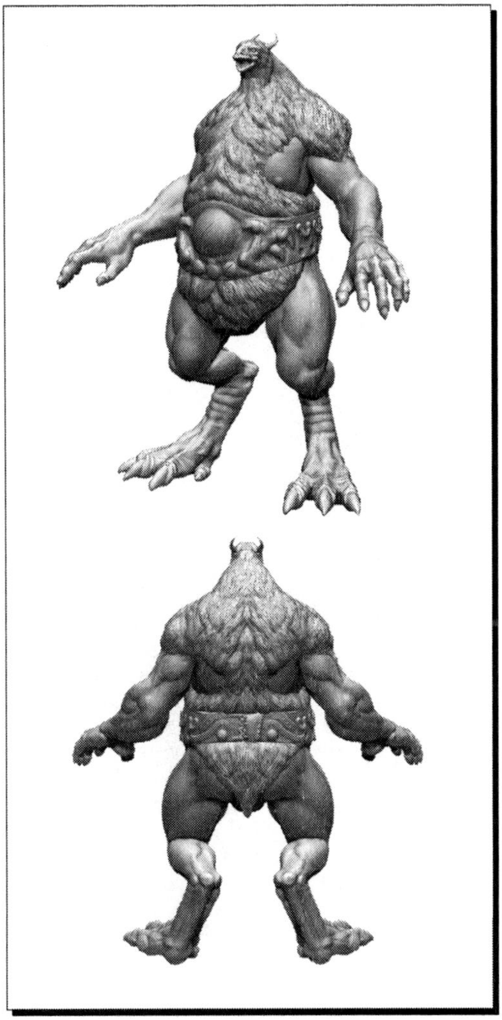

## Have a go hero – adding a weapon

Our creature is now finished. But it would look a lot more dangerous with a weapon in his hands, right? So what's the quickest way to do a hollow trunk?

Actually, it's quite easy with ZSketching. It works like creating hollow objects with paper mâché. You need to have something that fills out the volume to place your material on top. When done, you remove the volume and what's left is a hollow object:

1. Create a trunk with some ZSpheres. Don't add branches, only the volume of the trunk.
2. Switch to sketch mode with *Shift + A* and sketch thin strokes onto the volume, as shown in the next screenshot. The thickness of these strokes will be the thickness of the trunk's hull:

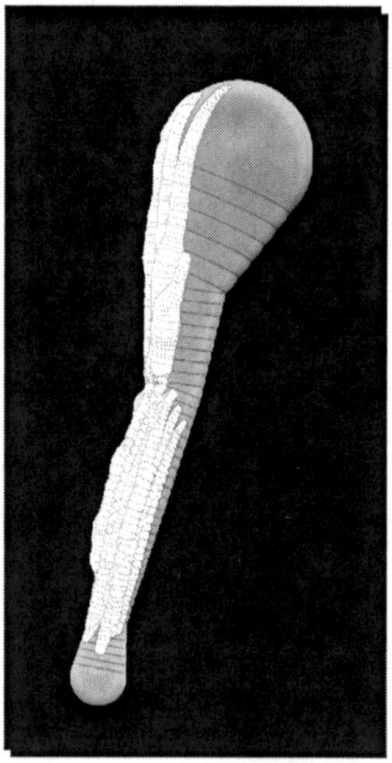

3. When we press *A* now, we get a hollow object. If the object gets filled, try a higher resolution like 256 in the **Tool | Unified Skin** palette. That's all.

# Summary

In this chapter, we've finished sculpting our first character and learned quite a lot about the creation of alphas and how to apply them. Specifically, we've covered:

- How to add final polish to complete a character
- How to create custom alphas, especially for overlapping structures such as feathers and fur
- How alpha grayscales refer to the depth of our brush strokes, allowing us to create rich surface structures
- How to sculpt and detail materials such as fur/hair of our characters at different stages
- How to add and sculpt various accessories like a belt or a weapon as subtools

Hooray! we've now completed our third model, "The Brute". Let's see how we can prepare him for games in the next chapter.

# 13

# Preparing the Creature for Games

*Now that we have finished the sculpting of our creature, let's make it ready for the game.*

*When working on the drone, we created the in-game mesh up front. But because our creature was created from ZSpheres, we will now follow a different workflow where we build the in-game mesh at the very end of the process. So in this chapter, we will learn about creating an in-game mesh from our high-poly reference and about transferring the details afterward. After that, we will delve deeper into unwrapping, which is the next step after the modeling is done.*

We'll cover the following topics in detail:

- Building a low-poly in-game mesh with retopologize
- Projecting the details onto our new topology
- Fixing potential errors that may pop up
- Extending ZBrush's capabilities with plug-ins
- Unwrapping our mesh with UV Master

[ You can download the finished creature by following the download link provided in the preface. ]

# Retopologizing for games

Okay, we've got our high-poly mesh ready. But in order to bring it into a game engine, we need to build a low-polygon mesh from it. Because we used ZSketch in the beginning, we now create the low-poly mesh at the end of the process. This step is called **retopologizing**, or in most cases just **retopo**, because it creates a mesh with a new topology and projects the details from the high-poly onto it. In this way, we end up with a mesh with a clean and optimized topology and all of the high resolution details that we sculpted in earlier.

This process can also be done in other major 3D applications such as Blender, 3ds Max, and so on. Honestly, I would prefer the retopologizing in Blender over that of ZBrush, as I find it a bit more robust. Nonetheless, the results are the same. So let's see how we can do this in ZBrush.

Before retopologizing, we should be clear about these points:

- **Polycount**: Think of how many polygons the character should have; this always seems tricky, but after some time you get used to it. Ask yourself how many polygons your platform and engine can handle for a character and how big will it be seen onscreen. Let's say our Brute will be used on a PC and console title, he's a few meters high and is visible fullscreen. So we're heading roughly for something around 5000 polygons. This is a very rough estimate and if we need less polygons for it, that's fine too. The fewer the better.
- **Animation**: How will the character be animated? If there's elaborate facial animation going on, the character should have enough polygons in his face, so the animator can move something. Ideally, the polygon-flow supports the animation.
- **Quads**: Always try to establish as many quads as possible. Sometimes, we just need to add triangles, but try to go for quads wherever you can.

With these three points in mind, let's start retopologizing.

## Time for action – creating an in-game mesh with retopologize

1. First, lower the subdivision levels of all the subtools to get increased performance.
2. Append a ZSphere as a subtool and make it the active one.
3. Name it something meaningful like Retopo.

4. Activate **Transparency** and place the ZSphere inside the mesh so that it is hidden, as shown in the next screenshot. Appending a ZSphere to the model gives us the advantage to easily hide subtools or adjust their subdivision level as we need it:

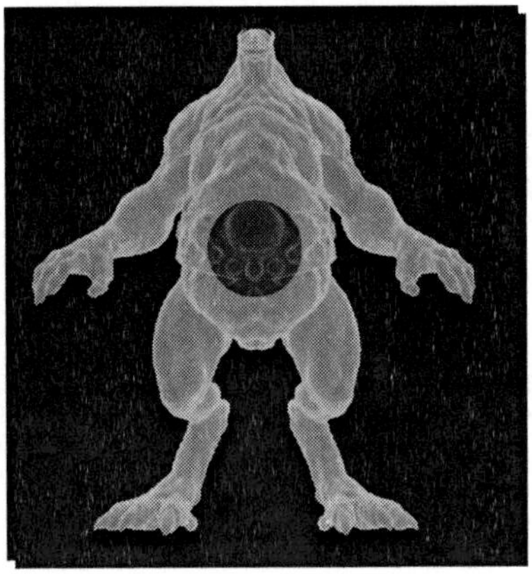

5. Deactivate Transparency and go to **Tool | Topology** and click on **Edit Topology.**
6. Activate **Symmetry**.
7. Pick the **SkinShade4** material and choose a darker color, so that we can see the orange lines of the retopologizing better. The **SkinShade4** material offers very low contrast, which is what we need here.

8. Begin drawing edges by *left-clicking* on the mesh. They will automatically snap to the underlying high-poly surface. Start out by laying in two circles around the eyes, as explained in the next image:

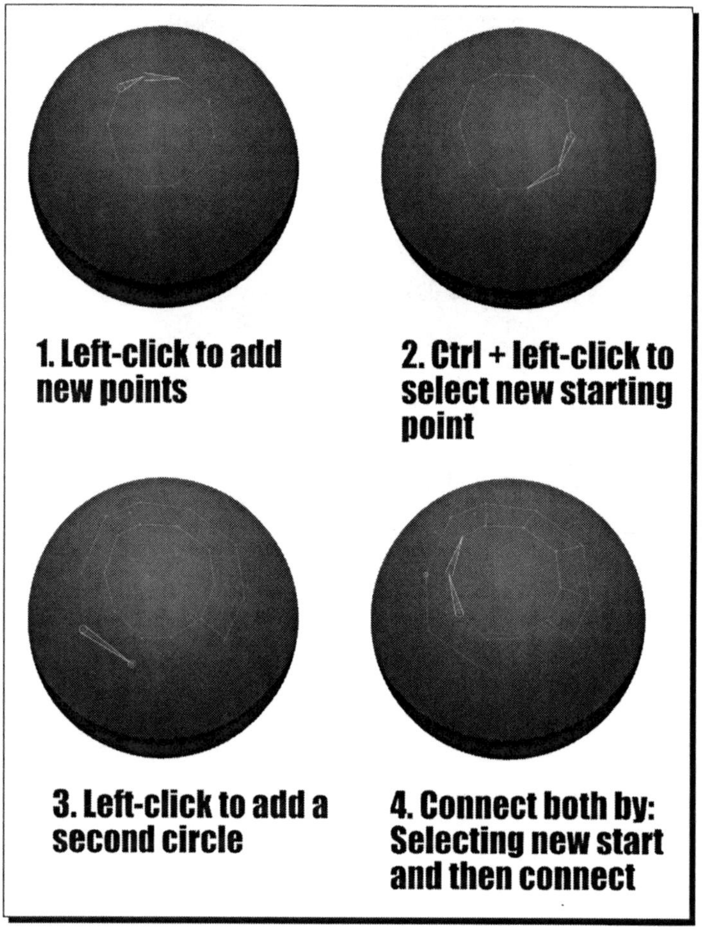

1. Left-click to add new points
2. Ctrl + left-click to select new starting point
3. Left-click to add a second circle
4. Connect both by: Selecting new start and then connect


**Retopologize commands**

When in *retopologize mode*, *left-clicking* adds a new vertex and an edge connecting it to the last selected vertex.

If we want to start out from a different vertex, we can select a new starting point by *Ctrl + left-clicking*.

Deleting points can be done by *Alt + left-clicking*. When you miss the point you wanted to delete, the last selected one gets deleted instead, so be careful about that.

9. Continue spreading new points over the head, as shown in the next screenshot. Try to place the points so that they capture the underlying form well:

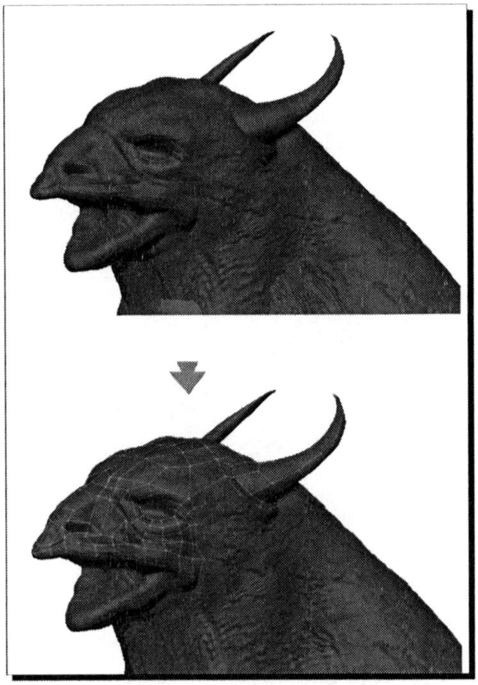

10. When adding the horns, start with a circle around their origin and then work your way up to the tip, as shown in the next screenshot. You may need eight vertices for the base, but only four at the tip, so you can simply join two lines on their way up:

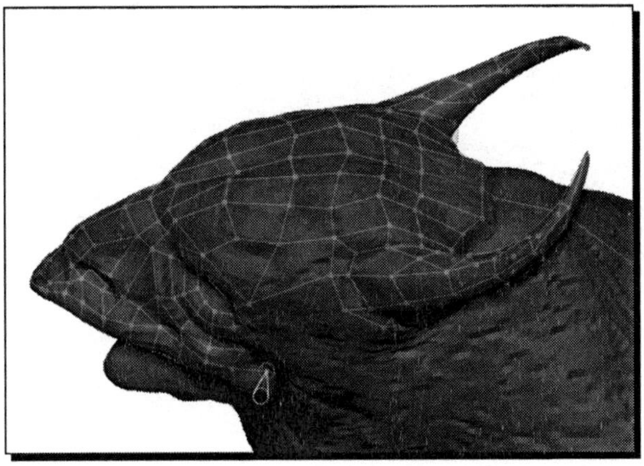

11. Spread the net around the neck, the shoulders, and the torso, as shown in the next screenshot. At the shoulder joint, we should add at least two edge loops, so the mesh can deform better in that area when animated. The same counts for other joints, such as the elbow-, wrist-, and knee-joint:

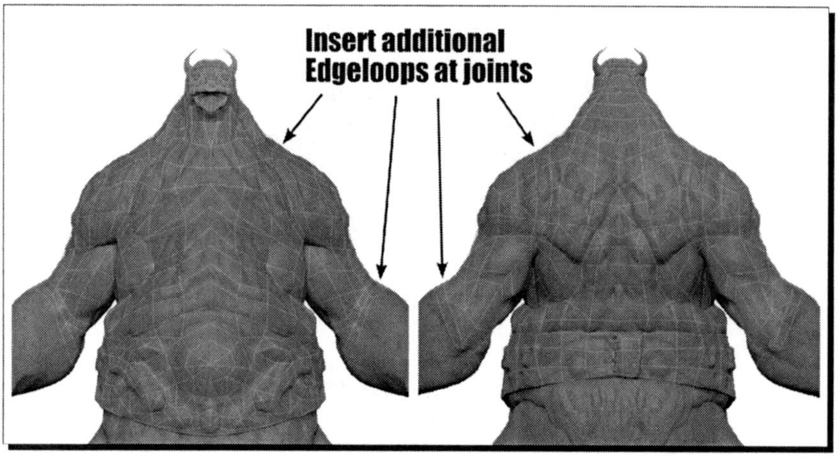


12. The hands may seem a bit tricky at first, but when you've got one finger down, it goes quite quickly for the others. The main question is how many sides the fingers should have. In this case, choose six sides, which is quite detailed for a finger and allows each to be fairly rounded. As shown in the next screenshot, at every joint, there's one edge loop for animation:

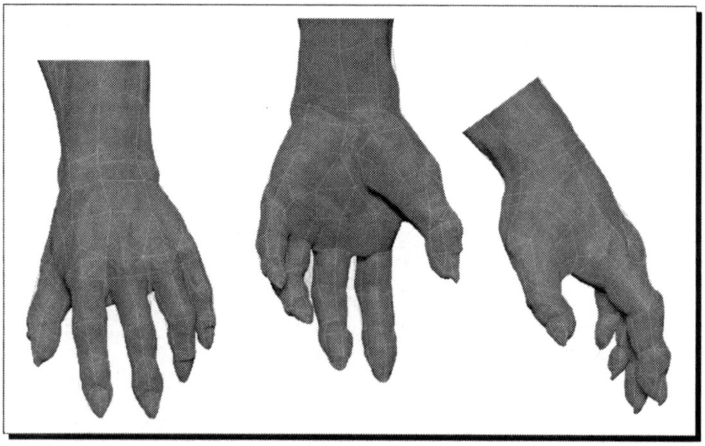

13. Don't forget to save regularly.

**14.** When working in retopologizing mode, for some reason, the navigation area gets ignored. To still be able to zoom when the model fills the whole screen, we can zoom out our canvas and use the gray border area to navigate. This is located under **Zoom | Zoom** or directly in the shelf.

**15.** Finish the lower part of the body and the belt, using the same techniques and procedures described earlier.

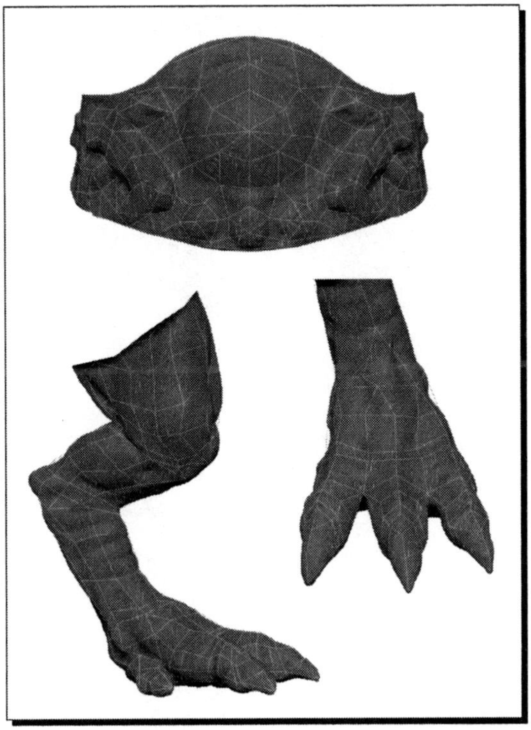

***16.*** That's it, we just retopologized our mesh, which would now look like this:

## What just happened?

We've just learned how to create a low-poly mesh from a high-poly one in ZBrush using retopologize.

# Polycount

The Brute ended up as a low-poly mesh that has 2618 polygons and 2256 points. Beware! ZBrush counts a quad as well as a triangle as one polygon. But game meshes always get triangulated when exported to a game engine. So what we need to know is the triangle count, which is 4495, roughly twice the vertex count. Luckily, this is below 5000 polygons, and exactly what we were heading for. You can find out the exact value by exporting it to an application like Blender and then triangulating it. Nonetheless, doubling the point-count should be sufficient for rough estimates.

At this point, we could already unwrap the low-poly and bake a normal map from the high-poly one in other applications. In most cases, this simply works by putting both meshes in the same location and lets the computer try to match areas from the high- and the low-poly to create a normal map. In ZBrush, this takes one more step, but gives us more control over the result. We'll subdivide the low-polygon mesh and project the high-polygon details onto it, so we have a mesh with clean topology and all the details in one. Because this is then one mesh only, ZBrush already knows which high-poly details belong to which low-poly-vertex, so we get a cleaner normal map from it. Let's try that out.

## Time for action – projecting the details onto the new mesh

Let's project all the details from the high-poly mesh onto our new low-poly one:

1. Select your retopologized mesh, making it the active subtool.
2. Projection can be done only with polygon meshes, not with ZSpheres, so we have to create an adaptive skin from it first. Go to **Tool | Adaptive Skin** and click on **Make Adaptive Skin** with the **Density** set to **1**. This will add a new tool of the mesh named **Skin_nameofthesubtool**.
3. Append this subtool to your high-polygon mesh, so your list of subtools looks similar to this:

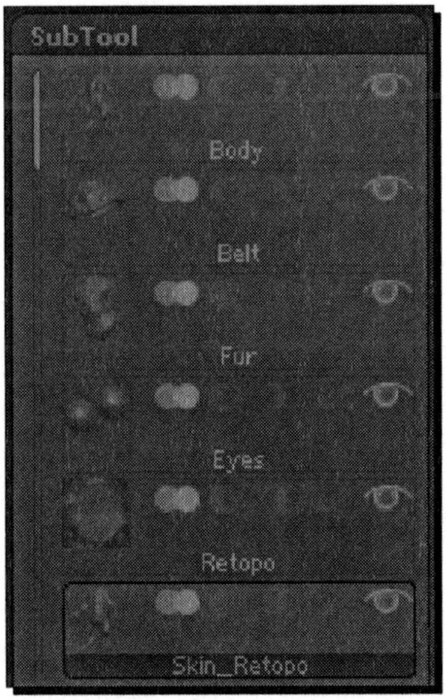

4. Turn off **Smt** and divide two times.

5. Turn **Smt** back on and divide a few times until you reach a reasonable polygon count of a few million polygons.

6. Store a morph target by navigating to **Tool | Morph Target** and click on **StoreMT**.

7. Hide the **Retopo-ZSphere-SubTool**, leaving only the high-poly meshes and the low-poly one visible.

8. Projecting details from one mesh to another works only on meshes with the eye icon turned on in the **SubTool** list. If it's too heavy for your machine to handle all high-polygon meshes at once, there's a little trick: We can enter **Solo mode**, hiding all the other subtools, regardless of whether their visibility is turned on or off in the **SubTool** list. In this way, the high-poly meshes are hidden, but the projection will still work. We can enter Solo mode by navigating to **Transform** and clicking on **Solo**, which can also be found in the shelf.

9. It's always a good idea to save before starting an intensive calculation, like a projection.

10. With a morph target stored and the tool saved, go to **Tool | SubTool** and click on the **ProjectAll** button with the default settings. Depending on your hardware, this may take a few minutes, so this is the perfect moment to get yourself another cup of coffee!

11. The projection did a quite decent job with only some small areas that we have to fix by hand now:

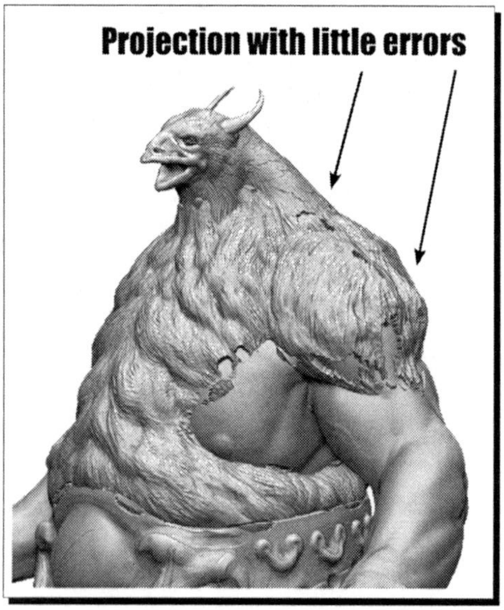

12. Now, simply pick the **Morph brush** and erase the errors.

13. Exit Solo mode, otherwise the **ZProject** brush won't work.

14. Turn off symmetry or the **ZProject** brush will project one side onto another, which can really mess things up.

15. Then pick the **ZProject** brush, turn on **Zadd**, set the **Intensity,** and reproject the missing details by hand. Pressing *Alt* will invert the direction of the projection. You get the best results if you project an area and then go over it again with *Alt* pressed. In this way, everything below gets pulled and everything above gets pushed into place. If this goes wrong, we can always pick the morph brush and start all over again.

## What just happened?

That's it! We just projected all the details onto our new topology.

Another way of doing this is to project the details with **ProjectAll**, one subdivision level at a time. Although, this is a little bit more accurate, it is also a bit more time-consuming. The choice is up to you.

When we divided our low-poly mesh, we had to make sure that **Smt** is turned off, so the form stays as it is. Because the low-poly was created exactly on the surface of the high-poly one, smoothing it would result in a form that matches the high-poly less.

If you like, you could also do the whole projection by hand by using the ZProject brush. For a plane this could be easier, but the more complex the mesh gets, the faster it is to use the projection function.

The ZProject brush will always project from the viewing angle. The more the mesh points away from the camera, the worse the brush will work because it can't look around edges. So, try to project details on faces that roughly point into the camera.

You will also note that the new projection can have fewer polygons, but still have the same amount of detail in it. This comes from the more optimized polygon placement, which we did when retopologizing. In my case, the retopologized version has only a quarter of the polygons of the high-poly mesh with the same amount of detail.

# Extending ZBrush with plug-ins: UV-Master

Okay, the last thing that holds us from baking a normal map, are the missing UV-coordinates. We could, of course, do that in an external application, but we can also use the new plug-in: **UV-Master**. Let's see how this can be done.

> We can browse and download plug-ins for ZBrush on `www.pixologic.com`. Once downloaded, plug-ins are installed by putting the downloaded files into the right folder of ZBrush. If successfully installed, the new plug-in will then be listed under **Zplugin** after the next restart of ZBrush.

## Time for action – unwrapping the creature with UV Master

UV Master produces decent UV-layouts for organic meshes in a very short time. It is a good starting point and you can still tweak the result in another application, if you like to.

For a quick UV-layout, follow these steps:

1. Go to `http://www.pixologic.com/ZBrush/downloadcenter/Zplugins/` and download UV Master for ZBrush.
2. Extract it and put its contents, the `UVMaster_4.0.zsc` and the `UVMasterData_4.0-folder`, into your installation path: `\ZBrush 4.0\ZStartup\ZPlugs` folder.
3. Restart ZBrush.
4. Open your new mesh with optimized topology and all the transferred details.
5. Switch to the lowest level of subdivision.
6. Open the Zplugin palette in a tray and expand the UV Master subpalette.
7. Go to **Zplugin | UV Master** and click on the **Work On Clone** button.
8. Go to **Zplugin | UV Master** and click on the **Unwrap** button, which will automatically unwrap your model.

9. Navigate to **Zplugin | UV Master** and click on the **CheckSeams** button to see where ZBrush cuts the model, as shown in the next screenshot:

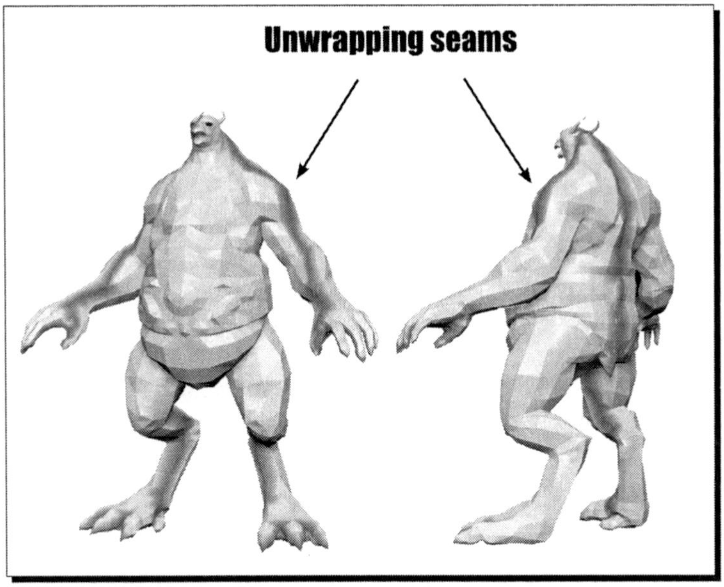


10. Alternatively, you can go to **Zplugin | UV Master** and click on the **Flatten** button to see the UV-coordinates as in other 3D programs. Pressing **Unflatten** will get you the model back. The following screenshot shows the flattened model with some annotations to make it more clear:

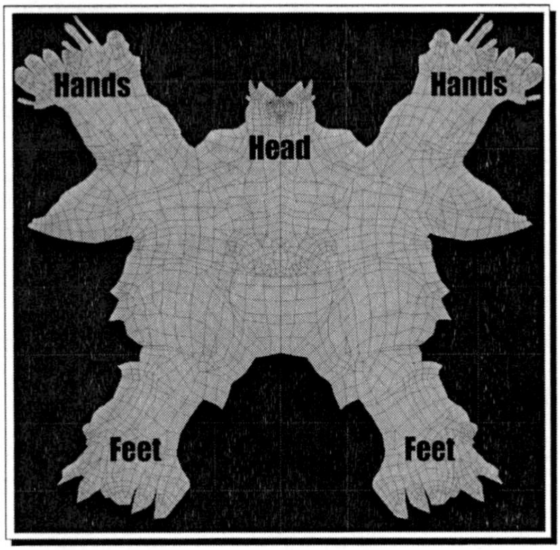

11. When you're done with unwrapping, navigate to **Zplugin | UV Master** and click on the **Copy Uvs** button.

12. Switch from your clone to the original mesh and go to **Zplugin | UV Master** and click on the **Paste Uvs** button, which will transfer the created UV-coordinates from the clone to the original mesh.

13. Now that we have UV-coordinates, we can bake a normal map like we did with the drone.

### *What just happened?*

We just created UV-coordinates for our mesh with only a few clicks. Let's talk a bit about what we did.

First, we chose to work on a clone, which is better, because it has no polypaint, subdivision levels, and other attributes that could bother us when creating a UV map.

## Fine control with control painting

Pressing **Unwrap** created a UV map for us in one click. This could be called a *quick and dirty* method, but it's fast. If we want more control, we can enable **Zplugin | UV Master | Enable Control Painting**. With control painting, we can attract **seams** or protect areas– like the face– from being cut. Just click on the **Attract** button and paint faces where you would like the seams to appear. You must have a brush selected that can actually apply paint, like the **Standard** brush. A good area for attracting seams could be in-between the legs, where the seam is hidden. Clicking **Protect** allows us to protect areas from being cut, for example, the face. Although this allows for better control, it's still a tradeoff. Painting attractive and protected areas will not guarantee that the algorithm will follow, but it's still much faster than cutting edges exactly by hand.

## The middle way—attract by ambient occlusion

A nice semi-automated way of creating UV Coordinates is the **Zplugin | UV Master | AttractByAmbientOcclusion** button, which will add attract painting based on ambient occlusion. This already gives some decent results for our character, which we can then fine-tune with control painting.

## Seams, what seams?

So why are we having seams anyway? Imagine peeling an orange—what would you do if you had to lay out the peel flat on a table?

As the orange represents a closed volume, you would have to cut it in order to make it flat. Now the question arises, how can you flatten an orange with as few cuts as possible, which is the first problem.

This also involves the stretching problem because no part of the orange's peel is really flat. So you have to press it down and squeeze it, the same goes for UV-layouts.

The third problem is painting. Imagine you had to paint a checker pattern on the laid out peel of the orange. If you form a sphere from it again, along the cuts, the pattern probably won't match. That's why fewer seams make painting in a 2D application easier.

So let's apply our orange-knowledge to 3D:

In general, it's better to have fewer seams. But fewer seams means more waste of space. A UV Layout that uses space most efficiently would lay out every single polygon as a separate island, but no one would be able to recognize or even paint anything inside of this map. So we have to find a middle way. Try to place seams where they can't be seen, for example, the armpits, between the fingers, the inner sides of the legs, and so on. If the character's wearing armor, this border would also do great as a seam.

The UV-layout that you need depends on the way you or your company work. If you sculpt and texture everything in ZBrush, you only need an efficient UV-Map to bake to. If you or others texture in a 2D-application such as GIMP or Photoshop, the UV-layout should be clearly readable and organized, which needs more adjustment in UV-mapping. Imagine you try to paint some jeans on a character's leg in Photoshop, and the leg is scattered in ten different islands across the texture, it will take forever and probably not look good anyway.

The best way to get a decent grasp on how UV-layouts can be done is to look at some reference. Just Google something like "uv-layout" and analyze them as to how easy they are to read and how efficiently they cover the texture space. If you do this, you will soon know how things work because unwrapping is no form of art. Once you get it, you just do it, like putting on your trousers every morning.

That's it; you just finished your third model and even unwrapped it. You can now go ahead and bake a normal map to view it in a game engine.

## Have a go hero – bake the polypainting into a texture

Now that you know how to retopologize and unwrap, you could even create a low-poly version of the tree, unwrap it, and bake the polypainting into a texture. To do this, you have to create a new texture in **Tool | Texture Map** and then bake the polypaint by clicking **Tool | Texture Map | from Polypaint**. In **Tool | UV Map**, you can set the texture's size.

## Pop quiz – unwrapping and retopologizing

1. If we have to lay out an orange's peel flat on a table, what would be the most elegant solution?
   a. Squeeze it with brute force until it's flat
   b. Place some cuts and flatten it
   c. Rip the peel into small pieces
2. What are the three problems when trying to unwrap a mesh?
   a. Model orientation and polygon count
   b. Texture resolution and Texture size
   c. Seam placement, stretching, and readability
3. What would be the best place for a texture seam on the head?
   a. Vertical along the nose and across the mouth
   b. Vertical along the back of the head
   c. Horizontal across the eyes
4. Why did we add edge loops at the joints of our character when retopologizing?
   a. So we can unwrap it better
   b. So it deforms better when animated
   c. To create more quads

# Summary

In this chapter, we learned a lot about creating a low-poly from a high poly and how to project the details back to our new in-game mesh. Most importantly, we learned how to make a high-polygon model first and do the low-poly afterwards, which gives us another workflow at hand we can choose from. Specifically, we learned:

- We get more creative freedom during the modeling process if we do the technical work like retopologizing and unwrapping at the end. Go wild first and clean up afterwards.
- To make models that work well in animation, we should add edge loops in important areas when retopologizing.
- To transfer details from one mesh to another, we can use projection.
- To get full control, we can even project details by hand using the ZProject brush.

- To apply a texture to a model, it needs UV-coordinates, which can easily be created with UV Master.
- When creating UV-layouts, we have to deal with three problems:
    - The amount and placement of cuts
    - Stretching
    - Readability of the layout

# 14
# Modeling the Harvester Ship

*Wow, we've already finished three models with ZBrush, covering a vast amount of sculpting techniques.*

*In this chapter, we'll start with our last model—The Harvester. For this task, we'll explore a new way of starting a mechanical model directly inside ZBrush. This is very similar to the workflow we used to build the creature—doing the sculpture first and then preparing it for games. At the end of the book, you will know many paths to complete a model, so you can choose the best according to your tasks.*

We'll talk specifically about:

- Quickly prototyping the major mechanical shapes with **ShadowBox**
- Creating crisp mechanical surfaces with the clipping brushes
- Creating perfect circles with the Circle brushes
- Assembling a complex model

Let's get on with it.

# The Harvester

The **Harvester** is the mother ship of the Pioneer Drone that we built previously. It is meant to control the drones and use them to harvest resources.

When creating the drone, we used a previously built base mesh we detailed afterwards. With The Harvester, we'll now explore a new technique, introduced with ZBrush 4.0—**ShadowBox**. This allows us to create a model by painting a cross section of all three sides. The next screenshot illustrates this principle. It may look confusing at the beginning, but once you get your head around it, blocking out mechanical models has never been easier. And it's tons of fun, really:

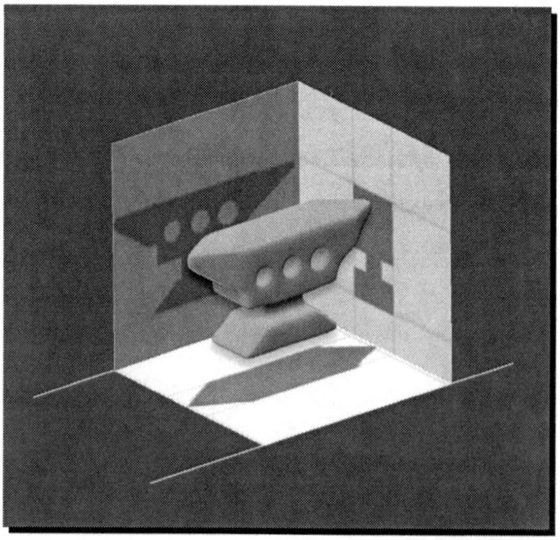

As you can see, the model is created by painting masks on all three sides of shadow box. Drawing masks goes quite fast, allowing us to do quick iterations in design. Let's see this technique in action.

## Time for action – blocking out the body of the ship

1. Pick the **Sphere3D** tool, draw it on the canvas, and enter Edit mode.
2. Go to **Tool** and click on the **Make PolyMesh3D** button.
3. Open the **SubTool** subpalette and click on **ShadowBox**, which is somewhat hidden below the big **ReMesh All** button, as shown in the next screenshot:

4. ZBrush will try to rebuild the sphere with three shadow box masks, as the following screenshot shows. As we don't want to keep that form, let's *clear the mask* by *Ctrl + dragging on the canvas*. Clearing the masking on the shadow box will also clear any mesh inside. Without masks, there is no cross section for ZBrush to build:

5. Let's start with the body of the ship. Such a large part requires a higher resolution. The three sliders shown in the next screenshot work for the **ReMesh All** as well as for the **ShadowBox**. Increase the **Res** to **256**. Changes to these sliders take effect, only if we exit and re-enter **ShadowBox** by pressing its button twice:

6. Snap to an orthogonal view with *Shift* and disable perspective.

7. Now that we've got our resolution set up, let's start the body. Select the **MaskRect** brush; as this is a masking brush, we have to hold *Ctrl* to activate it. Draw two rectangular masks on one side of the **ShadowBox**, as shown in the next image. Be careful to not draw over the edges of the **ShadowBox**.

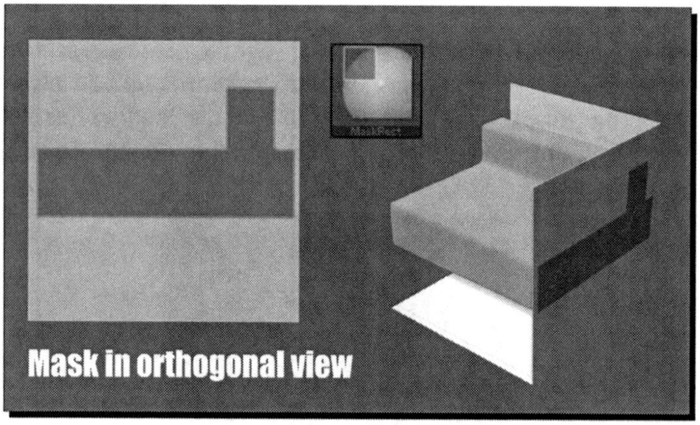


8. Move over to the side of **ShadowBox** and activate symmetry. Activate the respective axis—two red dots appear mirrored horizontally, as shown in the next screenshot:

9. Now we can draw the back of our ship symmetrically. Draw another rectangle, so we end up with an oblong cuboid, as shown in the next screenshot. The drawn rectangle will be mirrored the moment you let go to apply the mask:

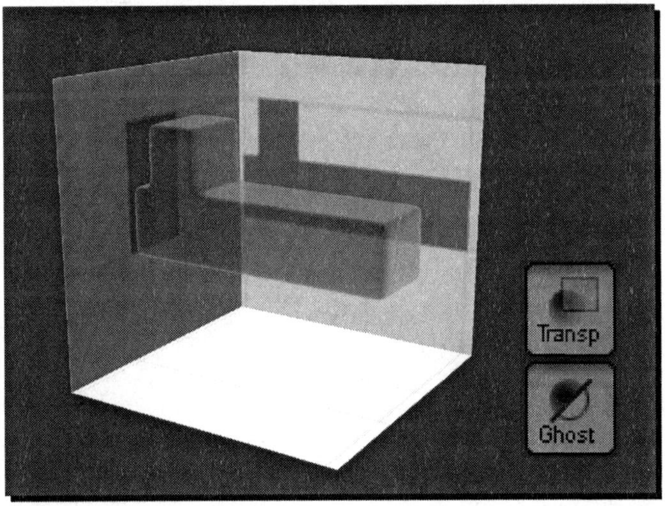


10. We can activate transparency to see through the mesh in **ShadowBox**, as the previous screenshot shows.

11. Select the **MaskPen** brush.

12. Open the **Stroke** palette.

13. Hold down *Ctrl* to switch to the **MaskPen** brush and activate **Lazymouse**.

14. Paint the masks on all three sides, so the body looks similar to the one shown in the following image. Press *Alt* to erase previous masking. Don't worry if the edges are not as sharp as they should be. We're only blocking out shapes now and we will refine them in the next step:

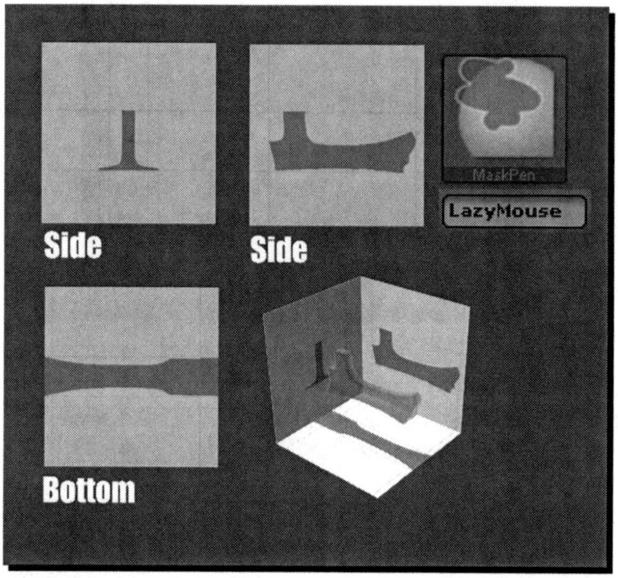


15. When you're satisfied with the result, exit **ShadowBox**. Now we'll work on the mesh outside of **ShadowBox**.

16. Make sure that **Perspective** is still disabled and you view the model exactly from the side by snapping the view with *Shift*.

17. Pick the **ClipCurve** brush. As a clipping brush, ZBrush notifies us that it can be activated with *Ctrl + Shift + Click*.

18. Let's use the **ClipCurve** brush to make our edges crisp. Press *Ctrl + Shift* and click to start a curve. Note that the line has a darker shade on one side, which indicates the side that will be clipped away. By pressing *Alt*, new points can be inserted in that curve. Pressing *Alt* twice adds a sharp corner. The next image illustrates these functions of the **ClipCurve** brush:

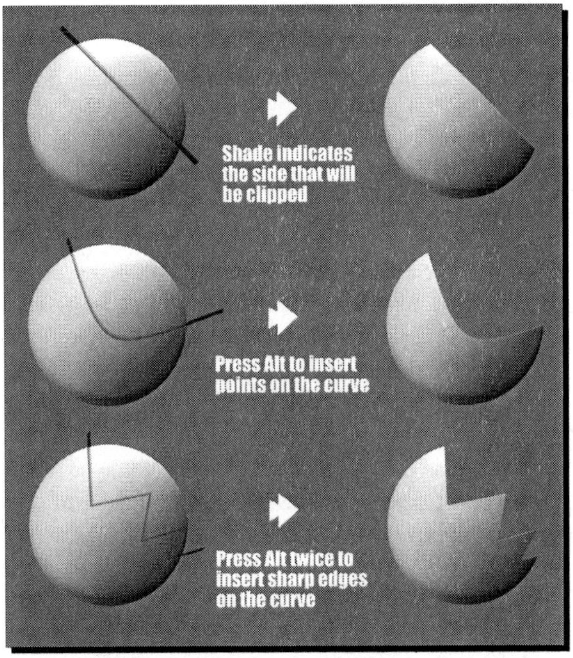


19. With the **ClipCurve** brush, clean up the corners of the model, as shown in the next image. As you can see, it's incredibly fast to block out and refine meshes with **ShadowBox** and the clipping brushes. We just have to get used to it:

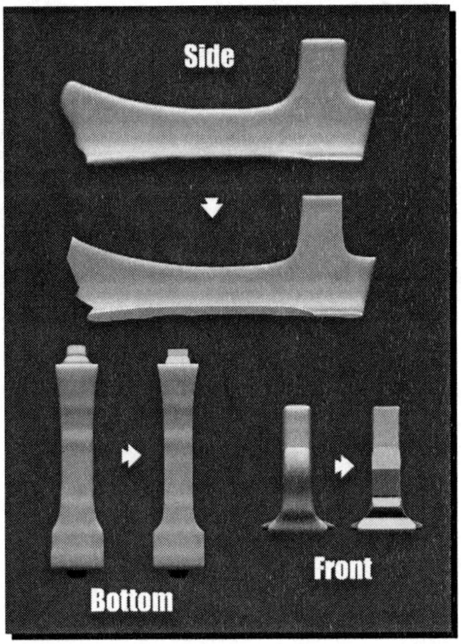

> When drawing a curve, before letting go, we can press *Space bar* to reposition it.
> When the shade is on the wrong side, we invert the clipping by holding *Alt* on release.

20. If we enter **ShadowBox** again on this subtool, we may lose some of the work we did outside of it, so we try to avoid that.

21. Let's create the wings in **ShadowBox**. Append another mesh as a subtool and enter **ShadowBox**. It doesn't matter which mesh we pick, as we delete it anyway.

22. Clear the existing masks.

23. Choose the **MaskRect** brush and draw a rectangle from the sides and the bottom to get a plane, as shown in the next screenshot.

24. Activate symmetry and **Lazymouse** (like we did before) and add a nice curve to the wings from the bottom. The result would look like this:

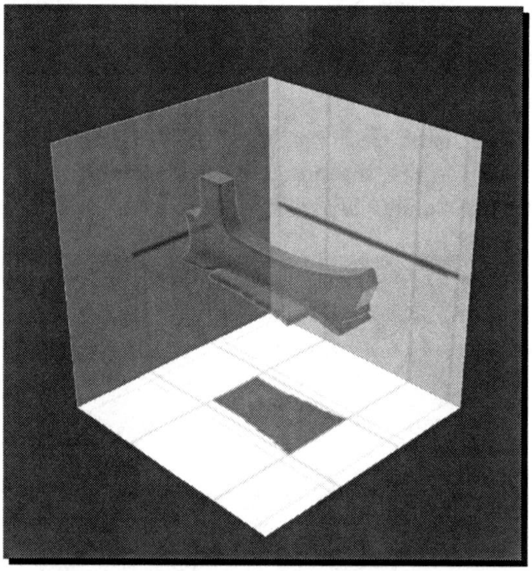

25. Exit **ShadowBox** and use the **ClipCurve** brush to clean up the edges—like we did for the body.

## What just happened?

We just blocked in the main form for the body of the ship. Let's have a closer look at some of the things we did.

# ShadowBox

The main idea behind **ShadowBox** is the ability to quickly create shapes. We'll use **ShadowBox** to block out and test our design in 3D, so that we can check if the concept transfers well into 3D. When we have all the proportions and main parts in place, we can step ahead and add detail in the next chapter.

## Entering and exiting ShadowBox

When entering **ShadowBox**, we saw that ZBrush tries to rebuild the selected mesh inside of **ShadowBox**. This is no problem if we create a mesh in **ShadowBox** and exit and re-enter, for example, to adjust the resolution. But if we exit, modify the mesh with sculpting tools, and re-enter again, we may lose parts of this work. The reason is that there are meshes that can't be built with **ShadowBox**, but sculpted, like concave objects. For example, a cave could not be rebuilt in **ShadowBox** by the intersection of three masks. So if we block out a hill in **ShadowBox**, sculpt in a cave, and re-enter ShadowBox, we would probably end up with a hill again.

So once we have decided to leave **ShadowBox** and work further, we probably don't want to re-enter again on this subtool.

Another thing worth mentioning is that **ShadowBox** always recreates meshes with even polygon distribution, somewhat similar to remesh. We can take advantage of that, for instance, when remeshing a stretched cube. After remeshing, it has an equal polygon distribution on all three sides, as the next image shows:

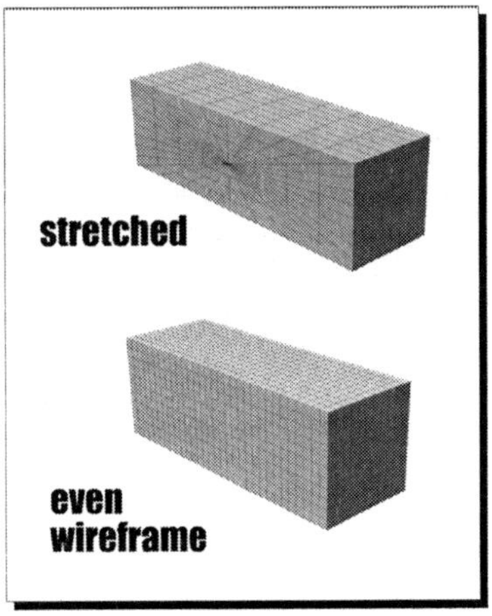

This works only on very simple meshes, which can be recreated easily within **ShadowBox**. For more complex ones, you should use **Remesh**.

# Working with ShadowBox

**ShadowBox** creates a mesh out of the cross section of three masks. Like with any other mask in ZBrush, they can be mirrored, blurred, sharpened, and created, or combined with alphas. Imagine you would like to create a coat of arms. Just create it as a two-dimensional alpha, set the resolution high enough, and apply it to one side of the **ShadowBox**. Done. What about a mesh with rounded corners? Simply blur the mask. It's a really quick way of creating 3D shapes.

When working with **ShadowBox**, we should avoid drawing masks over the edges of a side. A mask drawn over the edges could also affect the other sides, which may not be what we want. If we need to draw out a mask across the edges of a side, we can use a little trick and hide the others. If we turn on Polyframe, we can see that each side of **ShadowBox** is a separate polygroup. We can hide and isolate them individually like we did with other meshes. This is especially useful when masking with the **MaskCurve** brush, which masks or erases everything on one side of the curve. Due to this functionality, it will always affect the other sides, if they aren't hidden.

# Masking and clipping brushes

If we take a closer look at the masking and clipping brushes, we can see that they are not that different. In fact, they are built on the same stroke type. So there's a **MaskCurve** and a **ClipCurve** brush as well as a **MaskRect** and a **ClipRect** brush. If we want to adjust the stroke type for a masking brush, we have to hold *Ctrl* down as we set it up. The different masking and clipping brushes are an easy way to switch between the different stroke types quickly.

It's also recommended that you assign some hotkeys to the masking and clipping brushes because we will use them quite heavily throughout the next chapters. Assign a hotkey by pressing *Ctrl + Alt and clicking* on the desired brush or button.

## Pop quiz – shadowBox and clipping brushes

1. How can we access the settings for the clipping brushes?
    a. By holding down *Ctrl + Shift* for the clipping brushes
    b. By holding down *Alt + Shift* for the clipping brushes
    c. By holding down *Space bar* for masking and *Shift + Spacebar* for the clipping brushes

2. Why is the ShadowBox divided up into polygroups for each side?
    a. Because they can easily be hidden with polygroups
    b. Because colors make them easier to distinguish
    c. Because we can see the resolution of ShadowBox better with polygroups
3. What do we have to do to update ShadowBox when we change its resolution?
    a. Restart ZBrush
    b. Exit and re-enter Edit mode
    c. Exit and re-enter ShadowBox
4. What happens if we enter ShadowBox with a sculpted mesh?
    a. The mesh is replaced by a simple box
    b. The mesh is recreated inside ShadowBox
    c. The mesh is simply deleted

## Time for action – starting the engines

Okay, we've got the body of the ship ready. Let's move on to the second biggest part—the engines:

1. Pick the **Sweep3D** tool.
2. Open the **Tool | Initialize** subpalette.

3. In the **Initialize** settings, we can find a curve named **S Profile**, which stands for sweep profile. As its name says, this curve defines the profile of the mesh. We can alter the curve, as shown in the next image:

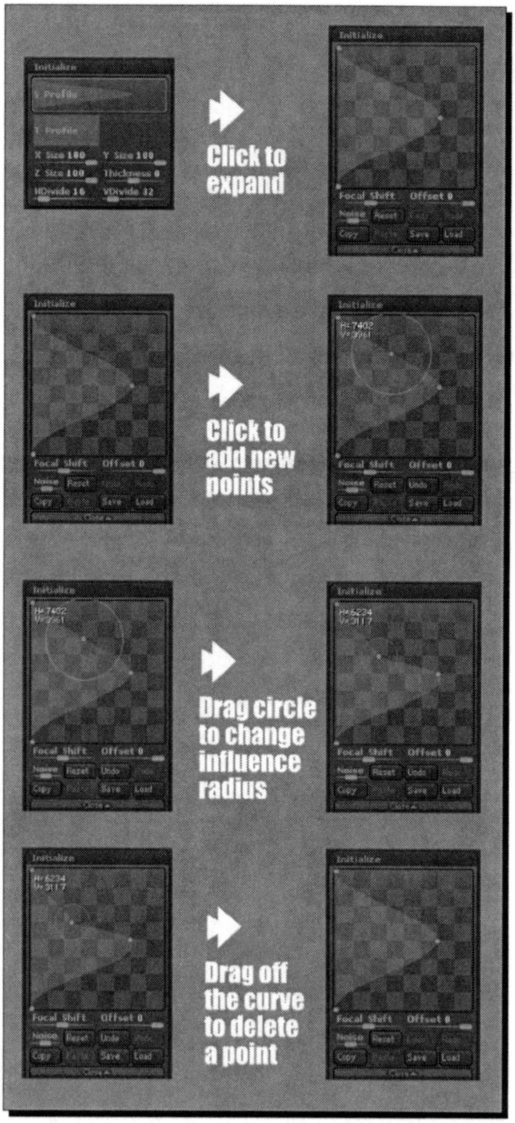


4. Create a curve with settings, as shown in the next screenshot:

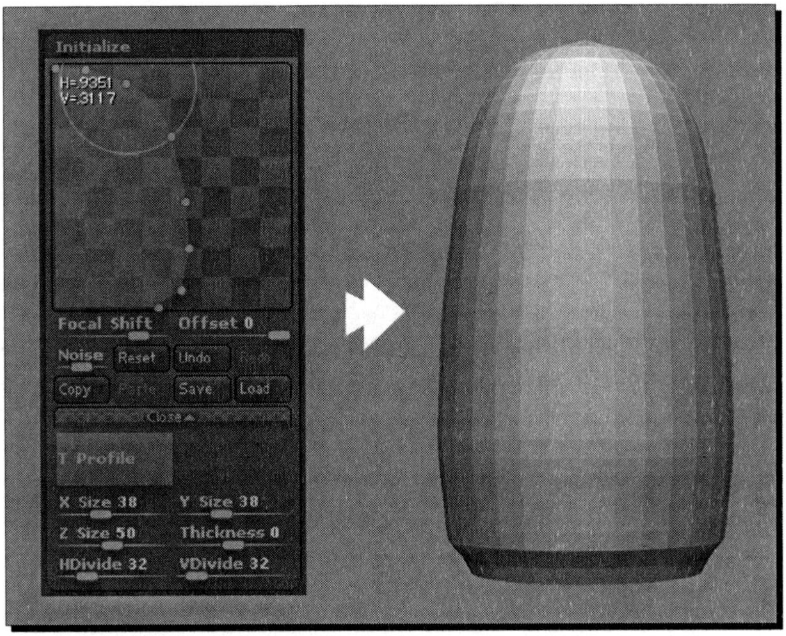


5. You may want to save the **Sweep3D** tool separately, in case we need it again. Once appended, it loses its initial settings.
6. When done, append the engine to the ship and position it accordingly. Be careful to only position the engine, not to rotate it.
7. We'll have a lot of subtools, so it's a good idea to name them.
8. Our ship would now look like this:

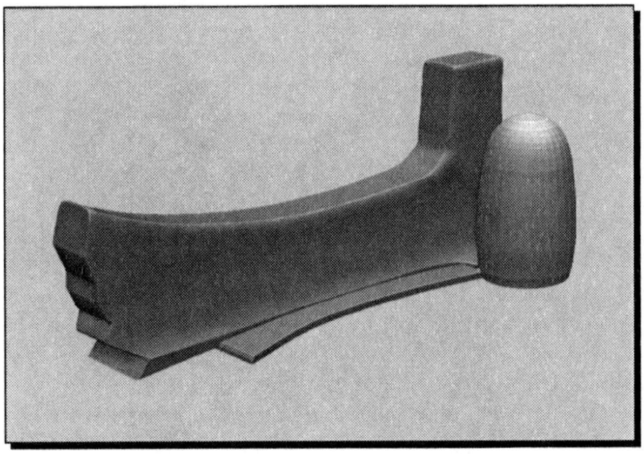

## What just happened?

We just created the rough shapes of the engines with the **Sweep3D** tool.

It's important to append the tool after we're finished with its initial settings. If we append the **Sweep3D** engines to our ship, they will automatically be converted to a polymesh3D and lose their initial settings. So we have to initialize them up front and append them at the end.

When creating objects, we didn't mirror and rotate them, but why? Because both would limit us in terms of symmetry. The engine, for example, can now be edited with radial symmetry. When we mirror them over, we can use symmetry only along one axis. The same counts for the turrets, which are spherical. So we'll create the objects first and mirror them at the end where needed. If we need to rotate, we can apply it as a layer, so we can always rotate it back to its original state.

## Time for action – blocking out the smaller parts

Let's block out some smaller props such as the wings and turrets, so we can finalize the overall placement:

1. Append a sphere. Duplicate and place it six times to determine the placements of the turrets.
2. If needed, use the **Transpose** tool to lengthen the body, as shown in the next image. Just mask off the rear part. You may also need to use the **ClipCurve** brush to correct the stretched shape a bit:

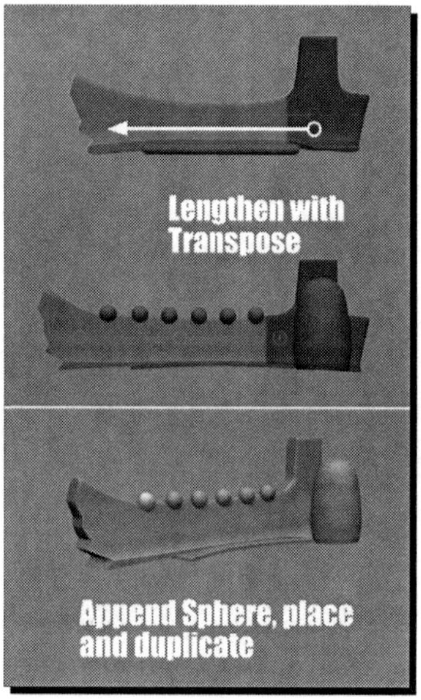

3. For the rear air inlets next to the engines, append a cube to the model. Scale and place it, as shown in the next image. Then clip it into shape from the front view:

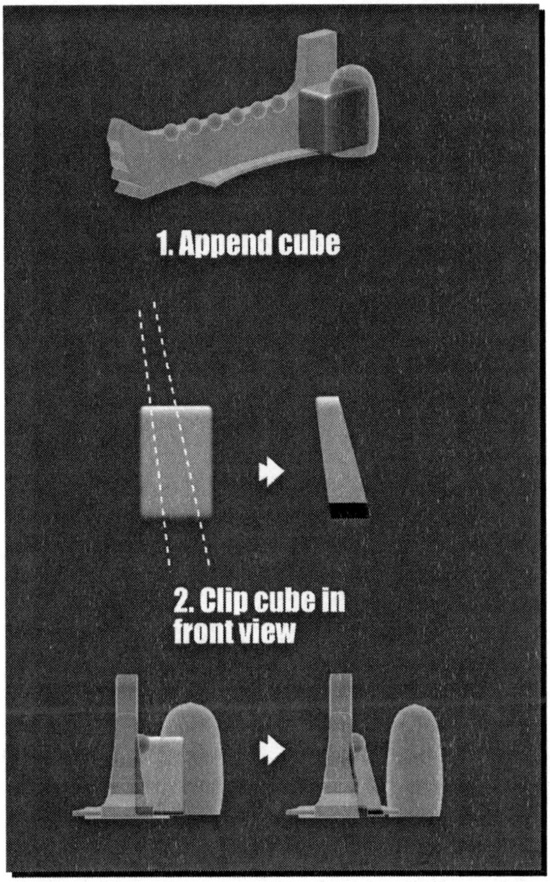

4. Pick the **MaskCurve brush** and mask the inlet, as shown in the following image. Then **offset** it by **2** on the respective axis, so that the unmasked part is pushed inwards:

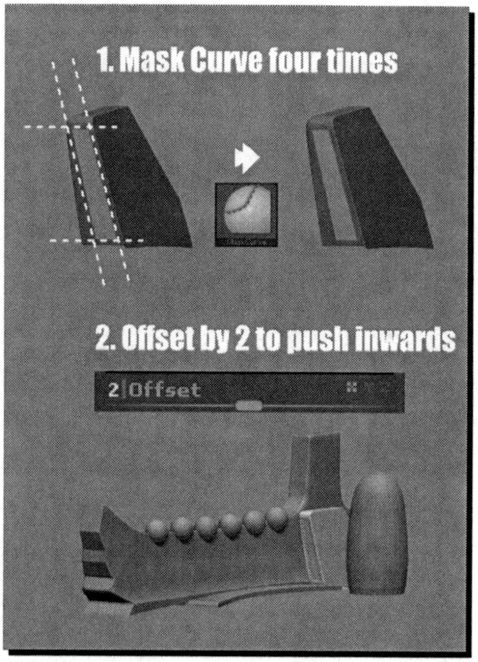


5. Let's continue with the front. Append another sphere and clip it with the **ClipCircleCenter brush**, to get a cylinder with rounded caps, as shown in the next screenshot. Flatten and place it at the front of the ship:

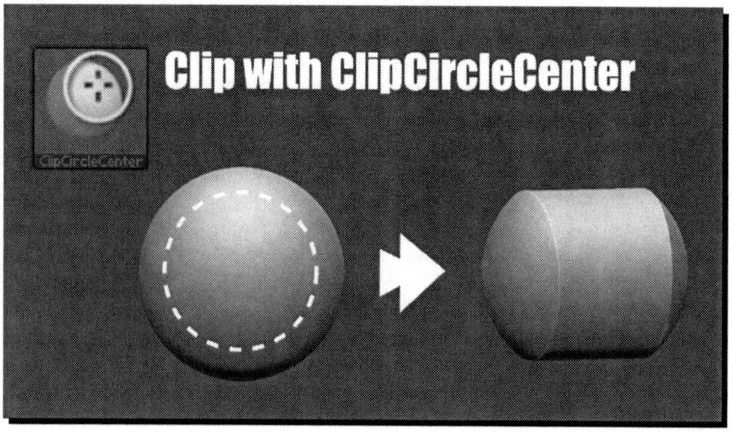

6. Continue to block in the forms of the little front engines and wings and finalize the proportions and the placement of the main objects on one side. If you would like to mirror parts, there's a **mirror** function in the deformation subpalette. The model would now look like this:

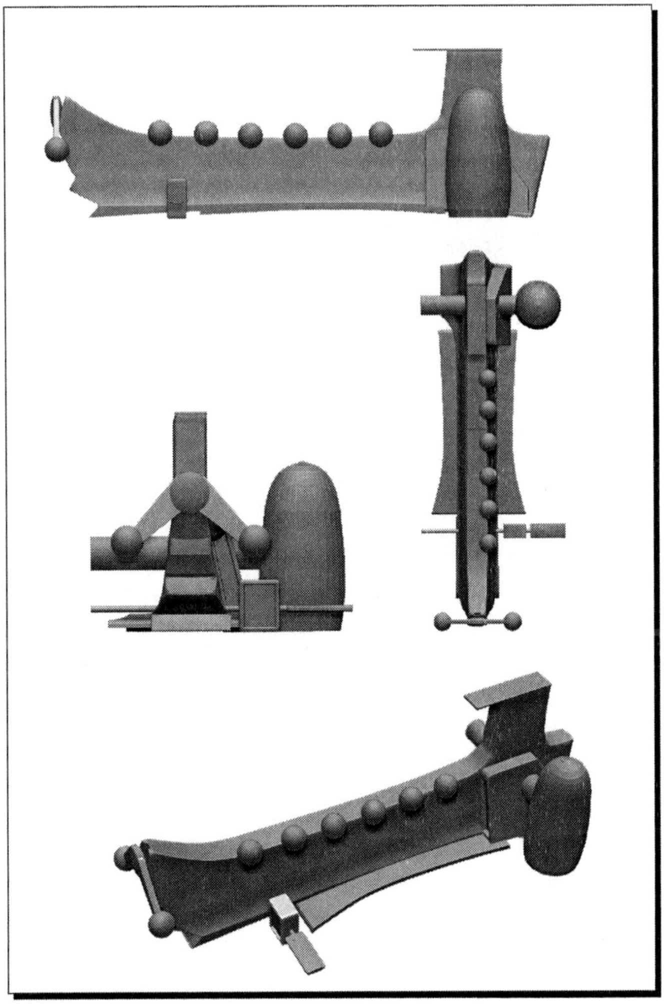

## What just happened?

We've just finished blocking in our harvester ship. It doesn't look that impressive at the moment, but it's rather important to get the proportions and positions right, so we can concentrate on the details in the next step. Let's look at some of the things we did more in-depth.

## The curve stroke type

As we discussed earlier, the behavior of the clipping brushes can also be used with masking brushes, as the curve stroke type is available for both.

When we don't add points to the curve, the curve stroke gives us a straight line, which is useful for masking things like the air inlets. The curve stroke type always tries to mask or clip away one side of the curve—this means that we can't create closed or intersecting shapes in one stroke. So to mask the air inlets, we have to mask each side individually to get what we intended. To mask or clip closed shapes in one stroke, we can use the lasso stroke or brushes, which work in a more freehand way.

## The ClipCircleCenter brush and behavior

The **ClipCircleCenter** brush works similarly to the other clipping brushes. The difference is that it starts from the center and always creates a perfect circle. The settings for that can be found in the stroke menu. If you hold down *Ctrl + Shift* to activate the clipping brushes, you can go to **Stroke** and click on **Center** and **Square** to change this behavior. Note that there is a **ClipCircleCenter** brush that comes with this behavior by default, but no corresponding **MaskCircleCenter** brush. So if you like this behavior, you can set it up for masking too.

## The undo history and subtools

When working with many subtools, it's interesting to know that there is no global undo history, but rather a per-subtool one. This means that pressing *Ctrl + Z* will only undo the last steps that we did on the active subtool, which may or may not be the order in which we applied them.

By now you should feel more familiar with **ShadowBox** and hopefully enjoy the easy way to create shapes.

# Summary

We've learned a lot about creating mechanical shapes inside of ZBrush in this chapter.

Specifically, we covered:

- How to quickly prototype ideas in 3D with **ShadowBox**
- How we can create nearly every shape in **ShadowBox**, except for concave and spherical ones
- How to finish mechanical surfaces with the various clipping brushes.
- How to create radial shapes with the **Sweep3D** tool

Now that we've blocked in our mesh, let's go ahead and add some details to the ship in the next chapter.

# 15
# Detailing the Harvester Ship

*We've explored another option of starting a mesh inside ZBrush, in the last chapter, which is* `ShadowBox`*. Now that we're more familiar with it and blocked in the most important elements on the model, we can step ahead and detail the harvester ship by working out the mechanical details. We will break down bigger parts into smaller ones and assemble them together, so that they can make up our complex ship.*

In this chapter, we will elaborate on how to:

- Break down complex parts such as the engines into smaller subtools
- Detail mechanical surfaces
- Create advanced objects such as the clamshell with ShadowBox and clipping brushes
- Combine and subtract meshes with Booleans
- Assemble and manage complex parts with subtools and polygroups
- Bring all the learnt techniques together

Let's get on with it.

> You can download the current state of the ship from the Packtpub website or by following the download link provided in the preface.

# Adding detail to our ship

We'll now start increasing the level of detail of our ship. It's the same process as with sculpting organic models. We work our way through from the largest parts, such as the engines, to the smallest ones—the bolts. We'll apply most of the learnt techniques in this chapter, such as masking, brushes, alphas, clipping brushes, subtools, and so on. As you already know how to use them, we'll only talk about new ways of usage. Let's start:

## Time for action – detailing the engines

1. Load the model that we built in the previous chapter.
2. Before we start with the engines, let's finish the form of the body, as shown in the next image. Increasing the volume of the body makes the ship more believable in its function as a cargo ship. Use the **Move** brush with a large brush size to widen the lower part of the body. Smooth out the result and fine-correct with the **Standard** brush and **Stroke | Lazystep** set to **0.1**. Lower values of **Lazystep** prevent dotted strokes. You can also mask off the top-most part to protect it from changes:

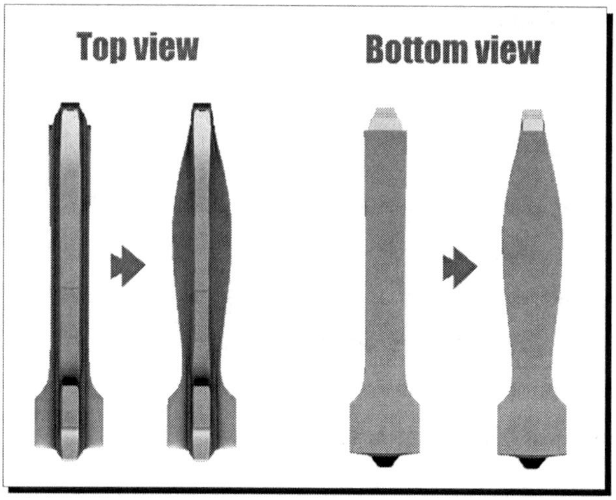


3. Now let's extract the hull for the engines. First, increase the subdivision level to have around 50,000 polygons, so that we can create clean masks.
4. Activate **Transform | L.Sym**, which stands for **local symmetry**. If this is activated, the center of the symmetry will be in the subtool's center instead of the one of the entire ship. This is important if we move something off the global center, as we did with the engines and still want to do symmetrical edits. Local symmetry can also be activated in the shelf.

5. Smooth out any irregularities with radial symmetry activated. Deactivate radial symmetry when finished.

6. Mask the engines with the **MaskRect** brush, as shown in the next image. When finished, extract the hull with **E Smt** set to **0**, **S Smt** to **5**, and **thickness** at **0.1**:

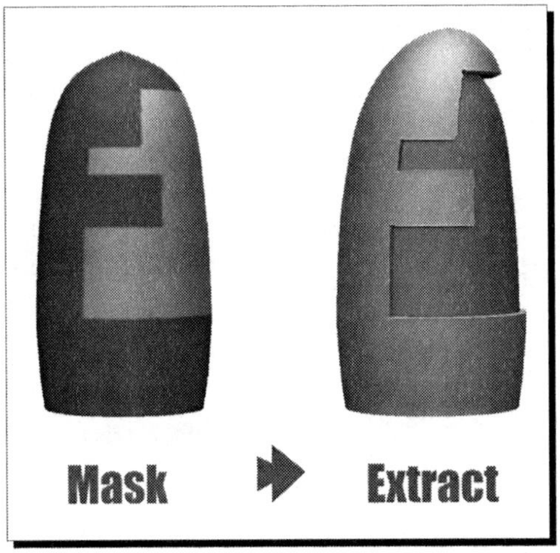


7. Duplicate and hide the inner engine part, in case you want to extract from it again. If you keep such backups in your subtool list, check if you still need them regularly because they increase the file size and decrease performance.

8. Sketch an engine-like structure on the inner part, as shown in the next image. Also add some inlets for the pipes shown in the concept. This stage is really rough; we can clean it up later if we want to. You can use rectangular or circular masks to keep some areas plain:

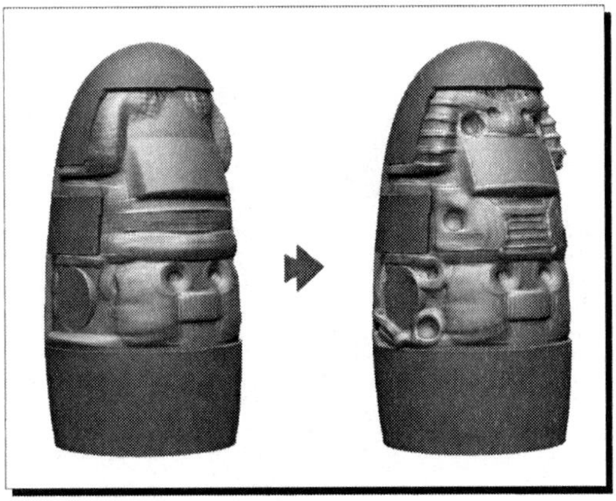

9. Append a **ZSphere** and create the pipes from it, as shown in the next image. In Draw mode, hold down *Shift* to add a **ZSphere**, which has the same size as its parent:

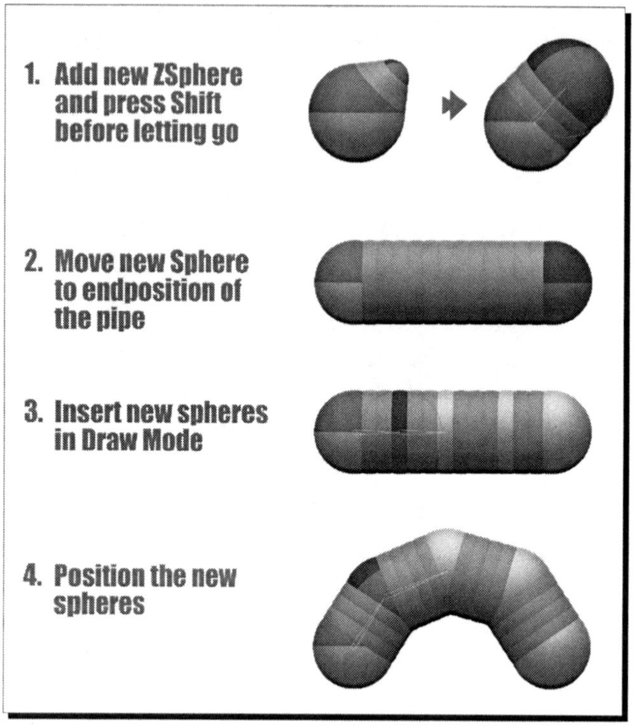

1. Add new ZSphere and press Shift before letting go
2. Move new Sphere to endposition of the pipe
3. Insert new spheres in Draw Mode
4. Position the new spheres


10. The added tubes could now look like the next image. Note that we mirror them over at the end:

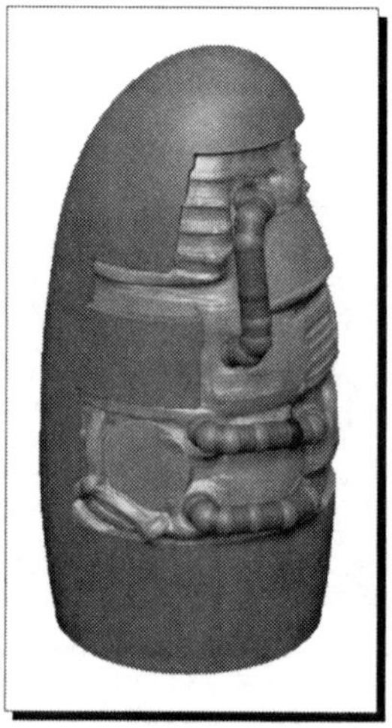

11. The new ZSpheres are automatically appended at the end of the list. We can rearrange our subtools with the arrow-buttons at the bottom of the subtools list, as shown in the next image. In this way, we can keep things organized:

12. Let's do the lamp on the engine's hull. Select the hull, activate symmetry, and mask a rectangle, as shown in the next image:

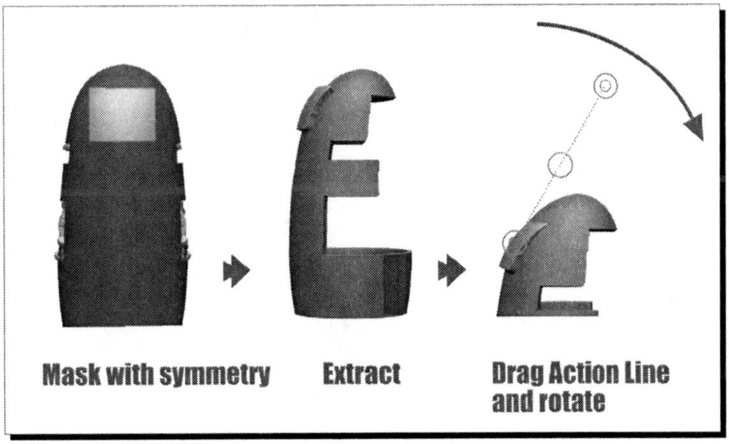


13. Paint erase any masking on the inside of the hull.

14. Extract with **E Smt 0**, **S Smt 5**, and **thickness 0.1**.

15. Snap your view with *Shift* and rotate the lamp with transpose, as shown in the previous image. If you drag out the Action Line from the model to the canvas, it will be perfectly parallel to the view. So if the view is aligned with the world axis by pressing *Shift*, the Action Line will be too.

**How to clean up mesh extracts**

Extracted meshes like our lamp often miss a good polygon distribution. Especially the sides which are stretched polygons and not divided, whereas the masked surfaces feature a lot of polygons. To get a more even distribution, we can simply use **RemeshAll** and **ProjectAll** in the **Subtool** palette, as shown in the next image. Just set the resolution and symmetry-axis, if needed, and press **RemeshAll**. When done, use **ProjectAll** to get the details back. You may want to project again after adding a new level of subdivision.

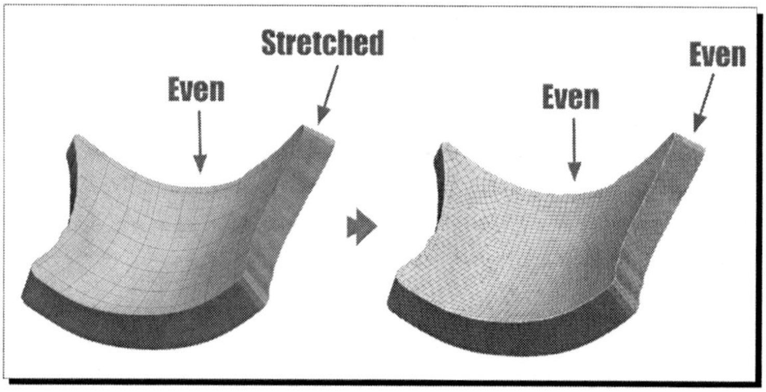


*16.* Use **radial symmetry** and a **Slash** brush to add horizontal cuts to the engines, as shown in the next image:

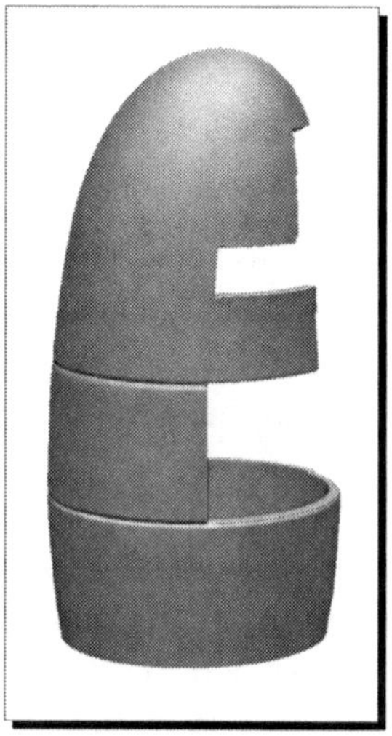

**17.** Refine the front with clipping and transpose, as shown in the next three images:

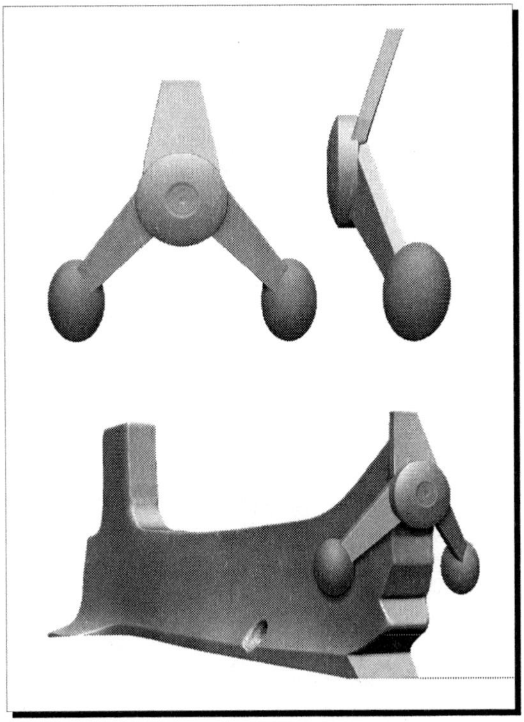

**18.** Start with appending a cube and clip it in front view, as shown in the following image:

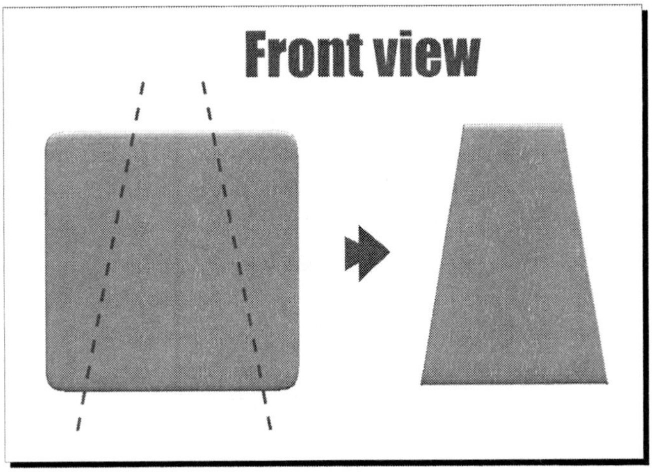

**19.** Use **Move** transpose instead of **Rotate** transpose, as shown in the next image. Opposed to rotate transpose, the top and bottom faces stay vertical with this technique:

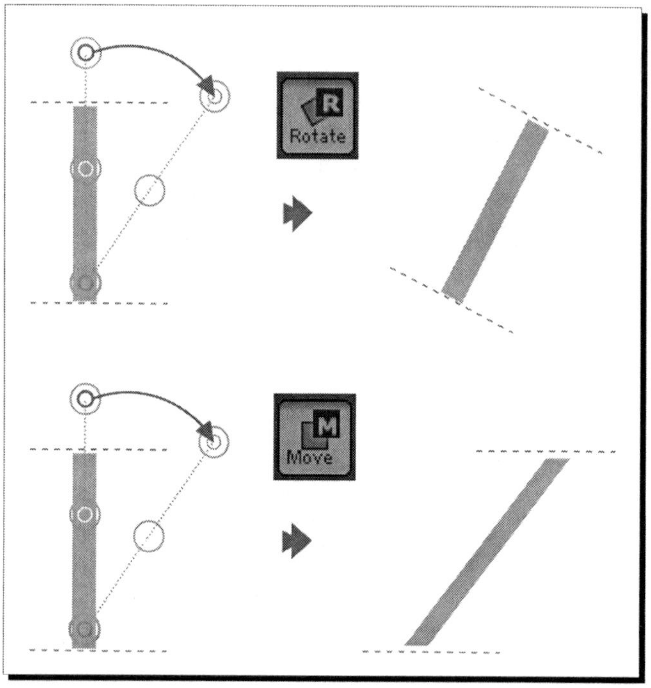


**20.** When building the front, you may want to reshape the body of the ship, as shown in the next image. Just move some parts and clip them again with the **ClipCurve** brush, as we did in the last chapter:

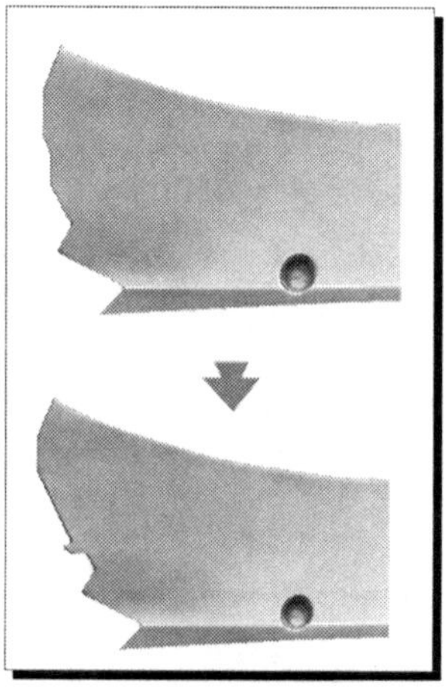

21. Now that we've established the front, we need a mount for the clamshell. Create it from a cylinder with radial and local symmetry, as shown in the next image. Radial symmetry also works with masking. When the masking is done, simply use **inflat**:

22. If we rotate the mount into place now, we can't use radial symmetry on it again. To avoid that, we can store the rotation on a layer. In this way, we can always turn it off and return the subtool into a position that's aligned with the world axis, so we can rely on radial symmetry again. Shape it with the **Move** brush, as shown in the next image, and add a layer before rotating it into place:

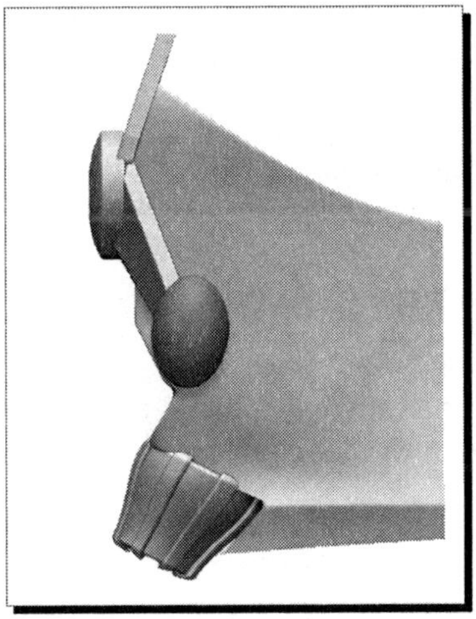

## What just happened?

We've just blocked in the engines and the front details of our ship. Let's discuss some major points again:

## Local symmetry

Local symmetry is useful for objects that were moved away from the center of the model. Off center, global symmetry along the global axis won't work anymore. Activating local symmetry picks the center of the subtool as a new origin of symmetry. This doesn't change the actual pivot of the subtool or object; it's just an option for our convenience.

What local symmetry can't take care of is "rotation". So if we rotate our object, local symmetry will not rotate the axis of symmetry along with it. So we have to work around that by storing the rotation on a layer.

## Subtool controls

Below the subtool list, we can find some useful buttons that can ease our workflow when having a lot of subtools. Apart from the **Move Subtool Up** and **Down** buttons, there are two buttons named **All Low** and **All High**, as shown in the next image. These two allow us to switch all available subtools to their highest or lowest level of subdivision, which can save us a lot of time.

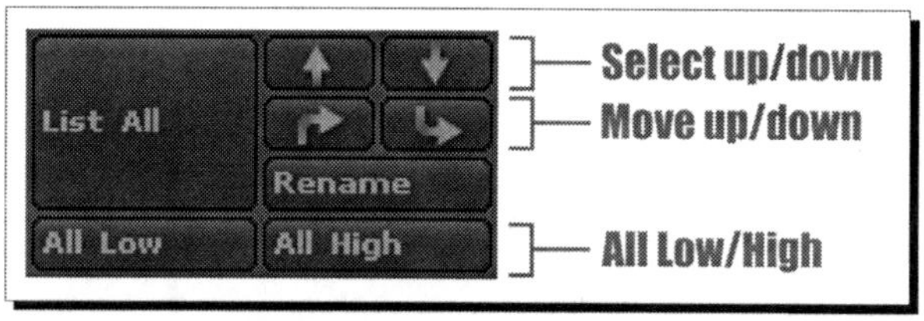


## Moving objects along one axis with the Action Line

To move an object exactly along one axis, we can do the following: Starting the Action Line on our mesh, but ending it on the canvas will create the Action Line parallel to the view. If the view is aligned with the world axis, the Action Line will be too.

Okay, now we've got our Action Line aligned with our axis of choice, but how do we restrict the object's movement along this axis? The trick is holding *Shift*. This will move the object only along the Action Line. In this way, we can even view the model from a different point of view and still move it exclusively along one axis because the Action Line stays in place.

## How clipping works

When clipping meshes, ZBrush will not remove any points of the mesh. Instead, it will move all points to the line we specified with the clipping brushes. That's the reason why we can just move the mesh and clip it again (if we want to) because we don't lose any polygons upon clipping. The only thing that may happen is polygonal distortion.

To relax such distortions, use the **Relax slider** in the **Deformations** subpalette. You can even mask specific areas to protect them from being relaxed, as shown in the next image:

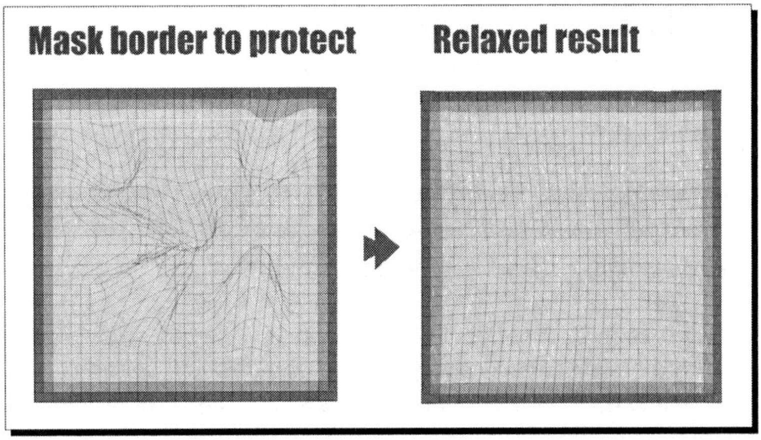


## Pop quiz – local symmetry, clipping, and moving

1. What does clipping do with the polygons that get clipped away?
    a. Delete them
    b. Flatten them to the clipping line
    c. Hide them
2. Imagine we would like to sculpt a column with radial and local symmetry, which action should we avoid?
    a. Moving the column up
    b. Moving the column to the right
    c. Rotating the column by 35 degrees in X
3. How can we create an Action Line parallel to the view?
    a. By starting the Action Line on the model and also ending it there
    b. By starting the Action Line on the canvas
    c. By starting the Action Line on the model and ending it on the canvas
4. For technical objects, it's sometimes important to move objects only along a specific axis. How can we achieve that in ZBrush if we have our Action Line already aligned and want to restrict the object's movement to the path of the Action Line?
    a. By holding down *Shift* as we move it
    b. By holding down *Ctrl* as we move it
    c. By holding down *Space Bar* as we move it

# Creating the clamshell

Now that we have finished the engines and blocked in the front details of our ship, let's continue with the clamshell. This part is quite complex in shape, so we have to break it down into several smaller subtools. To create the clamshell, we will mainly draw upon what we've learned about **ShadowBox** and clipping in the last chapter. So if you're unsure, you may quickly flip through it again.

## Time for action – creating the clamshell

Let's continue by creating the clamshell with **ShadowBox**:

1. Add a new subtool and work out the **shape in ShadowBox**, as shown in the next image. Use the **MaskCircle** brush and erase parts with *Alt*. In the second step, modify the masks by hand with the **MaskPen** brush and symmetry:

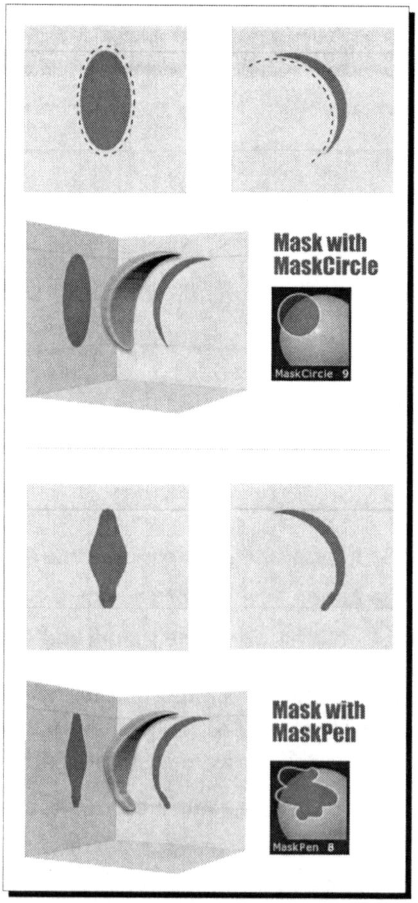

2. Duplicate the subtool that we just created and alter the masks, as shown in the next image to create a stabilizing element for the claw. Don't forget the small hole at the top:

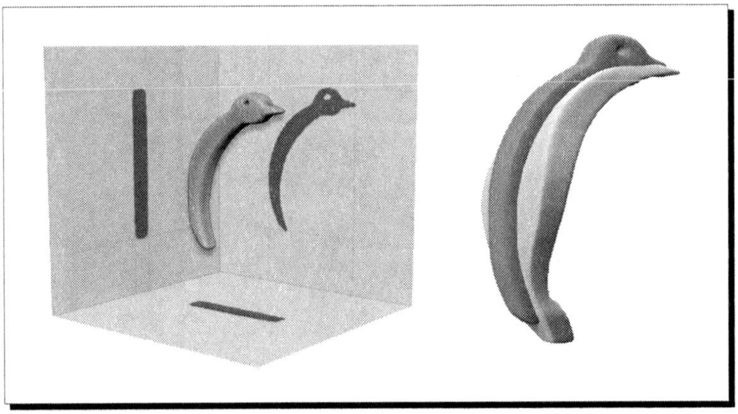

3. Exit **ShadowBox** on both meshes and make each mesh a polygroup by going to **Tool | Polygroups** and click on the **Group Visible** button.

4. Clean up the rounded edges of both with the **ClipCurve** brush, as shown in the next image:

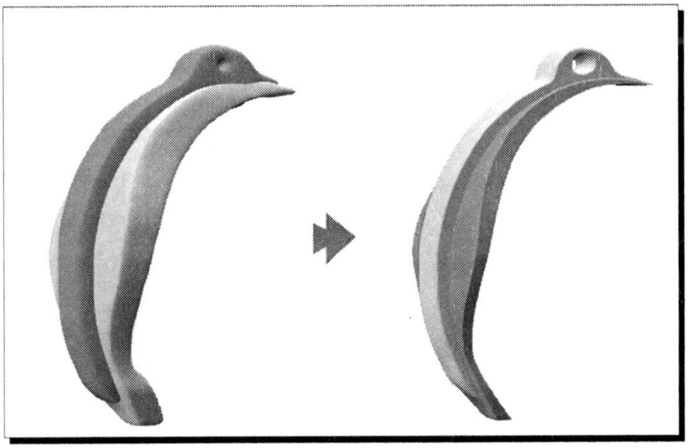

5. Clean up the hole with the **ClipCircleCenter** brush while holding *Alt*, as shown in the next image:

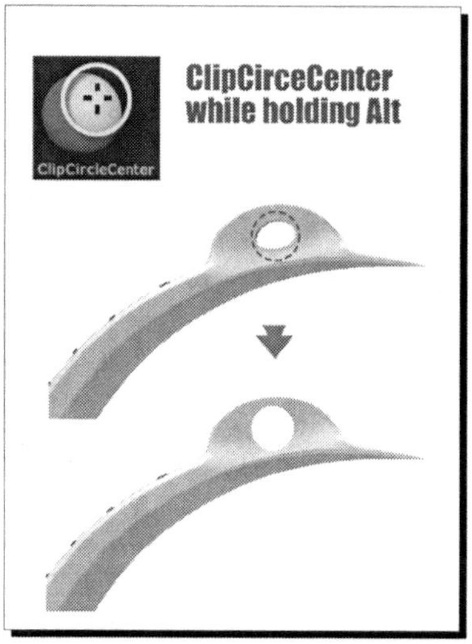


6. Let's add some details to the stabilizer. Add some subdivision levels, activate symmetry, and mask the topmost part, as shown in the next image. Clip it so that the unmasked area gets thinned out. After that, mask it again with a rectangular mask and **Inflat**, as shown in the second step of the next image. Keep the mask for the next step:

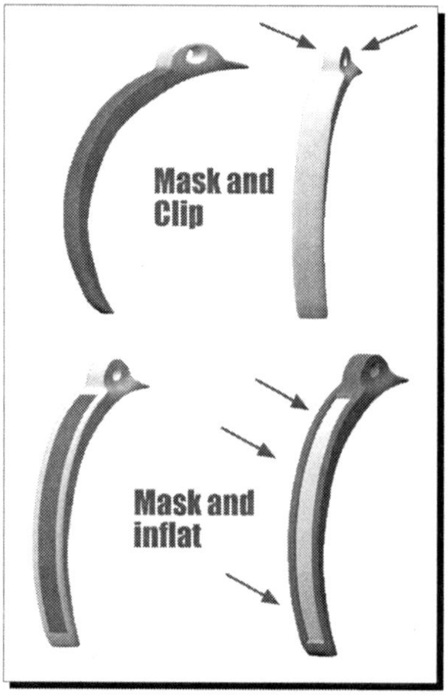

7. With the mask from the previous step, pick the **MaskRect** brush. Choose a rectangular alpha, such as **alpha 28** and set **Alpha | V Tiles** to **16**—this tiles the alpha 16 times vertically.

8. Set the stroke type of the **MaskRect** brush to **DragRect** and disable symmetry. Drag a mask, as shown in the next image and **Inflat** the result to get a nice pattern of small cross braces:

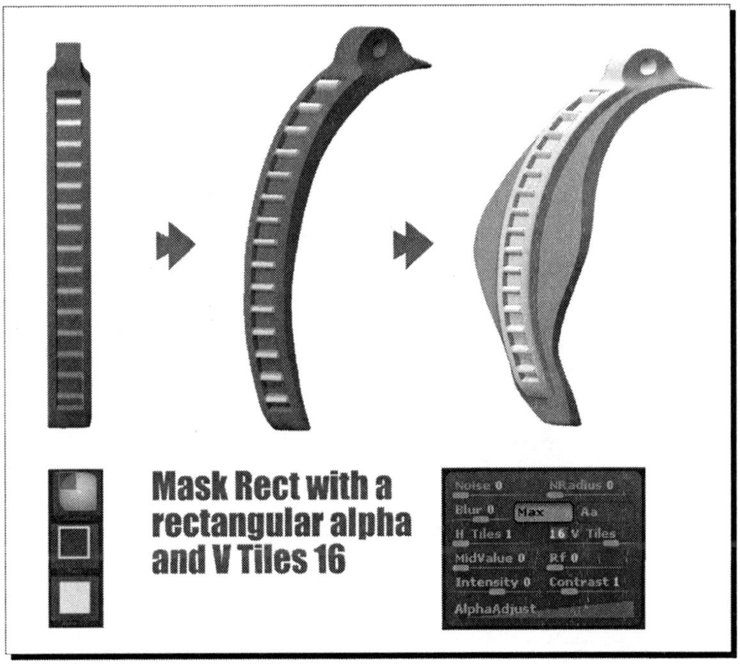


9. We've already made each mesh a separate polygroup, so we can now merge them by going to **Tool | SubTool** and click on the **Merge Down** button. We have to select the upper one in the subtool list to merge them. The button is grayed out, if there is no subtool below the active one.

**10.** With both merged, sculpt some connecting pieces to make the claw look more functional.

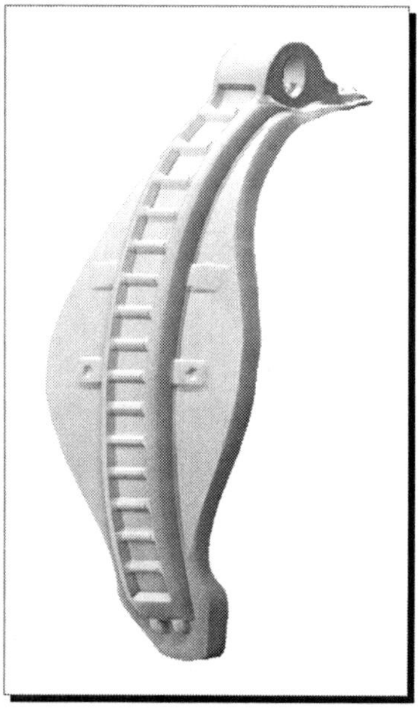

**11.** Finish the crane by sculpting and assembling smaller pieces, as shown in the next two images:

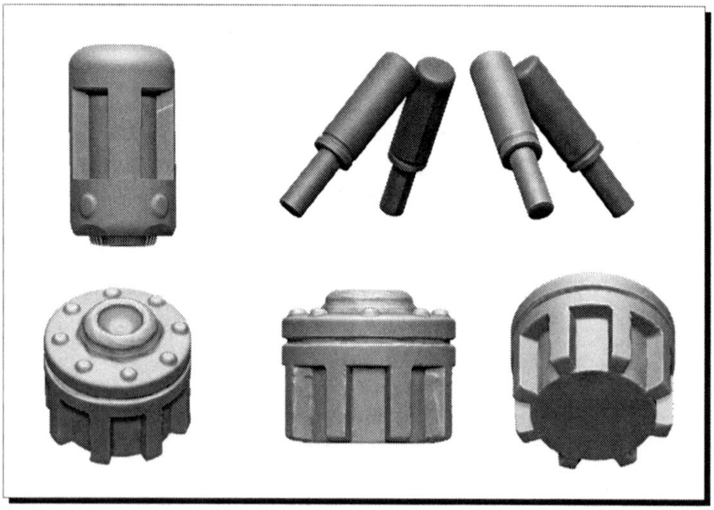

12. When you're done with one side, duplicate and transpose-rotate the duplicates with *Shift* by 90 degrees to finish the clamshell. Note that if you would like to animate the clamshell later, the cylinders that push it have to be made of two separate ones that can move into each other.

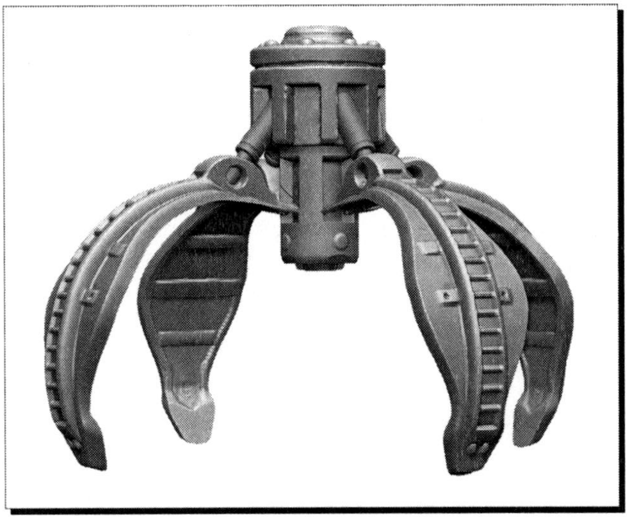

13. With the clamshell finished, don't forget to save.

## *What just happened?*

We've just finished the complex clamshell by assembling several pieces. Using simple techniques such as **ShadowBox** and masking, we can achieve amazing results in a short amount of time.

## Clipping holes

With the **ClipCircleCenter** brush, we cleaned up the hole on the claws of the clamshell. It's important to think of the placements of holes in the beginning because clipping can't cut holes in a mesh, it can only alter the existing ones. We'll talk about another way to cut holes inside existing meshes in the next example, but it's much more convenient to think about it in the beginning.

## Patterns with horizontal and vertical tiling

For the pattern on the clamshell, we used the **Alpha | V Tiles** feature, which is brand new in ZBrush 4.0. This allows us to create patterns from simple alphas and change the tiling on the fly, which is very useful. Using a simple rectangle is quite a simple example. Imagine using this for complex armor patterns or tiled floors.

Note that this is a global option. So once set, it will apply to all brushes that use an alpha.

## Merging subtools

To combine several smaller subtools, we used the **Merge Down** function. This combines two subtools into a new one, maintaining the polygroups. Giving each a separate polygroup helps when working on them separately after they were merged. Another advantage is that once combined, they can be split again by polygroups using the **Tool | SubTool | Groups Split** function.

Below the **Merge Down** button, there's also a **Merge Visible** button. The difference here is that **Merge Visible** will create a new tool that's appended to the list instead of adding a new subtool.

The second difference is that by default, the **weld** option next to it is activated. This will weld all points that overlap at the border where the meshes intersect. If we do this, we can't split them afterwards. The **weld** function is useful though; for example, if we mirror one half of the mesh over and would like to weld them in the middle. In our case, we should turn this option off.

# Time for action – adding some defences, the turrets

Let's add the turrets to our harvester ship, so that it can defend itself when the going gets tough:

1. To start the hull of the turrets, we need to select a new tool. Select the **Sphere3D** tool. Don't append it, just select a new one, we need to have a clean subtools list.
2. Make it a polymesh.
3. Duplicate it and shrink it down a little. We're going to subtract the smaller sphere from the bigger one to create a hollow shell. Place them inside each other, as shown in the next screenshot:

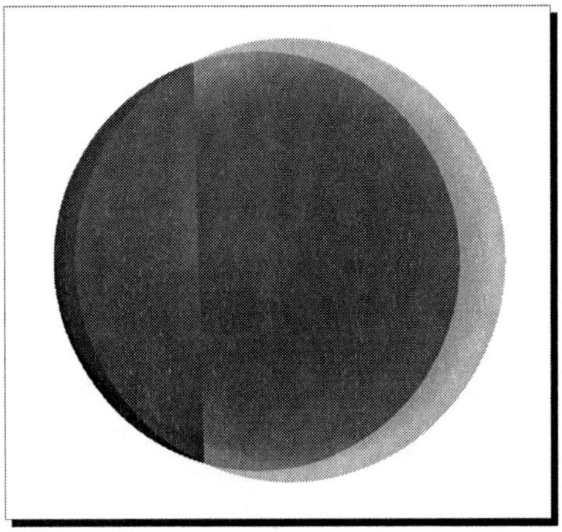

4. In the **subtool** list, set the **Boolean** icons, as shown in the next image. The bigger one should be set to **Add** and the smaller one to **Subtract**:

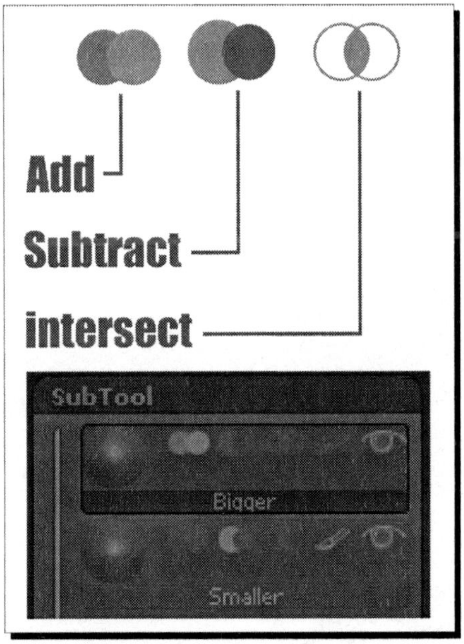


5. Make sure that the bigger sphere is the top-most subtool and also the active one. It's important that both are true; both subtools should be visible.

6. Let's set up the remeshing. Set **Polish** to **100** and activate remeshing symmetry on the correct axis. In my case, this is the Y-axis. The default resolution of 128 is fine.

7. Navigate to **Tool | SubTool | Remesh All**, which will create a new subtool based on the Boolean settings we did in the previous step.

8. Clip the resulting hull so that it forms half of a sphere, as shown in the next image. Smooth out the remeshing irregularities on the surface:

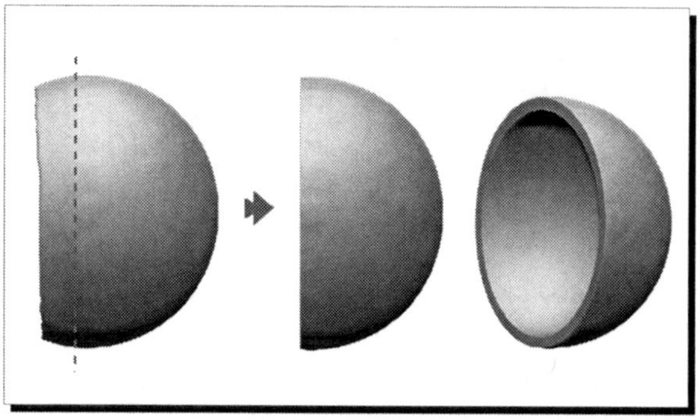

9. Mask the back side of the hull and clip a hole in the front, as shown in the next image. When using the clip circle brushes with the *Alt key*, make sure the cross in the center is not over the mesh, but over the canvas. Otherwise, it will push the surface outwards instead of clipping it:

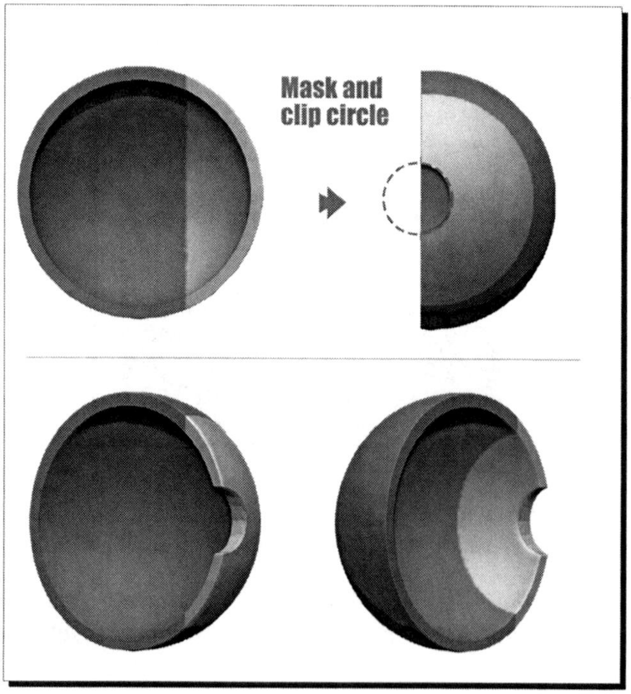

10. If you have distortion problems when clipping the hole, use the **Tool | Deformation | Relax slider** and clip it again.

11. Finish and assemble the turret with pieces, as shown in the next image. The smaller pieces are really no big deal, just radial symmetry over and over:

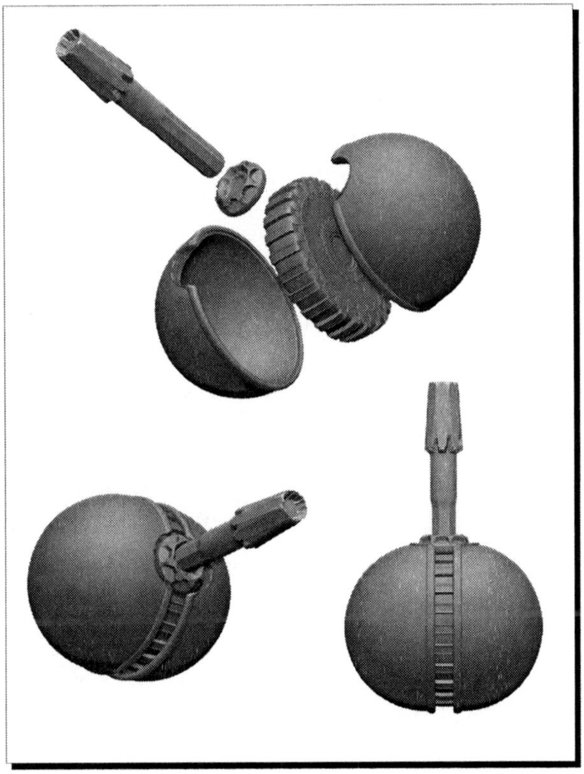

12. When finished, give each part a polygroup and merge them, like we did before. You can load the tool of the ship again and append the turret now.

## What just happened?

We've just created the turrets for our ship using ZBrush's Boolean functions. Let's discuss this more in depth:

# Combining meshes with Booleans

As we saw, Booleans allow us to combine different meshes into new ones. The important step is the remeshing at the end. In this way, we can cut holes into existing meshes by remeshing them. Simply project the details when the remeshing is done.

It's important to know that the Boolean operation evaluates the subtools list from top to bottom. So the order in which objects will be added, subtracted, or intersected is determined by their order in the subtools list.

The second important thing is that the Boolean operation starts with the active subtool downwards. Everything above the active subtool in the list will be ignored. This way you can exclude everything above the active subtool from the Boolean operation.

# Clipping with the Alt key

The **ClipCircle** and **ClipRectangle** brushes do have a little cross in their center. If we hold *Alt*, and the center-cross is over the canvas, the marked area gets clipped. If the center cross is over the mesh, it will be pushed out to match the marked area. This allows for interesting effects, not just limited to slicing away polygons.

## Pop quiz – Booleans

1. In which order does the Boolean function evaluate our subtools?
    a. From bottom to top
    b. From top to bottom
    c. In random order
2. What can't be done with Booleans?
    a. Creating a ring by subtracting two cylinders
    b. Creating a star by adding two triangles
    c. Creating a knot out of two cylinders

## Time for action – finishing the main parts of the ship

Let's finish this chapter by bringing it all together, starting with the placement of the turrets:

1. To place the turrets, we'll cut holes in the body of the ship. Select the main body, activate symmetry, mask, inflat, and clip it, as shown in the next image. Clip the holes holding the *Alt* key and the center-cross over the canvas, as we did in the previous example:

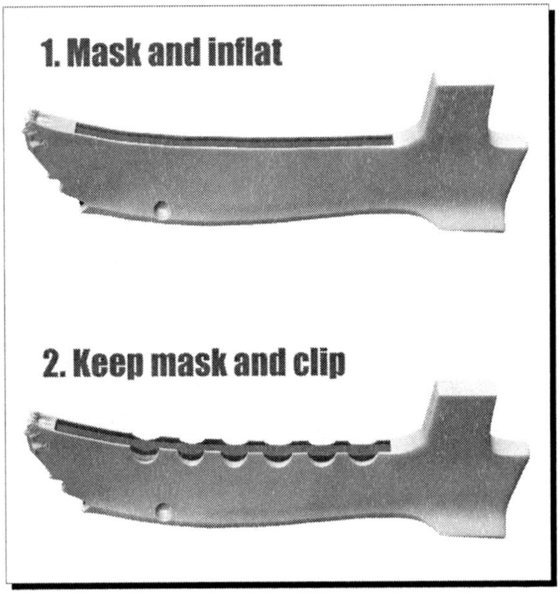


2. When finished with the clipping, cut lines into the body, starting at the indentations for the turrets, as shown in the next screenshot:

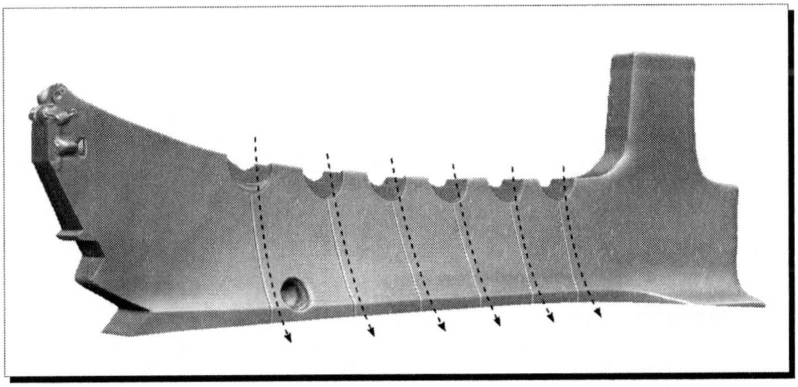

3. Duplicate the turrets and place them inside the holes, as shown in the next image. The hotkey for duplicate is *Ctrl + Shift +D*:

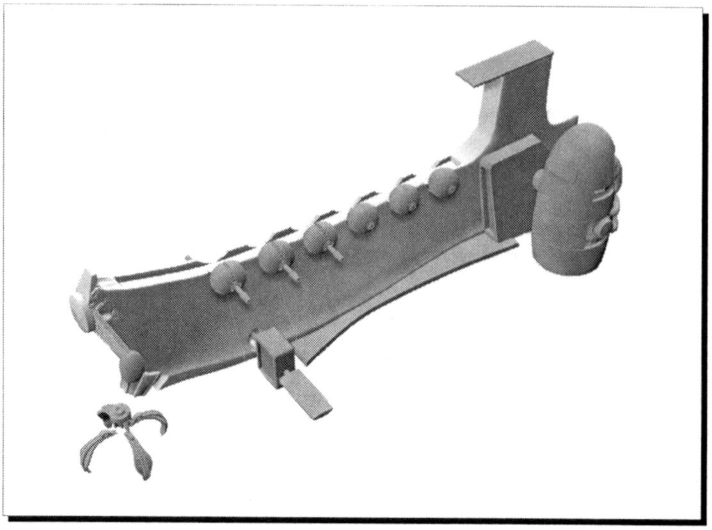

4. "Close" some turrets using polygroups, as shown in the next image. When moving both halves together, make sure that they don't overlap:

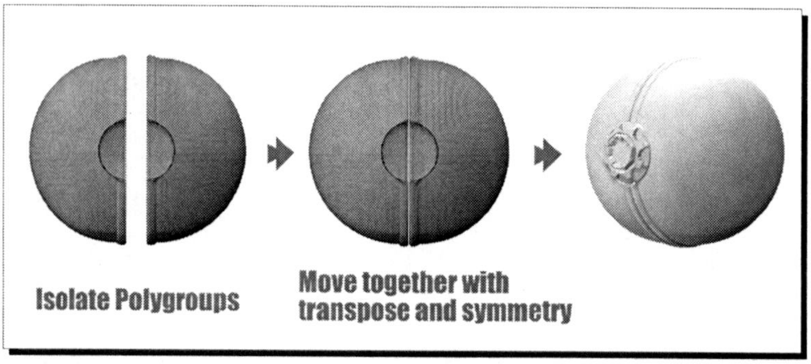


5. Let's continue detailing the front. Create a grille as shown in the next image. Use **ShadowBox** for the border object and standard cubes for the iron bars:

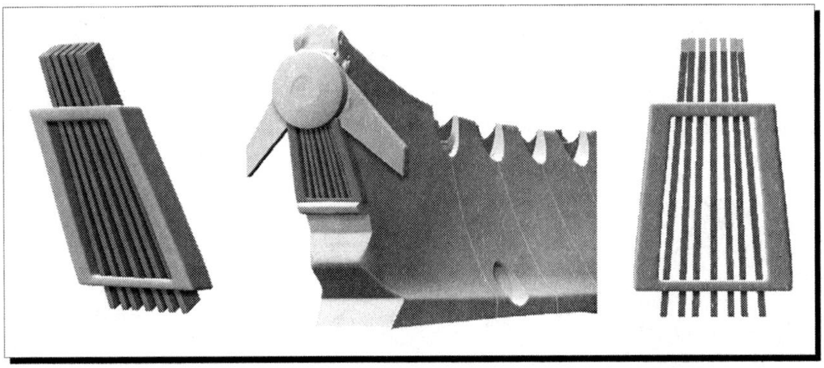

6. Let's finish the front part of the ship by adding the front turrets. Duplicate the turret we built earlier. **Groups Split** it to reuse the gear and the muzzle, as shown in the next image. **Groups Split** can be found under **Tool | SubTool | Groups Split**:

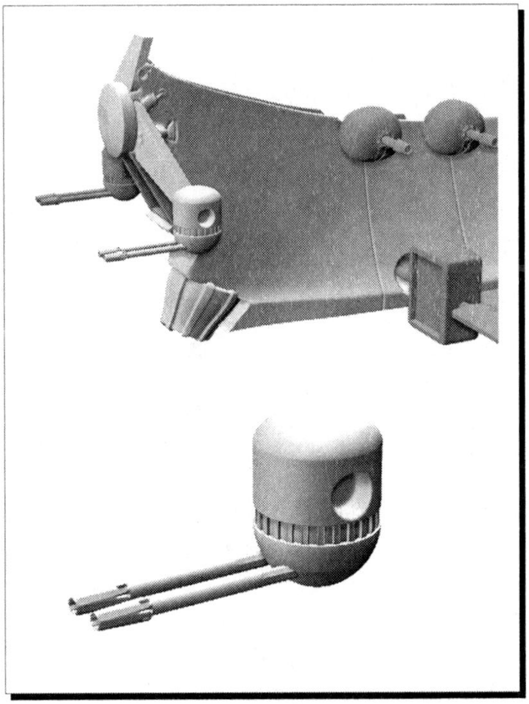

7. Now let's move ahead to the air inlets at the rear engines. Activate **Transform | BRadius** and clip the inlets with the **ClipCircleCenter** brush. If **BRadius** is active, the amount of clipping is determined by the brush size. Adjust the brush size until you're satisfied with the result.

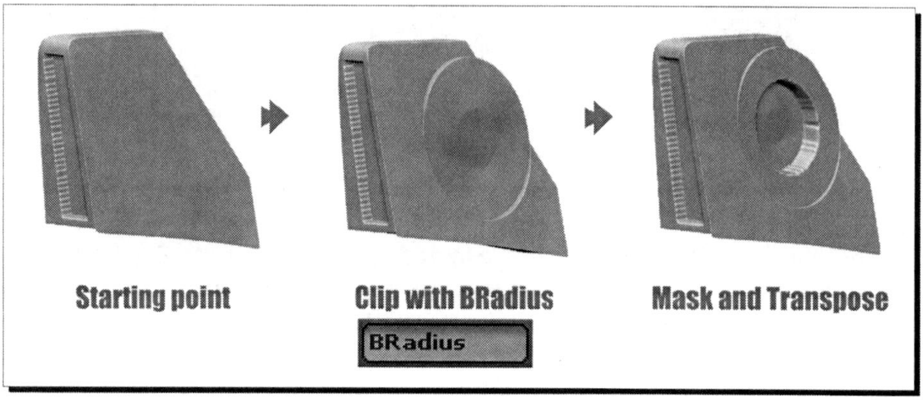


8. Add some details to the bar that holds the engines to make it look more believable. Sculpt the bar itself and add some more cylinders, as shown in the next image:

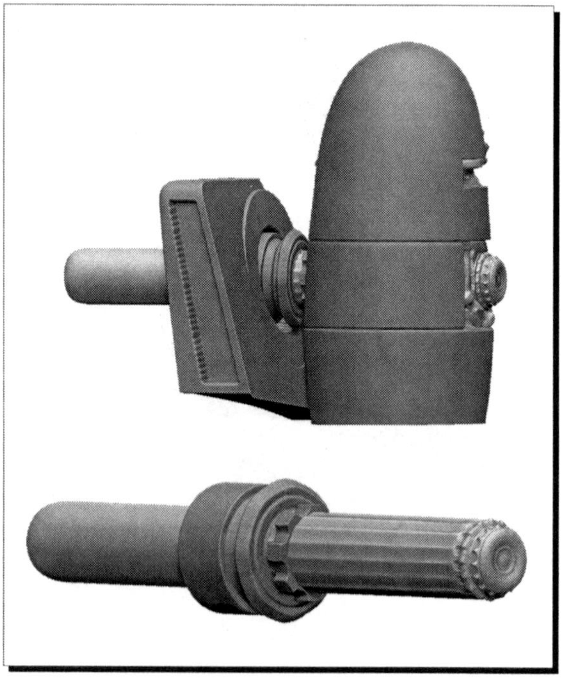

9. Finish the air inlets by adding some fins. Start from a cube—shape and duplicate it, as shown in the next image. Merge all so that you can clip them all in one go to fit the shape of the inlet:

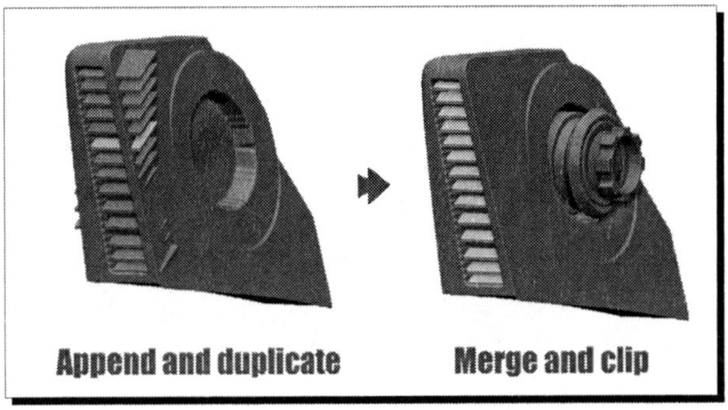


10. One last detail is still missing—the bottom. As this is a harvester and a cargo ship, it has tanks that can be accessed from the bottom. Switch to a **Sphere** tool and set **Tool | Initialize | Coverage** to **180,** so that you get a hemisphere to start from. Mask, extract, and sculpt it—as shown in the next image. For the sculpting of the technical inlets, activate symmetry on two axes, so that it is mirrored two times. This saves us a lot of time, getting four paint strokes out of one. The cables are done with ZSpheres, as we did for the pipes of the rear engines:

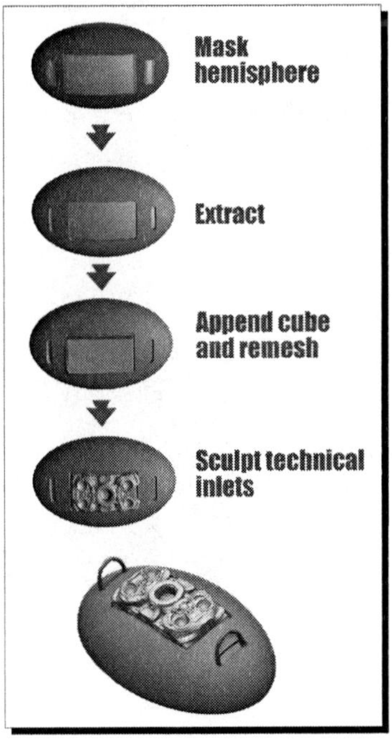

**11.** Finally, polygroup, merge, and duplicate them along the bottom of the ship, as shown in the following image:

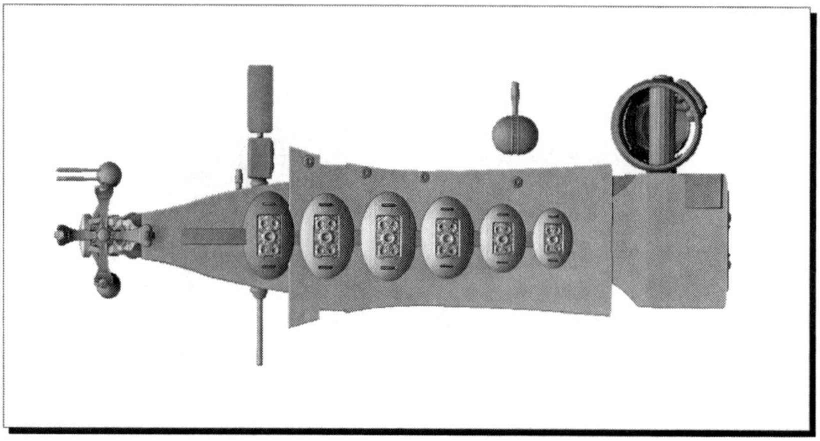

**12.** Our final model would now look like this:

## *What just happened?*

By now, the ship is nearly finished. Adding details to the ship went quite fast, considering how complex the model is. Let's discuss some key elements:

## Clipping again

Now we've seen how versatile clipping can be when combined with masks. If we press the *Alt* key, we can even push vertices to match the desired shape.

With **BRadius**, the amount of clipping depends on the brush size – the relative brush size, to be precise. Because zooming in and out also changes the brush size compared to the model, the amount of clipping also depends on the camera distance to the object. **BRadius** gives the most interesting results with the **ClipCurve** brush. Pick a sphere and give it a shot.

## Mirror axis

Merging subtools helps us to organize them better, while keeping them in separate polygroups for further editing. When using symmetry and polygroups to close the turrets, we have to be careful that they don't overlap in the middle. If they do, symmetry can't move them apart anymore. It will rather look like they were welded in the middle. Actually, they will still be independent parts and we can still separate them by polygroups. But local symmetry will only consider mesh parts that lie on one side of the axis of mirror. If something extends across that axis, it will cause problems.

Sculpting the tanks at the bottom of the ship with symmetry went really fast by using symmetry on more than one axis. If we do so, out strokes will be mirrored two times and be symmetrical on two axes. This also works with radial symmetry and looks really weird. But if you would like to sculpt a pattern on a sphere, it's the fastest way to go.

# Summary

That's it; all the main parts are fleshed out and have been put into place. The ship evolved quite a lot from the block-out of the last chapter, well done.

In this chapter, we've brought together nearly all techniques learnt, to create and to assemble a complex technical object. We've specifically covered:

- Our harvester ship consists of many subtools that can still be edited with (local-) symmetry.
- To cope with the complexity of our harvester, we can rearrange and merge subtools
- We can create any shape we want using either **ShadowBox**, **Booleans**, or **ZSketch**, or a combination of them
- Topology problems can quickly be resolved with a **Remesh All** | **Project All** workflow
- Patterns can be quickly created using the **H Tiles** and **V Tiles** options for alphas

Now that we've sculpted the main details, let's move on to the fine detail stage to make the ship look even more believable.

# 16
# Finishing the Harvester Ship

*We're almost there! Our most complex model we've built so far is near its completion. In this chapter, we'll finish the harvester by detailing it even more with a new focus on believability. Everything we create should obey certain rules, so that the viewers accept it visually.*

So in this chapter, we're going to cover:

- Assembling and connecting complex objects in a believable way
- Painting with grabbed geometry

Let's add the final polish.

## Believability

When creating models, especially for games, we always try to create a believable world for the players. Like the world itself, everything in it should follow certain rules. This doesn't necessarily mean that the player should be familiar with the rules. No, the main point is that there are consistent rules. In our case, it's a world with advanced technology, but familiar materials such as steel. So, the manner of manufacturing is similar to what we do when building machines. It's about stabilizing elements, connecting metal pieces with bolts, and cowling technical parts in a hull. That's what we're going to transfer to our model in this chapter.

# Time for action – finishing the engines

The bottom of our ship still looks very plain; let's go ahead and change that:

1. Finish the bottom side of the engines by creating several rings in **ShadowBox**, as shown in the next image. Sculpt them with radial symmetry. For the innermost part, use a circle as a base:

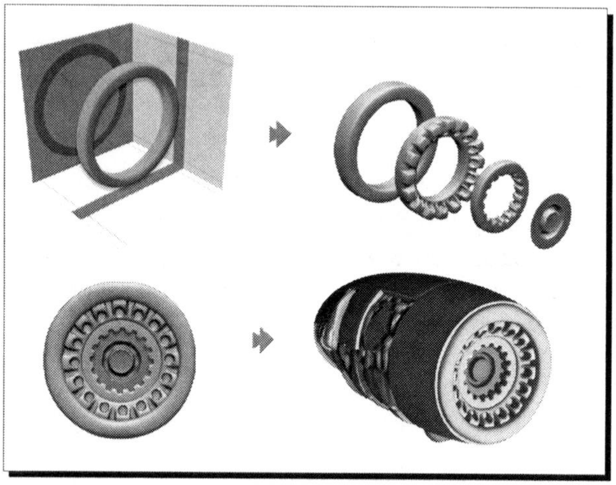

2. If we combine the **Tracks** brush with **alpha tiling**, we can sculpt a nice *cable pattern*, as shown in the next image. You can get an even cleaner distribution of the alpha if you activate **LazyMouse** with a high **LazySmooth** value:

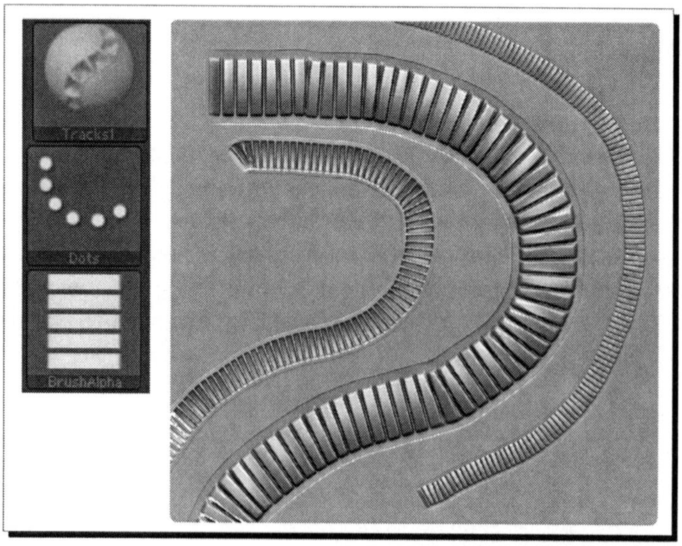

3. Add some cables to the engines and finish the mechanical parts with the **Trim Dynamic** and **Polish** brushes, like we did when sculpting the drone. When adding parts the viewers are familiar with (such as cables), it automatically affects the relative scale of our object. If we create something new, adding one common element helps to determine its relative size. That's why you see so many epic landscape pictures with a small human figure in the foreground. It's a matter of reference.

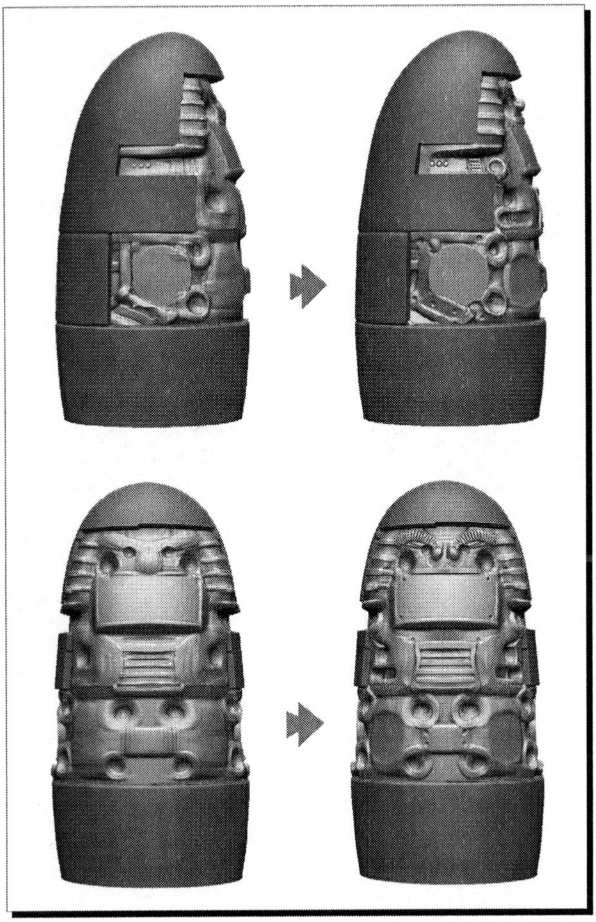

4. To finish the engines, we can now create adaptive skins from the **ZSphere** pipes and mirror them over.

5. Let's sculpt the bottom wings of our ship, as shown in the next image. Use the **ClayBuildup** brush in combination with **Stroke | Lazymouse | Backtrack**, **SnapToTrack,** and **Line** feature to create straight lines:

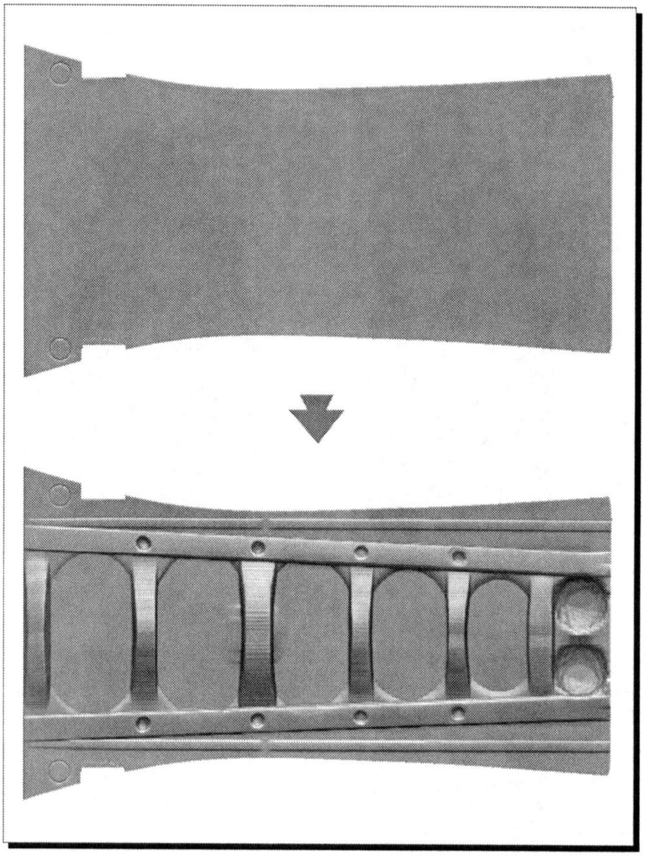

6. To repeat the pattern of the engines on the bottom of the ship, we will now grab the geometry of the engines and use it as an alpha. To achieve that, view the ship exactly from the bottom and turn off *perspective* and *edit mode*, as shown in the first step of the next image:

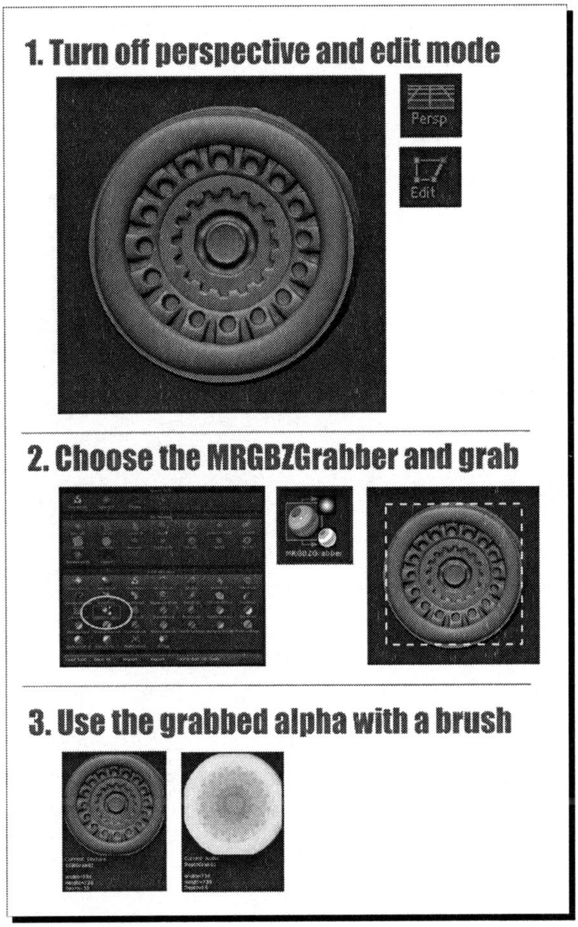


7. Choose the **MRGBZGrabber** from the tool list and grab the geometry, as shown in the second step of the previous image. The rectangle can be positioned with *Space bar*.

8. When letting go, we can see that we grabbed an alpha from the geometry, which we can now use on any brush to detail the bottom of our ship. Save the alpha by going to **Alpha | Export**.

9. To actually detail the bottom, we need only a few brushes. The following image shows how we can create several technical details with different brushes, strokes, and alphas. Don't forget that holding *Alt* inverses the direction of the brush:

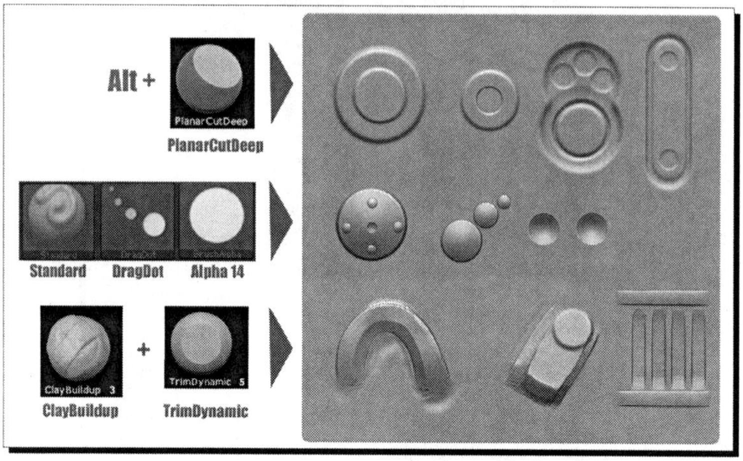


10. Use painted masks to create the rim around the bottom of the ship, as shown in the next image.

11. Use the techniques described earlier and the grabbed alpha to start adding detail to the bottom. Placing grabbed alphas works best with the **DragDot** stroke type, which allows for very accurate placement. Just make sure **LazyMouse** is off:

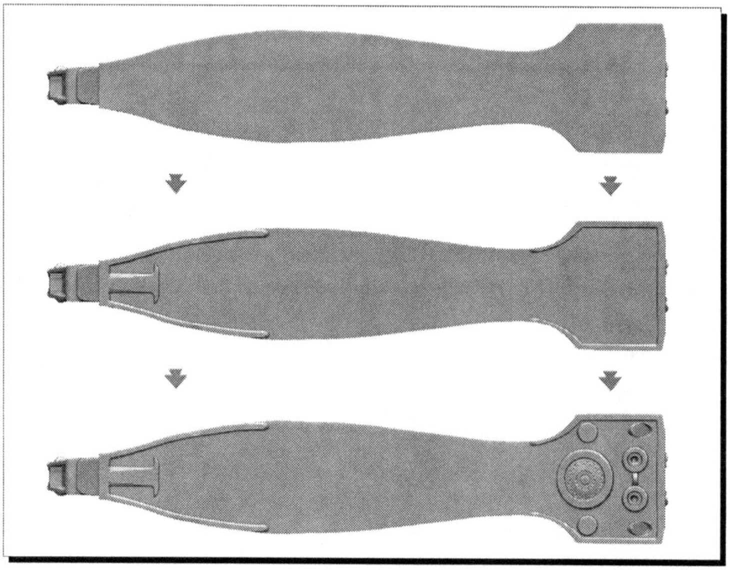

12. Continue with the bottom that reveals more technical parts to underline the complexity of the object. Sculpt in the little details, as shown in the next image, using the techniques described earlier:

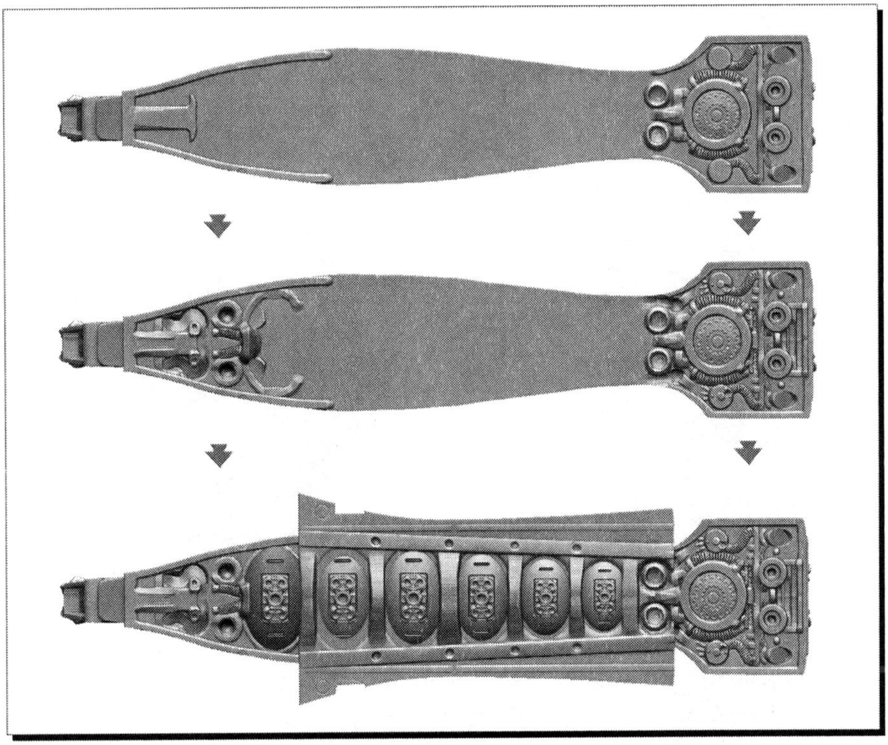

13. See how that little sculpting added so much sense and functionality to the bottom? It's a lot like sketching. You have to draw only the first lines of grass and the viewer will accept that everything behind it is covered in grass, too.

14. It's always a good idea to save your work.

## What just happened?

We just sculpted very fine technical details on the engines and the bottom of the ship, giving the viewer the impression of immense complexity.

For the cables, we used the **Tracks** brush in combination with the **alpha tiling** feature. What makes the difference between the **Tracks** brush and others is the **Stroke | Roll** feature, which tiles the alpha along the stroke. We can apply the roll feature to any brush we want.

# Paint with grabbed geometry

We've already learned how to create an alpha in a 2D image editor from scratch. Grabbing sculpted geometry is even faster. We can sculpt things and use it as a brush, which can be a huge timesaver. Imagine you would like to create a stone golem and add little rocks on his back. Sculpting each of them would take forever. Just create a stylized rock with clipping brushes and grab it, as shown in the next image. If we don't save the alpha, it will be gone upon the next restart of ZBrush:

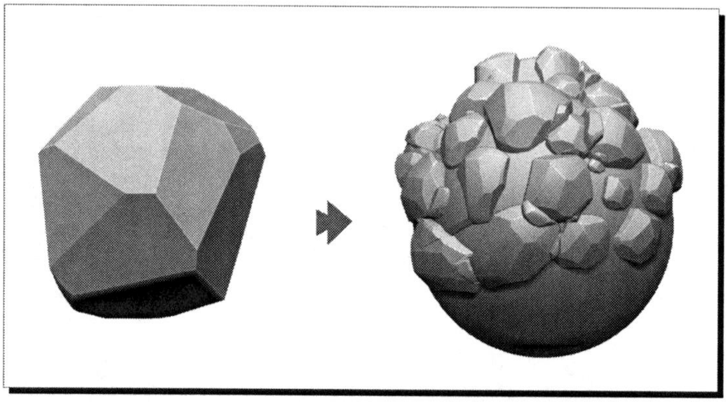

For alphas that are created from reference images, the 2D approach is still the method of choice.

If we need very accurate placements of the alphas, the **DragDot** stroke type is very useful. Opposed to the **DragRect** stroke, the DragDot's stroke position can be adjusted when placing it on the mesh. The **DragRect** can change only its size and rotation but not its position. As you can see, each has its own strengths and weaknesses.

The **MRGBZGrabber** has its name from the things that it grabs. It can grab **M** (material), **RGB** (color as a texture), and **Z** (depth as an alpha). Grabbing even includes textures, which means you can also paint something and reuse it as a texture for your brush.

Note that the size of the grabbed alpha and texture depends on the size the object occupies on the canvas when you exit *edit mode*. You can check the size of the alpha in pixels when hovering over its icon.

If we grab alphas from geometry, we even get 16-bit alphas, which have around 65,000 shades of gray, instead of 256. This means that the alphas are smoother and have less of a stair-stepping effect.

There are plenty of possibilities for what we can do with this. We can sculpt bolts, stones, pores, bullet holes, leafs, craters, eyes, and so on, and scatter them all over the mesh with this technique.

## Pop quiz – creating alphas from geometry

1. Which tool can grab geometry and create an alpha from it?

   a) The MRGBZGrabber

   b) The Cloner brush

   c) The Smudge brush

2. The size of the grabbed alpha depends on?

   a) The amount of polygons of the mesh

   b) The size the object occupies on the canvas in pixels

   c) The screen resolution

## Time for action – adding the final details

Let's finish our harvester ship by detailing the front wings and the command bridge:

***1.*** Starting with the front engine, first work on the case by clipping the sides, as shown in the next image:

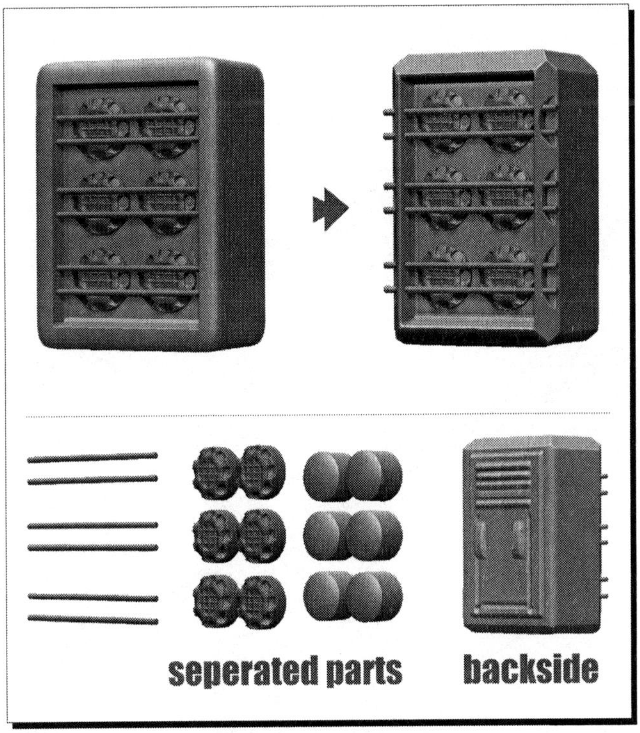

2. Add details to the backside, as shown in the previous image. This helps to suggest that the case contains technical elements that can be reached by opening a door on the back.

3. Continue by adding the lamps at the front, as the previous image shows. The grill on the lamps can be done with a rectangular alpha and **Alpha | H Tiles** at **8** and **Alpha | V Tiles** at **10.**

4. The front engines need a strong connection to the body, so they can lift the ship. Add a new cylinder and sculpt it with radial symmetry, as shown in the next image:

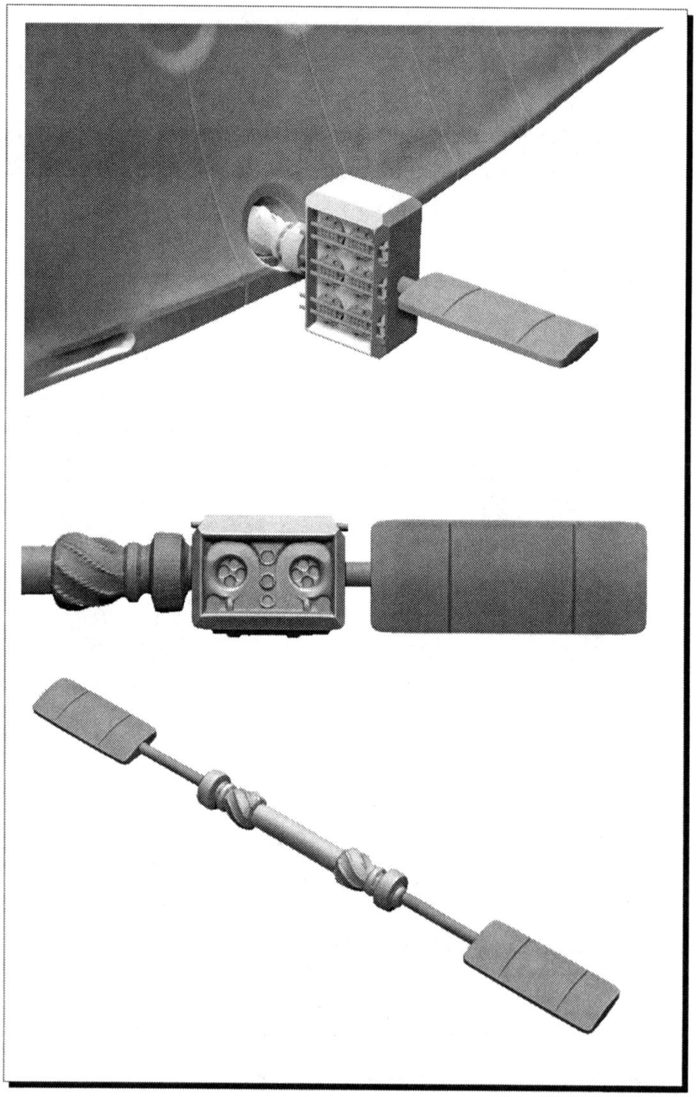

5. Also, inset the bottom of the front engines and add some exhausts.

6. Finally, add two slashes on the wings, as the previous image shows.

7. Let's continue with adding some detail to the command bridge, so it looks more believable. Start by clipping the back and roughing in some detail on the sides, as the next image shows. Use the **ClipCircle** brushes and hold *Alt* to create the prominent circles, as shown in the next image. Don't forget to mask the backside when using the clip brushes:

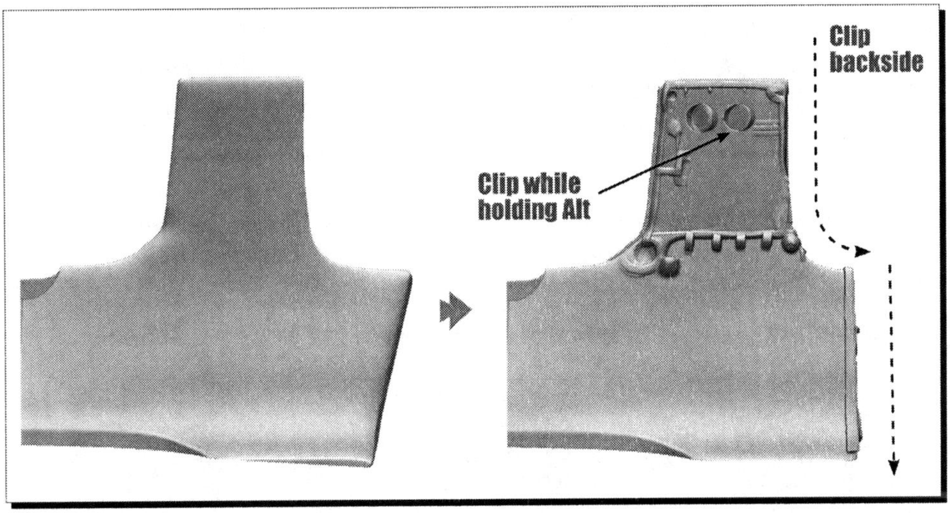


**How to speed up SmartReSym**

Using SmartReSym on polygon heavy meshes can take up quite some time. There are two ways of increasing the speed of the calculation:

First, the smaller the unmasked area is, the faster the ReSym will work.

The second possibility is to use it on lower subdivision levels, which is also a lot quicker.

8. Before we refine the command bridge, let's grab an alpha of a simple bolt so we can place it here and there. Start with a simple bulge and flatten the sides with radial symmetry to quickly shape a bolt, as shown in the next image. The grabbed alpha also works great as indentation when holding *Alt*:

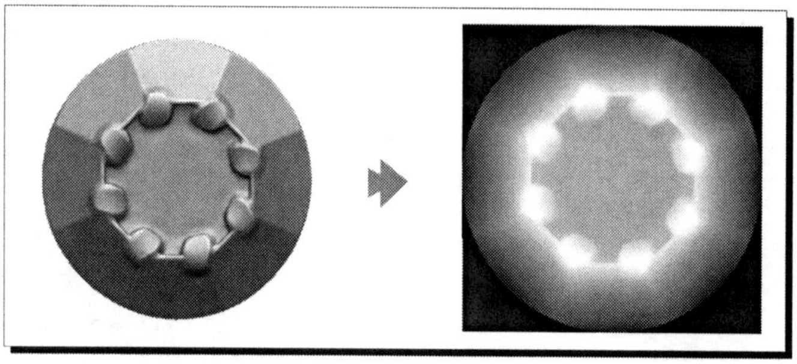

9. Continue refining the side view, as shown in the next image. The door allows the viewer to judge the size of the ship perfectly:

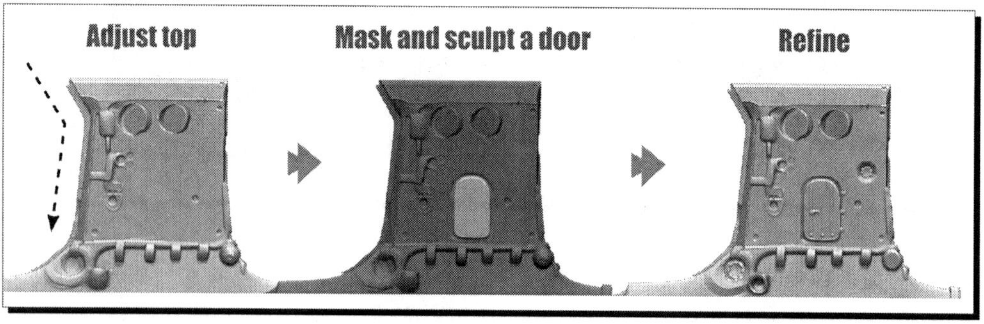


10. Create something that looks like a command bridge from the front by masking and transposing it, as shown in the next image:

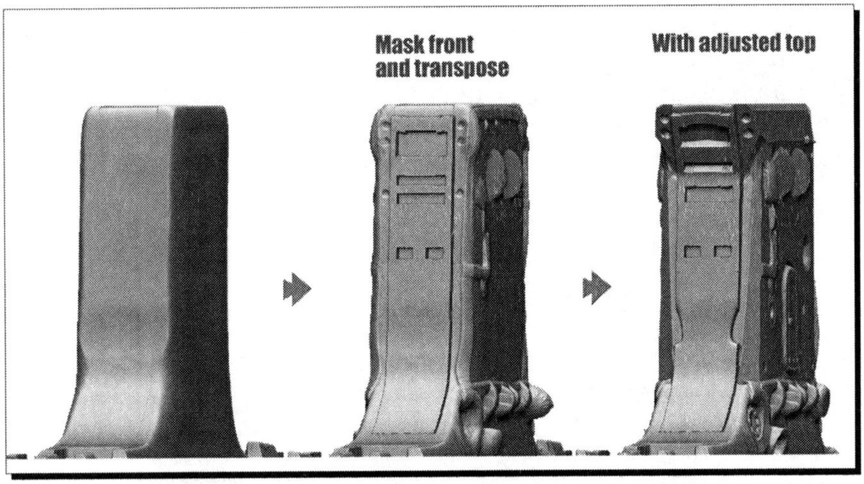


**11.** We are almost there! To finish the command bridge part, sculpt the backside as shown in the next image. Use **Masking** and **V Tiles** for the rolling gate:

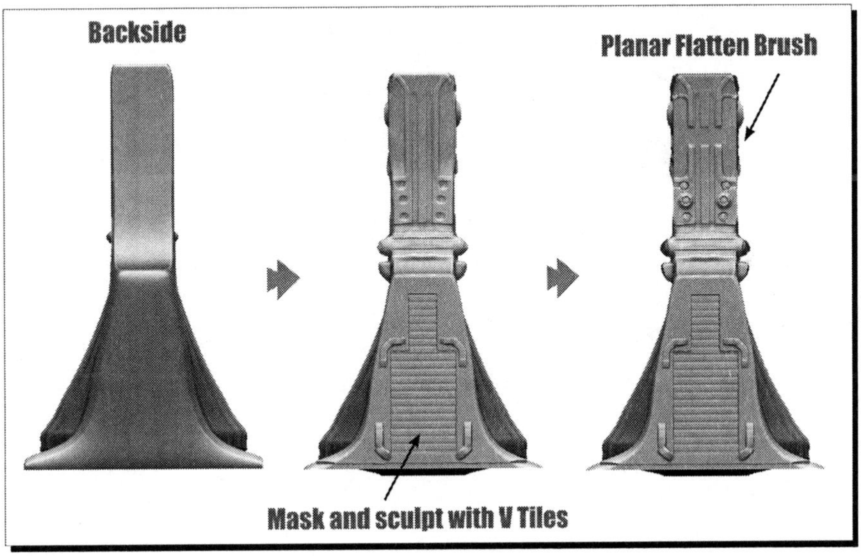

**12.** The area between the turrets is still a bit empty and the turret's gears should have something to hold on to. Let's deal with that by adding a stretched cube between the turrets, which resembles the technical parts that are connected to the turrets. After scaling, remesh it, so that it has an even polygon distribution. Sculpt it as shown in the next image. Finally, polish the hard edges of the sockets:

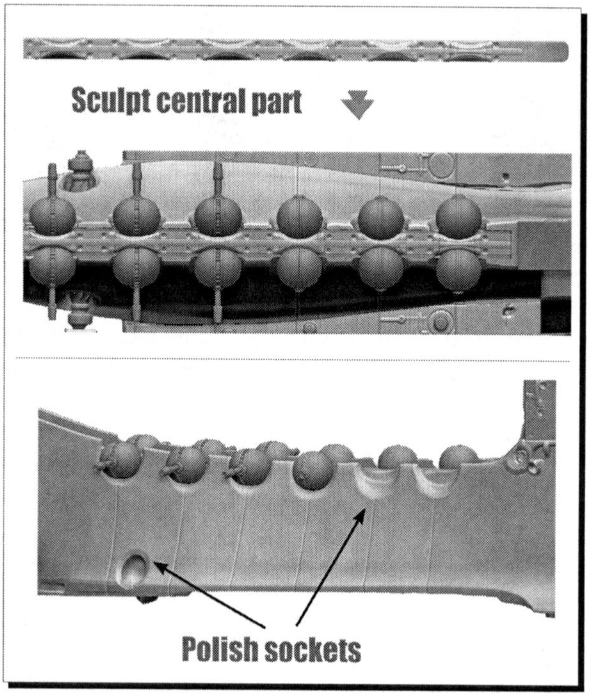


**13.** Save the final model.

**14.** Our final harvester ship would look like this:

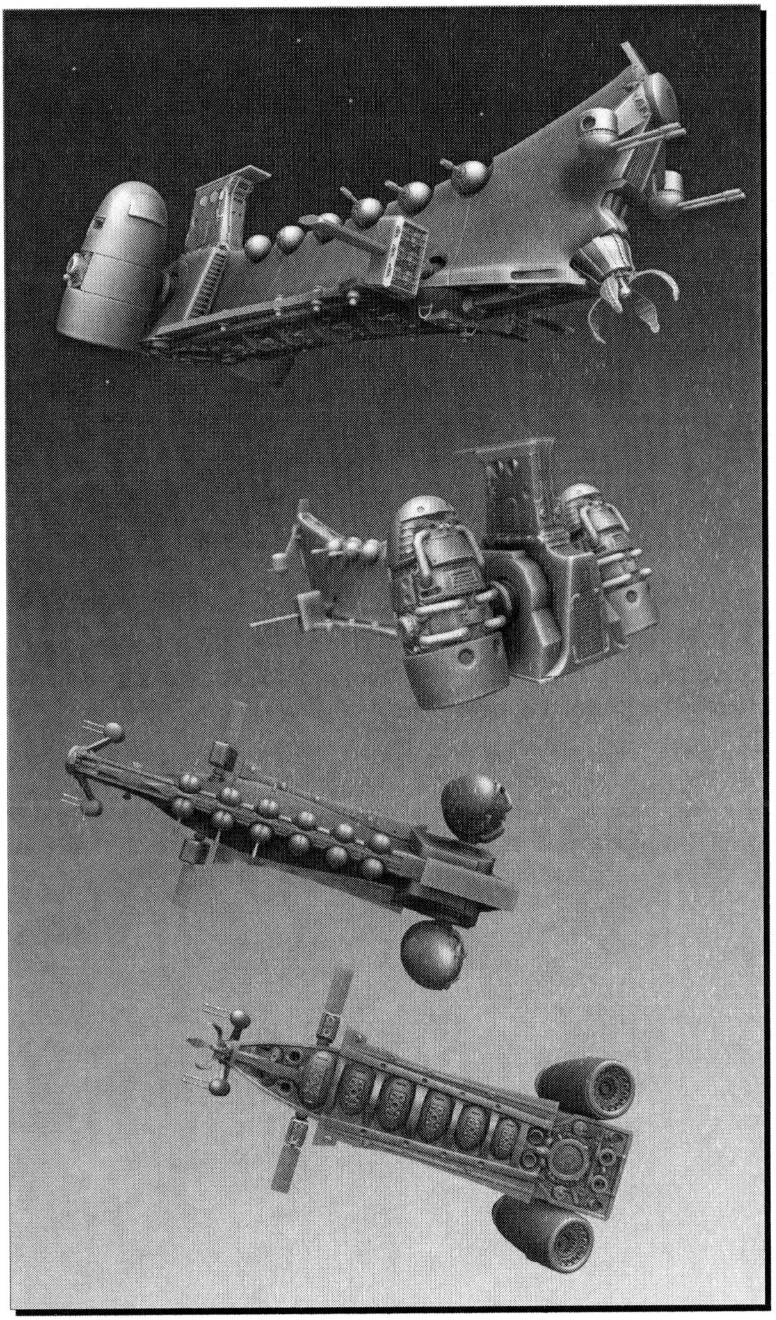

## What just happened?

Wow, we've finished our fourth and last model—the harvester ship. We didn't use any new techniques but rather applied all the learnt ones to create this heavily complex ship.

Basically we concentrated on bringing the same level of detail to each part of the ship by adding small details such as bolts, doors, and cables. We gave nearly each part a functionality that the viewer can understand and thus increased the believability of the final model.

To finally view this ship inside a game engine, we would have to follow the same steps as we did for the creature. First, create a low-poly with retopologize and then unwrap it, so that we can bake a normal map.

# Summary

In this chapter, we've brought together many techniques we learned earlier such as clipping, using masks, and how to sculpt mechanical surfaces. Specifically, we covered:

- When modeling semi-realistic mechanical objects, we tried to give each part an understandable meaning, so that the viewers will accept it.
- We've learned how combining techniques can lead to amazing results. Combine the **Tracks** brush with **alpha tiling** and get a cable brush.
- We can create impressive patterns in no time by painting with grabbed geometry.

That's it! You've successfully mastered the last tutorial of this book. Now you should have all the tools at hand to sculpt almost anything you could imagine. With ZBrush the sky is the limit.

# Epilogue

Congratulations, you've completed this book and are now familiar with the key concepts of using ZBrush for games.

You've learned how to tackle very different sculpting tasks and how to solve them, from organic to hard surface sculpting. Your future tasks as a game artist will deal with the same problems and solutions we did because it's either organic, inorganic, or a mix of both.

Remember the graphic of a game asset workflow with ZBrush from the first chapter? Let's look at it in retrospect:

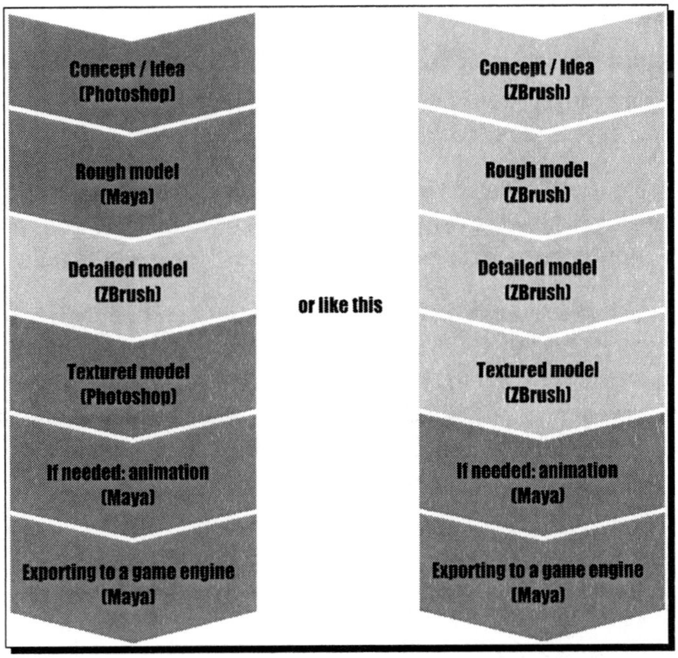

The first model we created was the haunted tree, which was modeled from **ZSpheres** and then detailed and even textured in ZBrush. This workflow is closer to the right one in the preceding image.

The second model, the drone, was started as a rough **base mesh** in Blender and detailed in ZBrush. This was the classical way of modeling before there was ZSketching or **Shadowbox**. This resembles the workflow example on the left in the previous image.

The third model, the brute, was created entirely in ZBrush with **ZSketch**. Like the tree, this is closer to the right example because it solely relies on ZBrush for modeling.

The fourth and last model, the harvester, was also entirely done in ZBrush introducing mesh creation with **Shadowbox.**

As you can see, with each model we explored another way of creating a mesh and learned when to choose which workflow. So, hopefully, this book gave you a solid understanding of the different workflows and how ZBrush can be used in a game pipeline.

By now, I hope you see ZBrush not only as a modeling tool but rather an extension to your creativity. It doesn't stop you, but rather encourages you to express yourself freely with as few technical restrictions as possible.

# Where to go next?

Go ahead and explore ZBrush more. With **UVMaster**, we already expanded ZBrush's capabilities by using a plug-in. You can find many more plug-ins at: `http://www.pixologic.com/ZBrush/downloadcenter/zplugins/`.

One of these plug-ins is called **Paintstop**, which allows you to use ZBrush as a 2D sketching application. It is useful if you want to quickly nail down an idea. Thus, you can even rely on ZBrush in the conception stage, as shown in the previous image on the right.

I would like to name two additional features that were out of scope for this book, but are still worth mentioning: ZBrush 4.0 comes with a **Timeline** feature. Combined with the rendering options, this allows you to render out turntables or complex camera movements for presentations or your portfolio, which is great. The second one is **Spotlight**, which is used to texture models from photo references really quickly. You can find more information about both on the official site at: `http://www.pixologic.com/ZBrush/features/ZBrush4/paint-and-show/`.

To further improve your skills as an artist, I encourage you to join a community or to enter some art contests. It's always fun and you'll get better each time.

Some good websites on Digital Art and Games are:

- `http://www.ZbrushCentral.com`: Focused on ZBrush
- `http://www.CGtalk.com`: Focused on CG in general, from drawing over sculpting to animation
- `http://www.GameArtisans.org`: Focused on Game Art
- `http://www.Gamasutra.com:` Focused on the business side of making games and Game Design

Let these sites inspire your future work.

I'm sure you're on the right track because by finishing this book, you've shown that you're really passionate and determined about what you do. That's the key to break into the industry.

I hope you enjoyed reading this book.

All the best

**Manuel Scherer**

# Pop Quiz

## Chapter 2: Pop quiz – 2D, 2.5D, and 3D mode

| | |
|---|---|
| 1 | By using the **Edit** button |
| 2 | Tool |
| 3 | Rotating |

## Chapter 3: Pop quiz – the root sphere and adaptive skin preview

| | |
|---|---|
| 1 | Because the root sphere can't be deleted without deleting the entire hierarchy. |
| 2 | Toggling Tool \| Adaptive Skin or pressing A will preview our mesh. |

## Chapter 4: Pop quiz – materials

| | |
|---|---|
| 1 | **MatCap** Materials |

# Chapter 4: Pop quiz – brush settings

| | |
|---|---|
| 1 | Pressing *Alt* inverts the brush direction. *Space bar* opens the quick menu; *Shift* is used for the **Smooth** brush. |
| 2 | This gives us a smaller brush size when zoomed in and a bigger size when zoomed out without having to change the size manually. |

# Chapter 4: Pop quiz – subdivisions

| | |
|---|---|
| 1 | Four times |

# Chapter 5: Pop quiz – Polypainting

| | |
|---|---|
| 1 | Rgb should be turned on. Zadd and Zsub are only used for sculpting. You can turn on Zadd and Rgb to sculpt and colorize the mesh simultaneously. |
| 2 | Because the resolution of Polypainting depends on the amount of vertices available. |

# Chapter 5: Pop quiz – masking

| | |
|---|---|
| 1 | **Masking** protects parts of the mesh from actions such as sculpting or painting. Although it looks like masking darkens parts of the mesh, the colors aren't changed. It is just for visualization. |

# Chapter 6: Pop quiz – subtools

| | |
|---|---|
| 1 | Meshes and ZSpheres. Everything that is considered a tool can be added as a subtool. As **ZSpheres** are also tools, this works too. |

# Chapter 6: Pop quiz – 3D primitives

| | |
|---|---|
| 1 | Converting it to a PolyMesh3D will make it sculptable. Converted primitives don't have initialize settings anymore. |

# Chapter 7: Pop quiz – in-game meshes

| | |
|---|---|
| 1 | Mesh information and UV-Coordinates |
| 2 | Because games are calculated in real-time we try to preserve resources wherever possible to ensure it still runs smoothly, even on lower hardware setups. |

# Chapter 8: Pop quiz – masking

| | |
|---|---|
| 1 | The opacity of the masking is controlled by the Rgb Slider, similar to Polypaint. |

# Chapter 9: Pop quiz – textures and Normal maps

| | |
|---|---|
| 1 | Color/diffuse maps |
| 2 | Sixteen times because it is four times bigger in width and height. |
| 3 | Yes, because it is not animated, we could do so. |

# Chapter 10: Pop Quiz – ZSketching a character

| | |
|---|---|
| 1 | For detached parts, the armature brush would be sufficient, but for connecting two shores, the sketch brushes would be more useful since they can rejoin on surfaces. A third option would be rejoining the armature stroke with a smooth brush. |
| 2 | Always have the mirrored parts visible, too, to prevent errors. |
| 3 | Reshaping the ZSketch can be done quickly by using Move, Scale or an armature. Starting all over is the worst option since it takes up the most time. Heavily changing the silhouette of a polygonal model isn't ideal either, because it provides us with less freedom than ZSketch. |
| 4 | For the rigging process, a relaxed pose is better than the T-pose. The reason for this is that the model will deform better, when it is modeled in-between its motion extremes. |

# Chapter 11: Pop quiz – masking and Polygroups

| | |
|---|---|
| 1 | Either close ZBrush and discard the changes on exit, or go to **Preferences \| Hotkeys \| Load** and load the startup hotkeys. |
| 2 | Polygroups allow us to hide parts of the body with a single click. Creating Polygroups is worth the time spent, because we need to hide parts quite often in the modeling process. |
| 3 | If they weren't symmetrical, working on one side would not mirror over to the hidden parts. By painting Polygroups symmetrically, this can't happen when hiding by Polygroups. |
| 4 | A leg could easily be masked by using the topological masking from the Transpose Tool. Since the Navel is only a spot on the mesh, painting it would probably be the easiest way. The upper half of the body could be masked quickly by dragging a mask.. |

# Chapter 12: Pop quiz – layers and alphas

| | |
|---|---|
| 1 | By using a morph target and the **Morph** brush, we can erase parts from the layer. |
| 2 | It would create a rivet-like bulge, because only white parts get elevated. When pressing *Alt*, it would create a hole. |
| 3 | Because the source image had too many artifacts, which lead to noisy alphas of bad quality. Painting them by hand, gives us full control and the cleanest results. |

# Chapter 13: Pop quiz – unwrapping and retopologizing

| | |
|---|---|
| 1 | Placing some cuts and flattening it would be the most elegant solution. Unwrapping a mesh works the same way |
| 2 | Seam placement, stretching, and readability |
| 3 | There's no definite rule of unwrapping a character's head, but the seam should not be placed in the face, so the back of the head is a good idea. |
| 4 | The mesh will deform better in animation if there are additional loops at the joints. |

# Chapter 14: Pop quiz – shadowBox and clipping brushes

| | |
|---|---|
| 1 | By holding down *Ctrl + Shift* for the Clipping brushes. |
| 2 | Because they can easily be hidden when using brushes that would influence other sides, like the MaskCurve Brush for example. |
| 3 | Exit and re-enter ShadowBox will update it according to the settings. |
| 4 | ZBrush will recreate the mesh in ShadowBox with masks. Since this can't recreate all shapes available in sculpting, there can be a loss of detail. |

# Chapter 15: Pop quiz – local symmetry, clipping, and moving

| | |
|---|---|
| 1 | Clipping will flatten polygons to the clipping line. |
| 2 | We should avoid to rotate objects in order to work with local- and radial symmetry. We can store the rotation on a layer instead. |
| 3 | By starting the Action Line on the model and ending it on the canvas, the action line will be parallel to our view. If our view is aligned to a world axis, the action line will be, too. |
| 4 | Holding *Shift* will move the object only along the path of the Action Line. Another option would be to use the **Offset slider** in the Deformation Subpalette. |

# Chapter 15: Pop quiz – Booleans

| | |
|---|---|
| 1 | From top to bottom, starting with the active subtool |
| 2 | Creating a knot can't be done with Booleans, since it will not deform the meshes but only add, subtract or intersect them. |

# Chapter 16: Pop quiz – creating alphas from geometry

| | |
|---|---|
| 1 | The MRGBZ grabber can grab geometry and create an alpha from it. |
| 2 | The size of the grabbed alpha depends on the size the object occupies on the canvas (in pixels). |

# Index

## Symbols



## A



## B



## C

## Q



## R



## S

## T



## U



## V



## W



## X



## Z

# Thank you for buying zBrush 4 Sculpting for Games: Beginner's Guide

## About Packt Publishing

Packt, pronounced 'packed', published its first book "Mastering phpMyAdmin for Effective MySQL Management" in April 2004 and subsequently continued to specialize in publishing highly focused books on specific technologies and solutions.

Our books and publications share the experiences of your fellow IT professionals in adapting and customizing today's systems, applications, and frameworks. Our solution-based books give you the knowledge and power to customize the software and technologies you're using to get the job done. Packt books are more specific and less general than the IT books you have seen in the past. Our unique business model allows us to bring you more focused information, giving you more of what you need to know, and less of what you don't.

Packt is a modern, yet unique publishing company, which focuses on producing quality, cutting-edge books for communities of developers, administrators, and newbies alike. For more information, please visit our website: `www.PacktPub.com`.

## Writing for Packt

We welcome all inquiries from people who are interested in authoring. Book proposals should be sent to `author@packtpub.com`. If your book idea is still at an early stage and you would like to discuss it first before writing a formal book proposal, contact us; one of our commissioning editors will get in touch with you.

We're not just looking for published authors; if you have strong technical skills but no writing experience, our experienced editors can help you develop a writing career, or simply get some additional reward for your expertise.

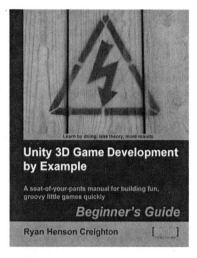

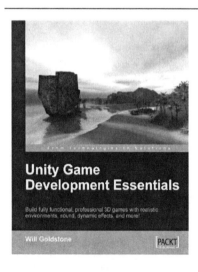